Lingua Cosmica

Lingua Cosmica

Science Fiction
from around the World

Edited by
DALE KNICKERBOCKER

**UNIVERSITY OF
ILLINOIS PRESS**
Urbana, Chicago, and Springfield

Library of Congress Cataloging-in-Publication Data
Names: Knickerbocker, Dale, 1962– editor.
Title: Lingua cosmica : science fiction from around the
    world / edited by Dale Knickerbocker.
Description: Urbana : University of Illinois Press, [2018]
    | Includes bibliographical references and index.
Identifiers: LCCN 2018003407 | ISBN 9780252041754
    (hardback) | ISBN 9780252083372 (paperback)
Subjects: LCSH: Science fiction—History and criticism.
    | BISAC: LITERARY CRITICISM / Science Fiction &
    Fantasy. | BIOGRAPHY & AUTOBIOGRAPHY / Literary.
Classification: LCC PN3433.5 .L56 2018 | DDC
    809.3/8762—dc23
LC record available at https://lccn.loc.gov/2018003407

Contents

Introduction

DALE KNICKERBOCKER

Two friends—let's call them Boutros and Wei—converse. Boutros asks, "What do you call a person who speaks three languages?" Wei replies, "Trilingual." Boutros continues with the query, "What do you call a person who speaks two languages?" Wei responds, "Bilingual." Finally, Boutros inquires, "What do you call a person who speaks one language?" He receives the reply, "Monolingual." "No," Boutros retorts, "American." This hoary jest, well known among those of us who teach languages and literatures from outside the English-speaking realm, illustrates two important challenges faced when trying to promote the understanding of other cultures—and their science fiction. The first is obviously linguistic: in the context of science fiction (sf), one can walk into a bookstore in virtually any non-Anglophone country in the world and, if there is any sf at all, it will consist mostly of translations of English-language works. The opposite is also true: as the Serbian sf author Zoran Živković laments, "If you enter a bookshop in the U.S. or the U.K., the chances of finding a translated book are less than 3 percent."[1] Not only does the translation river run in only one direction, it tends to drown local authors, who find it difficult to publish their work (much less have it translated into English), as local thirst has already been quenched by imports.

The second is the arrogance and myopia implicit in the conflation of the word "American" with a citizen of the United States of America, a practice that illustrates perfectly a sort of cultural chauvinism that extends beyond the borders of any single country. As Donald Wolheim observes, "In our conventions and our awards and our discussions we slip into the habit of referring to our [English-language] favorites as the World's Best this and the World's Best that."[2] Or one could cite the persistent belief that any science fiction worthy of the name can only be written in the most technologically advanced nations—after all, sf is only about science, right?—or that because we haven't heard of sf from, say, Africa or South America, it must not exist. These attitudes are rather ironic in a genre in which the themes of exploration and encounters with others (extraterrestrial, technological, etc.) are so important: what better vehicle for understanding our terrestrial others than a genre inseparably intertwined with questions of otherness?

The first conundrum I faced when preparing this volume could be summarized by paraphrasing Istvan Csicsery-Ronay Jr.'s observation that everyone knows what global science fiction is until they have to define it.[3] Simply put, how was I to define a "center" against which an "other" science fiction (or science fiction of the "other[s]") could be defined? By language? By nationality? Neither seemed to work entirely, so I decided to "Kobayashi Maru" the question;[4] in fact, the title of this book is itself misleading, as one chapter focuses on works entirely in English, by the Nigerian American filmmaker Olatunde Osunsanmi. Since the United States, United Kingdom, and Anglophone Canada comprise the predominant center of production of sf literature, film, and television, I searched for scholarship on sf from outside this group, to which I shall henceforth refer as the "Anglophone axis" (with sincere apologies to other English-speaking peoples).

In recent years, there has been a rapid growth in interest by scholars within the Anglophone axis that gives cause for hope that sf from other regions is gaining the attention it merits, as evidenced by numerous phenomena. First, there is the publication of several anthologies that either include or are entirely dedicated to sf from outside the Anglophone axis: 1989's *Science Fiction from China*, edited by Patrick D. Murphy and Dingbo Wu; Nalo Hopkinson's 2000 *Whispers from the Cotton Tree Root: Caribbean Fabulist Fiction* (2000) and her 2004 *So Long Been Dreaming: Postcolonial Science Fiction and Fantasy* (coedited with Uppinder Mehan); Andrea Bell and Yolanda Molina-Gavilán's 2003 collection *Cosmos Latinos: An Anthology of Science Fiction from Latin America and Spain*; Ivor W. Hartmann's 2012 *AfroSF: Science Fiction by African Writers* and his 2015 *AfroSFv2*; Yvonne Howell and Anne O. Fisher's *Red Star Tales: A Century of Russian and Soviet Science Fiction* and Horea Gârbea, Magda Groza, Mihaela Mudure, and Samuel W. Onn's anthology of Romanian sf, both published in 2015; and Julia Novakova's compilation of Czech speculative stories in 2016.[5] The 2016 publication of the Polish novelist Jacek Dukaj's *The Old Axolotl* and the Finnish author Johanna Sinisalo's *The Core of the Sun*, as well as the forthcoming translation of the complete works of the Serbian author Zoran Živković announced by Cadmus Press, are also heartening developments.[6]

This increased attention is further substantiated by the publication of international-, area-, or nation-themed special issues by genre-specific journals such as *Science Fiction Studies*, which has produced the special issues "Global SF," "Afrofuturism," "Japanese SF," "Soviet SF: The Thaw and After," "Latin American SF," and "Chinese Science Fiction"—with issues on Italian, Spanish, and Southeast Asian sf reportedly in the works. *Paradoxa* has also made major contributions, with "Three Asias: Japan, S. Korea, China" and "Africa SF"; and the *Cambridge Journal of Postcolonial Literary Inquiry* devoted its September 2016 issue to African Science Fiction. Even mainstream journals have begun to consider the topic worthy of study: *World Literature Today* has published an issue on international sf, and the Latin American–studies journal *Iberoamericana* even dedicated a two-issue volume to sf from that region. Furthermore, in 2012, a special issue of *Renditions* introduced eight authors of the Chinese "New Wave" to Anglophone readers.

Organizations dedicated to science-fiction and fantasy literatures worldwide have sprung up outside the Anglophone axis, such as the Gesellschaft für Fantastikforschung in Germany and the Finnish Society for Science Fiction and Fantasy Research (both of which maintain English versions of their websites). New multilingual, peer-reviewed journals continue to appear—for example, the Finland-based *Fafnir: Nordic Journal of Science Fiction and Fantasy Research*, *Hélice: Reflexiones críticas sobre ficción especulativa* (Spain), *Alambique: revista académica de ciencia ficción y fantasía* (United States), and *Abusões* (Brazil)— as do English-language portals dedicated to non-Anglophone or multilingual science fiction.[7]

In addition, a number of awards have been established to promote and reward literature, translation, and scholarship in the field. The International Association of the Fantastic in the Arts began offering the Jamie Bishop Award for the Best Non-English Language Essay on the Fantastic (which includes sf) in 2007 and the Walter James Miller Memorial Award for Student Scholarship in the International Fantastic at its 2015 conference. The Association for the Recognition of Excellence in Science Fiction and Fantasy began awarding the Science Fiction and Fantasy Translation Award in 2010. This prize was strangled by its own success: nominations became too overwhelming in number to be considered, and it was last granted in 2013.

Despite such interest, scholarship on the topic is still in its infancy and thus, as is to be expected, has taken a broad historical or thematic view of national or regional science fiction (such as M. Elizabeth Ginway's study of Brazilian sf from the 1960s through the 1980s, Rachel Haywood Ferreira's survey of the genesis of the literary species in Latin America during the early modern period, Anindita Banerjee's study of Russian and Soviet sf, or Walter Smyrniw's book on the development of the genre in the Ukraine), or has examined it broadly through a particular theoretical lens (e.g., Jessica Langer's 2011 *Postcolonialism and Science Fiction*). Most articles also either take a wide perspective or are focused on specific works; for instance, among all the articles on Latin American sf in the two special issues of *Iberoamericana* mentioned above, only three are author-themed articles focusing on contemporary writers, none among those covered in this collection. The same can be said of book-length scholarly anthologies on international sf: for instance, M. Elizabeth Ginway and J. Andrew Brown's 2012 *Latin American Science Fiction: Theory and Practice* contains only one such article.

Lingua Cósmica: Science Fiction from around the World came about as the result of a discussion with Willis Regier at the Thirty-fifth International Conference on the Fantastic in the Arts in March 2014, in which he expressed the University of Illinois Press's desire to increase its offerings on recent non-Anglophone authors in its Modern Masters of Science Fiction series, which publishes studies of single writers. I suggested that, due to the unknown status of virtually all such contemporary creators, a collection of essays to introduce figures worthy of belonging to an international sf canon might help to create a market for studies of individual authors. The goal would be to offer essays that would fill the gap between the survey-type studies noted above and articles focusing on one work. As a result of that conversation, I contacted numerous scholars in the field with the following query: if you had to choose *one* post–World War II author or filmmaker of primarily sf who works in a language other than English, or who publishes from the English-speaking "periphery" (e.g., Anglophone India or Africa), as the most important, who would it be? Abstracts were solicited, a proposal was written, and, with the very capable collaboration of the people at the University of Illinois Press, you now hold the result in your hands.

The main objective of this project is to identify major contemporary authors of science fiction outside the English-speaking world and present them to students and scholars within its boundaries. It aims to answer questions such as: Who are these authors and why are they important? What innovative thematic material or formal elements do they offer? What unique characteristics from their culture do they bring to the genre? How do they dialogue with the history of the genre? And how do they fit into the contemporary sf scene worldwide? Contributors were tasked with making a case for the importance of their writer or filmmaker, contextualizing their work within the contexts of national and international sf traditions (themes, tropes, tendencies, subgenres, etc.), and offering an in-depth analysis of a major work or works.

Another obstacle to overcome when preparing this volume was to identify qualified scholars of a type of fiction not generally taught in doctoral programs; moreover, they had to be willing to write the essay in English. The greatest challenge, however, was attempting to ensure the widest possible geographic representation. For example, my attempts to have representation on authors and filmmakers from the Middle East and sub-Saharan Africa were unsuccessful, and, in addition to the present chapters, the project originally included essays on a Brazilian and a Bengali-language Indian author that unfortunately were fated not to be. Perhaps someone will take up that work in a not-too-distant future. It is hoped that the value of what is included will lessen readers' discontent with what is not.

Many of the creators whose work is examined here are also known—perhaps even more well-known—as fantasists, and their works frequently include elements of sf and fantasy. I believe that this reflects the evolution of the genre globally as well as the literary traditions of the cultures themselves. It would have been ironic to demand generic "purity" (if one were to claim the existence of such a species, it would no doubt be a white male Anglo animal anyway) in a collection intended to cross borders and break down walls. In any event, the essays make clear why and how each figure participates in the genre.

The authors and filmmakers studied are Daína Chaviano (Cuba) by Juan Carlos Toledano Redondo, Jacek Dukaj (Poland) by Paweł Frelik, Jean-Claude Dunyach (France) by Natacha Vas-Deyres, Andreas Eschbach (Germany) by Vibeke Rützou Petersen, Angélica Gorodischer (Argentina) by Yolanda Molina-Gavilán, Sakyo Komatsu (Japan) by Tatsumi Takayuki, Liu Cixin (China) by Mingwei Song, Yves Meynard and Jean-Louis Trudel writing under the pseudonym Laurent McAllister (Francophone Canada) by Amy J. Ransom, Olatunde Osunsanmi (Nigerian American) by Alexis Brooks de Vita, Johanna Sinisalo (Finland) by Hanna-Riikka Roine and Hanna Samola, and Arkady Strugatsky and Boris Strugatsky (USSR/Russia) by Yvonne Howell.. These authors possess one thing in common: there is little or no scholarship in English on their work.[8]

Juan Carlos Toledano Redondo's "Daína Chaviano's Science Fiction Oeuvre" examines Chaviano's opus, paying particular attention to her novel *Fables of an Extraterrestrial Grandmother* in the context of the pro-Soviet Cuba of the 1980s. Toledano Redondo identifies Chaviano as part of Cuba's "New Wave" of the 1980s, whose combination of the conventions and tropes of sf, fantasy, folklore, and mythology, while in consonance with much of what was going on in sf in the rest of the world (as several of the essays in this collection demonstrate), were quite unique in the Cuba of the time. Toledano Redondo argues that the popularity of Chaviano's work is due to her use of language, characters, and tropes usually associated with fantasy, folklore, and myth in a narrative in which they can be interpreted as referring to modern scientific concepts and devices (an ambiguity he also cites as the reason her writing escaped censorship). He furthermore finds that Chaviano's opus displays a "cosmovision" or concept of the universe coinciding with theories of quantum mechanics and the multiverse, one in which the borders between science and magic are porous. Toledano Redondo analyzes her most important work, the aforementioned *Fables*, as examplary of her techniques and cosmovision. He also uncovers its political content, seeing in its depiction of the opening of the borders between alternate universes an allegorical criticism of "the Cuban authorities' inability to open up their country to the world and even to their own society."

In "Jacek Dukaj's Science Fiction as Philosophy," Paweł Frelik audaciously asserts that Dukaj, still little-known outside his native Poland, is not only "a true heir to Stanisław Lem" but, arguably, "overshadows" the Polish master "in terms of narrative complexity and intellectual density." Frelik notes three basic characteristics in Dukaj's fiction: He participates, in his own unique way, in the genre-bending common to many of the authors studied in this collection. His narrative also critiques numerous aspects of Polish politics, society, and culture. Frelik focuses, however, on "the unusual dynamic between the practice of worldbuilding and narrative plotting" in which the former is dominant, unusual in sf. Frelik argues that, like Lem and authors such as William Gibson, China Miéville, and Kim Stanley Robinson, Dukaj manipulates generic conventions "as tools for thinking through philosophical and political issues." In this way, he maintains "a critical attitude towards the science fiction tradition at large and specific scientific, intellectual, and political discourses."

In "Jean-Claude Dunyach, Poet of the Flesh," Natacha Vas-Deyres discusses an author whom she places in a generation of French sf writers who began their careers from 1980–85, including Roland C. Wagner, Emmanuel Jouanne, Sylvie Lainé, and Jean-Marc Ligny, among others. Influenced by Samuel Delany, Ray Bradbury, and even more so by J. G. Ballard, Dunyach takes his work in a direction similar to that of Johanna Sinisalo, Daína Chaviano, and Angélica Gorodischer, mixing hard sf with the fantastic.

Vas-Deyres proposes to answer the question, "What makes contemporary French sf truly French?" by analyzing Dunyach's "AnimalCities" cycle, which consists of several short fictions and two novels: *Dead Stars* and *Dying Stars*. These AnimalCities "are living extraterrestrial city-shaped animals, made of flesh and cartilage, traveling through space from node to node on the web of the universe," who develop a "symbiotic liaison with humanity [that] gradually leads humans to understand the global nature of reality." Tracing this "French urban imagination" back to Emile Zola's 1873 *The Belly of Paris* or his 1872 *The Kill*, among other influences, Vas-Deyres posits that themes such as "time, death, memory, relativity, mutations, and relationships with the machine or extraterrestrials, are always considered from the angle of a sensorial materiality," concluding that Dunyach "offers a perfect example of what is uniquely 'French' about French sf during this period": it is "a sensualist form of science fiction."

In "Andreas Eschbach's Futures and Germany's Past," Vibeke Rützou Petersen analyzes five of Eschbach's novels published from 1995 to 2011 as exemplary of the thematic interests common to his narratives and, at the same time, of the internal diversity of his work. She characterizes his narratives as being in the tradition of hard sf and space opera, but hybridized with subgenres including the thriller and detective novels. Petersen observes that, while many of Eschbach's works reflect historical concerns of Germany such as the Holocaust, his tropes also correspond to those common in Western sf in general (time travel, cyborgs, galactic empires), as well as to themes of worldwide interest such as capitalism, power, religion, global terrorism, climate change, and ecology. Technology is central to Echsbach's work, but his use of it is rarely radically innovative, and while Eschbach constructs fictional worlds, he does so "not the way we know it from Ursula K. Le Guin, Kim Stanley Robinson, or even William Gibson." Petersen suggests that what makes Eschbach's fictions unique is precisely that "the worlds he builds are ours, and we recognize them without estrangement."

Yolanda Molina-Gavilán's "Angélica Gorodischer: Only a Storyteller" locates this difficult-to-categorize writer—it could easily be argued that she has as much in common with the New Weird as Sinisalo—in a constellation with an eclectic cluster of stars, including Italo Calvino, Franz Kafka, Umberto Eco, Philip K. Dick, Arthur C. Clarke, Isaac Asimov, Hans Christian Andersen, J. R. R. Tolkien, Virginia Woolf, and Jorge Luis Borges but, above all, Ursula K. Le Guin. Molina-Gavilán credits Le Guin and Gorodischer with "infusing an enduring feminist sensibility into the genre." She analyzes stories in the collections *Trafalgar*, *The Republics*, and *Imperial Kalpa*, describing the Argentine author's writing as characterized by playful metafictional features and the blending of fantastic and science-fictional elements "with a metaphysical core." Molina-Gavilán explains how Gorodischer takes full advantage of the defamiliarizing possibilities of these genres to comment on power and to interrogate and problematize sex and gender and their relationship to that power in order to undermine patriarchal thought, while also reflecting on "universal philosophical concerns such as the selfish nature of human beings or the meaning of human evolution."

Takayuki Tatsumi's "Sakyo Komatsu's Planetary Imagination: Reading *Virus* and *The Day of Resurrection*" offers an analysis of Sakyo Komatsu's 1964 novel *The Day of Resurrection* and its film adaptation by Kinji Fukasaku, *Virus* (1980). He places these works squarely within the post–Cuban Missile Crisis surge in apocalyptic literature and film worldwide (such as Eugene Burdick and Harvey Wheeler's bestselling 1962 novel *Fail Safe*, turned into the eponymous 1964 film by Sidney Lumet; Kurt Vonnegut's 1963 novel *Cat's Cradle*; or Stanley Kubrick's 1964 movie *Dr. Strangelove or: How I Learned to Stop Worrying and Love the Bomb*). He also reminds the reader that Komatsu's novel preceded Michael Crichton's very similar *Andromeda Strain* (1969) and points out interesting parallels between *The Day of Resurrection* and Herman Melville's *Moby-Dick* (1851).

Tatsumi details Komatsu's key role not only as one of the founding figures of Japanese sf but as one of the first and primary promoters of a relationship between Eastern and Western sf writers as chair of the Executive Committee of the International Science Fiction Symposium held in Japan in 1970, among other activities.

Tatsumi observes that "Komatsu's story [*The Day of Resurrection*] gives a keen insight into the possible coincidences between natural disaster and artificial disaster, which we were to witness nearly fifty years later than the original publication of the novel; that is, in the multiple disasters in eastern Japan on March 11, 2011"—the earthquakes and consequent Fukushima nuclear catastrophe—foreseeing "the total apocalypse to be caused by a coincidence between a natural disaster such as a tremendous earthquake and artificial disaster as represented by full-scale nuclear war."

It is perhaps a sign of the times that the first non-English-language work to win the Hugo Award for Best Novel (2015) is from China: Liu Cixin's *The Three-Body Problem* (published in English by Tor in 2014). In "Liu Cixin's Three-Body Trilogy: Between the Sublime Cosmos and the Micro Era," Minwei Song analyzes the *Remembrance of Earth's Past* trilogy of which *The Three-Body Problem* forms the first part, and which also includes *The Dark Forest* (English translation 2015) and *Death's End* (English translation 2016).

The author claims for Liu the status of the leading figure of what he identifies as the "New Wave" of Chinese science fiction and posits that the fundamental characteristic of Liu's writing is his experimentation with "changing the physical rules of the universe," then rigorously following through the consequences. He describes the trilogy as an attempt "to render the [Kantian] sublime visible": "infinite, formless, boundless, overwhelming, with a magnitude beyond the human ability to measure and grasp," yet "created out of precise details."

Song proposes that the central theme unifying the trilogy is "whether the human beings who are morally conscious can survive in a universe that has no place for morality. In other words, can humanity be preserved in a world that only obeys the inhuman principles of 'hard science'"? Nor is the political dimension overlooked: the trilogy begins during the bloody days of the Cultural Revolution (1966–76), and the question posed is directly related to "Mao's ideal for a permanent revolution . . . the foundational belief in the possibility of revolutionizing humanity through dehumanizing the revolutionaries." Song nonetheless observes a fundamental ambiguity in the trilogy: "The most magical power of the trilogy may still come from the sustaining of humaneness that can be found even in the coldest moments and places."

The subject of Amy J. Ransom's contribution is Laurent McAllister, nom de plume of the Québécois writers Yves Meynard and Jean-Louis Trudel writing collaboratively. Ransom places their joint efforts within the panorama of Québécois franco-nationalism and the rise of the Québécois French sf movement in the 1970s, as well as in the broader context of hard sf space opera and cyberpunk. Ransom then analyzes the *Suprématie* cycle, which tells the story of an alliance of interstellar races resisting the "evil empire" of the Supremats, beings attempting to assimilate and subjugate peoples by suppressing all freedom and difference. Making use of Gilles Deleuze and Félix Guattari's concept of the "rhizome," a metaphor for a theoretical nonhierarchical or "horizontal" form of resistance to power capable of generating a similarly nonhierarchical society, Ransom proposes that the *Suprématie* cycle portrays such a resistance through its representation of the starship *Doukh/Harfang* and its crew, its conception of the use of art as resistance, and its depiction of the rebel alliance. She concludes that, through its representation of a multitude of sentient races that cooperate rhizomatically, McAllister suggests a model of the future in line with what Stefan Herbrechter called "critical posthumanism," putting the cycle in consonance with the fiction of writers such as Margaret Atwood, Octavia Butler, Ursula K. Le Guin, and Kazuo Ishiguro.

While Alexis Brooks de Vita's "Olatunde Osunsanmi and Living the Trans-atlantic Apocalypse: *The Fourth Kind*" looks at a screenwriter/filmmaker who works in English, the topic may be the most international in this collection, dealing as it does with the Transatlantic Human Trade that changed the destiny of Africa and the Americas. De Vita draws attention to the African/Diaspora screenwriter, director, and producer by addressing the question of why relatively few African Americans or Africans (apparently) write science fiction. First, she debunks the validity of the question, demonstrating that Africans and their U.S. descendants have a long tradition of addressing science-fictional themes. Then, echoing Namwali Serpell, she points out that "African Americans are, historically and in reality, descendants of people who were abducted by aliens" and that, as such, they are living the results of one sf's most classic narratives: alien abduction/invasion, the main theme of Osunsanmi's *The Fourth Kind*.

De Vita not only analyzes the film's treatment of the devastating effects of the encounter between different civilizations (slavery, coloniality, cultural indoctrination, and control of dominated peoples), she also examines white Western audiences' and critics' discomfort with the film, concluding that "Osunsanmi portrays an African/Diaspora reality, in a genre and via a medium created by and of interest to Europeans and Americans, exposing a reality the latter may not have explored from the candid perspectives of the peoples traumatically affected"—the Transatlantic Human Trade—a portrayal that "forces its audience to acknowledge potential socially taught biases by first querying, then overturning, and finally undermining them." The answer to the question of why more Africans do not write science fiction, she suggests, is that in so many of the genre's classic narratives, their own traumatic history is rewritten with the historical persecutor usurping the role of the oppressed. They thus may not be eager to adopt the colonizers' generic vehicle to express their own reality.

Hanna-Riikka Roine and Hanna Samola's "Johanna Sinisalo and the New Weird: Genres and Myths" identifies the predominant trait of the Finnish author's work as "the crossings of generic boundaries and the casual combinations of various types of texts as well as the radical mix of real and fictional." The authors observe that Sinisalo draws on influences as varied as Tove Jansson, H. G. Wells, Ursula K. Le Guin, Margaret Atwood, Michael Tournier, and Ray Bradbury, as well as fairy tales and Finno-Ugric mythology and folklore, placing her among a group of writers who have come to be known as practitioners of the Finnish Weird, a sort of Nordic counterpart to the strain of fiction identified by Jeff Van-derMeer and Ann VanderMeer in their groundbreaking 2008 anthology *The New Weird*. Roine and Samola affirm that writers of the Finnish Weird attempt "to challenge the tradition of realist writing that has dominated the Finnish literary canon for a long time." The authors pose the following questions: "What kind of elements does Sinisalo's technique make use of, and what do they bring to the readerly interpretation? Is there something unique to the way Sinisalo uses these elements?" Examining Sinisalo's opus in general and her satirical, dystopian, alternative-future novel *The Core of the Sun* in particular, they posit that she is unique among Finnish Weird authors because not only do her works always begin with the type of "what if?" proposition characteristic of sf, her writing persistently *works through* these thought experiments—while also making use of elements taken from other narratives types. The resulting literature offers not unequivocal answers but is characterized by ambiguity and polysemia.

If Africans historically lived the invasion and abduction narrative, in her chapter on the brothers Arkady Strugatsky (1926–91) and Boris Strugatsky (1933–2012), Yvonne Howell asserts that Soviet ideology itself was science-fictional: "There was something essentially 'science fictional' about the Soviet project, which superimposed a hyperrational, materialist, and stridently future-oriented official ideology onto deeply embedded premodern epistemologies." She poses the question: "How can we attribute the Strugatskys' once and future relevance to the way in which their understanding of science fiction continued to evolve in the space between local and global developments?" Howell lays out the trajectory of the Strugatskys' opus and the sociopolitical history of the USSR and post-Soviet Russia as two rails of the same track, tracing their work from the early utopias of their "Nooniverse" cycle that reflected postrevolution optimism, through their engagement with concerns equally relevant to East and West during the cold war, and into their post–Prague Spring disillusionment with the "progressive" values of modernity. Howell concludes with an analysis of the Strugatskys' 1966 novella *Snail on the Slope*, which presents a sentient matriarchal forest in advance of Ursula K. Le Guin's 1972 *The Word for World Is Forest,* and its counterpart, *Tale of the Troika* (1967), which presents a "harshly hierarchical . . . male-dominated" society run by the "Bureau" and "committed to overcoming all obstacles with technological fixes." She demonstrates the contemporary relevance of the brothers' work by showing how these novellas have been appropriated for ideological use: "Today's Russian neoconservatives reread the Strugatskys as a vindication of the necessary 'third way' that Russian transhumanist philosophy offers the world. . . . [W]hereby science allows us to have . . . superpowers . . . , Russian Orthodox Christian philosophy gives us all the right spiritual values."

Distance provides perspective, and proximity provides knowledge. So let us cross frontiers to seek out new commonalities, as well as the differences that offer new meaning to the already familiar.

Acknowledgments

I would first like to thank Gary K. Wolfe for recommending me to Willis Regier, director of the University of Illinois Press, as the person to talk to regarding non-Anglophone authors of science fiction. I'd also like to express my gratitude to the acquiring editor for science fiction studies, Marika Christofides, for her invaluable advice and infinite patience during the preparation of the manuscript.

I thank Linda E. McMahon for her generous endowment of the chair that bears her name in the Department of Foreign Languages and Literatures at East Carolina University, which allowed me the time necessary to carry out this project.

I dedicate this work to my parents, Harold "Bud" and Lorraine C. Knickerbocker.

Above all, I would like to thank my soulmate, Purificación Martínez Escamilla, without whom nothing would make sense.

Notes

1. Živković, "Writing in Languages Other Than English."

2. Wolheim, Introduction.

3. See Csicsery-Ronay, "What Do We Mean," in which he insightfully problematizes the terms "global," "cultural," and "science fiction."

4. Most readers will recognize the reference to the fictional world of the *Star Trek* franchise, in which Starfleet Academy cadets are required to undergo a test consisting of a computer simulation in which they captain the *Kobayashi Maru*—no matter what they do, the vessel will be destroyed. Cadet James T. Kirk reprograms the computer, allowing him to save the ship and thus defeat the "no-win" scenario. It was first introduced in the second film of the movie series, *Star Trek II: The Wrath of Kahn* (1982).

5. This book will employ the endnote and bibliography system contained in the *Chicago Manual of Style*, sixteenth edition. In the text, the first mention of each non-English language work will give the title in the original language (or its Western transcription in the case of Chinese-, Japanese-, and Russian-language works), followed by the English translation. Subsequently, titles will be given in English. Since the bibliographies contain all works cited and referred to, notes will contain abbreviated references to works cited directly, or be informational. Works only referred to may be found in the bibliography at the end of each chapter. In consideration of the intended readership, all works currently translated into English for each author will also appear there.

6. See Rachel Cordasco's extremely useful website, "Speculative Fiction in Translation," on which she posts news of new sf translations as they become available.

7. To offer just a few examples: http://scifiportal.eu/ (Europe), www.srsff.ro/ (Romania), http://sfmag.hu/ (Hungary), and http://www.haikasoru.com/ (Japan).

8. At the time of this writing, criticism on the Strugatsky brothers leads the way, with about a dozen articles in English—hardly in line with their vast opus published over more than thirty years. Daína Chaviano and Angélica Gorodischer are the subject of three articles each, and Johanna Sinisalo, Andreas Eschbach, Jean-Claude Dunyach, and Laurent McAllister are each the subject of one. Olatunde Osunsanmi and Jacek Dukaj have been heretofore completely ignored, and the only attention garnered by Liu Cixin and Sakyo Komatsu has been by the scholars contributing to this volume.

Bibliography

"African Science Fiction." Special issue, *The Cambridge Journal of Postcolonial Literary Inquiry* 3.3 (September 2016).

Ares, Silvia Kurlat, ed. "La ciencia-ficción en América Latina: entre la mitología experimental y lo que vendrá [Science fiction in Latin America: Between experimental mythology and what will come]." Special issue, *Iberoamericana* 78.238–39 (January–June 2012).

Ayerdhal, and Jean-Claude Dunyach. *Etoiles mourantes* [Dying stars]. Paris: Réédition Mnémos, 2014.

Banerjee, Anindita. *We Modern People: Science Fiction and the Making of Russian Modernity.* Middletown, Conn.: Wesleyan University Press, 2012.

Bell, Andrea, and Yolanda Molina-Gavilán, eds. *Cosmos Latinos: An Anthology of Science Fiction from Latin America and Spain.* Middletown, Conn.: Wesleyan University Press, 2003.

Bould, Mark, ed. "Africa SF." Special issue, *Paradoxa* 25 (2013).

———, and Rone Shavers, eds. "Afrofuturism." Special issue, *Science Fiction Studies* 102.2 (July 2007).

Chaviano, Daína. *Fábulas de una abuela extraterrestre* [Fables of an extraterrestrial grandmother]. Havana: Letras Cubanas, 1988.

"Chinese Science Fiction." Special issue, *Science Fiction Studies* 40.1 (March 2013).

Cordasco, Rachel. "Speculative Fiction in Translation." June 4, 2016. Accessed July 26, 2017. http://www.sfintranslation.com.

Crichton, Michael. *The Andromeda Strain.* 1969; reprint, New York: Harper, 2008.

Csicsery-Ronay, Istvan Jr. "What Do We Mean When We Say 'Global Science Fiction?' Reflections on a New Nexus." *Science Fiction Studies* 39 (2012): 478–93.

———, and Erik Simon, eds. "Soviet Science Fiction: The Thaw and After." Special issue, *Science Fiction Studies* 31.3 (November 2004).

Dr. Strangelove or: How I Stopped Worrying and Learned to Love the Bomb. Dir. Stanley Kubrick. United States: Columbia Pictures, 1964.

Dukaj, Jacek. *The Old Axolotl* [Starość axolotla]. Trans. Stanley Bill. Poznań: Allegro, 2015.

Dunyach, Jean-Claude. *Etoiles mortes* [Dead stars]. Paris : J'ai lu SF, 2000.

Fail Safe. Dir. Sidney Lumet. United States: Columbia Pictures, 1964.

Ferreira, Rachel Haywood. *The Emergence of Latin American Science Fiction.* Middletown, Conn.: Wesleyan University Press, 2011.

The Fourth Kind. Dir. Olatunde Osunsanmi. United States: Universal Pictures, 2009.

Gârbea, Horea, Magda Groza, Mihaela Mudure, and Samuel W. Onn, eds. *Worlds and Beings: Romanian Contemporary Science Fiction Stories.* Bucharest: Romanian Cultural Institute Press, 2015.

Ginway, M. Elizabeth. *Brazilian Science Fiction: Cultural Myths and Nationhood in the Land of the Future.* Lewisberg, Pa.: Bucknell University Press, 2004.

———, and J. Andrew Brown, eds. *Latin American Science Fiction: Theory and Practice.* New York: Palgrave, 2012.

Gorodischer, Angélica. *Kalpa Imperial: The Greatest Empire That Never Was.* Trans. Ursula K. Le Guin. Northampton, Mass.: Small Beer Press, 2003.

———. *Las repúblicas* [The republics]. Buenos Aires: De la Flor, 1991.

———. *Trafalgar.* Trans. Amalia Gladhart. Northampton, Mass.: Small Beer Press, 2013.

Hartmann, Ivor W., ed. *AfroSF: Science Fiction by African Writers.* N.p.: Story Time, 2012.

———, ed. *AfroSFv2.* N.p.: Story Time, 2015.

Hopkinson, Nalo, ed. *Whispers from the Cotton Tree Root: Caribbean Fabulist Fiction.* Montpelier, Vt.: Invisible Cities Press, 2000.

———, and Uppinder Mehan, eds. *So Long Been Dreaming: Postcolonial Science Fiction and Fantasy.* Vancouver: Arsenal Pulp Press, 2004.

Howell, Yvonne, and Anne O. Fisher, eds. *Red Star Tales: A Century of Russian and Soviet Science Fiction.* Montpelier, Vt.: RIS Publications, 2015.

Komatsu, Sakyo. *Virus: The Day of Resurrection* [Fukkatsu no Hi; 1964]. Trans. Daniel Huddleston. San Francisco: Haikasoru, 2012.

"Japanese Science Fiction." Special issue, *Science Fiction Studies* 29.3 (November 2002).

Langer, Jessica. *Postcolonialism and Science Fiction.* New York: Palgrave, 2011.

Le Guin, Ursula K. *The Word for World Is Forest.* 1972; reprint, New York: Berkley Books, 1976.

Levy, Michael. "Science Fiction in Australia." *Science Fiction Studies* 27.1 (March 2000): 124–31.

Liu Cixin. *The Dark Forest.* Trans. Joel Martinsen. New York: Tor, 2015.

———. *Death's End.* Trans. Ken Liu. New York: Tor, 2016.

———. *The Three-Body Problem.* Trans. Ken Liu. New York: Tor, 2014.

McKitterick, Christopher, ed. "International Science Fiction." Special issue, *World Literature Today* 84.3 (May/June 2010).

Melville, Herman. *Moby-Dick; or, The Whale.* New York: Harper and Brothers, 1851.

Murphy, Patrick D., and Dingbo Wu, eds. *Science Fiction from China.* New York: Praeger, 1989.

Novakova, Julia, ed. *Dreams from Beyond: Anthology of Czech Speculative Fiction.* 2016; accessed July 26, 2017. https://www.julienovakova.com/dreams-from-beyond/.

"On Global Science Fiction, Part 1." Special issue, *Science Fiction Studies* 26.3 (November 1999).

"On Latin American SF." Special issue, *Science Fiction Studies* 34.3 (November 2007).

Rottensteiner, Franz. "Recent Writings on German Science Fiction." *Science Fiction Studies* 28.2 (July 2001): 284–90.

———. "SF in Germany: A Short Survey." *Science Fiction Studies* 27.1 (March 2000): 118–23.

Santoro Domingo, Pablo. "Science Fiction in Spain: A Sociological Perspective." *Science Fiction Studies* 33.2 (July 2006), 313–31.

Sinisalo, Johanna. *The Core of the Sun*. Trans. Lola Rogers. New York: Black Cat, 2016.

Smyrniw, Walter. *Ukrainian Science Fiction: Historical and Thematic Perspectives*. Bern: Peter Lang, 2013.

Song, Mingwei, ed. "Chinese Science Fiction: Late Qing and the Contemporary." Special issue, *Renditions* 77/78 (November 2012).

Star Trek II: The Wrath of Khan. Dir. Nicholas Meyer. United States: Paramount, 1982.

Strugatsky, Arkady, and Boris Strugatsky. *Noon: 22nd Century* [Polden' XXII veka]. Trans. P. L. McGuire. New York: Macmillan, 1978.

———. *Snail on the Slope* [Ulitka na sklone]. Trans. A. Meyers. London: Bantam Books, 1980.

———. "Tale of the Troika" [Skazka o troike; 1967]. In *Roadside Picnic / Tale of the Troika*. Trans. Antonia Bouis. New York: MacMillan, 1977. 147–244.

Tatsumi Takayuki, Jina Kim, and Zhang Zhen, eds. "Three Asias: Japan, S. Korea, China." Special issue of *Paradoxa* 22 (2010).

Vandermeer, Ann, and Jeff VanderMeer. *The New Weird*. San Francisco: Tachyon Publications, 2008.

Virus. Dir. Kinji Fukasaku. Japan: Kadokawa, 1980.

Vonnegut, Kurt. *Cat's Cradle*. New York: Holt, Rinehart and Winston, 1963.

Wolheim, Donald. Introduction to *Science Fiction: What It's All About*, by Sam J. Lundwall. New York: Ace Books, 1971. 7–11.

Zola, Émile. *La Curée* [The kill]. Paris: Charpentier, 1872.

———. *Le ventre de Paris* [The belly of Paris]. Paris: Charpentier, 1873.

Živković, Zoran. "Writing in Languages Other Than English." *Europa SF*, April 24, 2014. Accessed July 26, 2017. http://scifiportal.eu/writing-in-languages-other-than-english-zoran-zivkovic/#comment-119095.

Lingua Cosmica

Daína Chaviano's Science-Fiction Oeuvre

Fables of an Extraterrestrial Grandmother

JUAN CARLOS TOLEDANO REDONDO

"On the 3rd of March of 1999 I discovered that Gabriel, after announcing to Mary that she was the chosen one, made love with her and left her pregnant with a baby that she would call Jesus, and who would become, in Gabriel's words, 'great because his blood will contain the spirit of the gods.'"[1] This is the way Daína Chaviano recounts the ancient gospel narrative in her short story "La anunciación" (The annunciation), published in 1983 in the collection *Amoroso planeta* (Loving planet). This is Chaviano's only science-fiction (sf) story translated into English, and one of the most widely read and studied, together with the collection *Los mundos que amo* (The worlds I love; 1980) and her only sf novel, *Fábulas de una abuela extraterrestre* (Fables of an extraterrestrial grandmother; 1988, henceforth *Fables*). Yolanda Molina-Gavilán identifies in "The Annunciation" a "recurrent characteristic of Spanish [sf] literary production" that distorts religious stories and reorganizes them in a way that makes the modern reader question their veracity and recategorizes them as new historical myths.[2]

The use of fantasy and sf[3] to question certain general established prejudices, with special focus on Cuba's cultural prejudices, is also a recurrent characteristic in Chaviano's stories. To achieve this, she creates plots and characters that move away from what is called "hard sf." In fact, she is considered, together with Chely Lima and Alberto Serret, the frontrunner of the Cuban new wave of the 1980s, a wave that did not appear without controversy on the island. A few authors and critics called this style in Cuba "ciencia ficción rosada" (pink science fiction),[4] diminishing it by equating it to a "feminized" version of a putative "pure sf." However, Chaviano has achieved great prestige in Cuba and overseas with her work. I argue in this essay that it is precisely for that reason—the use of a style that broke with the tenets of both hard and social-realist sf—that her work was so well received in Cuba and abroad in the 1980s and 1990s. Her work is distinctive because most of it reflects a consistent view or concept of the universe, or *cosmovision*, with recurrent leitmotifs. I am aware of the difficulty of proving such a premise, but I intend to show that by looking at the time and place in which Chaviano's work is published, and the literary context of sf/f production in Cuba, it is possible to connect her style to her success.

Daína Chaviano was born in Havana in 1957, four years before Fidel Castro announced that the Cuban revolution was a socialist one. Therefore, she grew up in a society marked by the utopian project of creating what came to be known as "el hombre nuevo," the new man—which, needless to say, also meant a new woman. This "new man" represented a sort of dedicated superman who was always fighting, working, writing, and thinking in the name of socialist principles.[5] Unavoidably, a new kind of human required a new kind of cultural production, one aligned with the tenets of the new socialist man. Consequently, a kind of novel also appeared that was called "new" (the so-called novel of the revolution);[6] however, this novel did not really change the principles of the bourgeois novel. It was still a literary artifact written in prose that narrated the story of one or several people who try to resolve a given conflict. The aesthetic changes introduced in Cuba were neither radical nor permanent enough to accept today that a truly new novel was even created.

It was not until 1971, with the proclamation of socialist realism as the main cultural pattern during the First National Conference on Education and Culture, that the new revolutionary principles were debated and imported from the Soviet Union. In 1971, Chaviano was already a teenager, so we can infer that her future craft would be affected by the decisions made by the cultural authorities in that year. Perhaps the most relevant consequence of the new literary norms was the suspension of publication of local sf on the island until 1978 and the substitution of that local production by translated texts from the Soviet Union and the Communist bloc.[7] It was Chaviano who in 1988 published a seminal study of sf in Cuba from the 1960s to the 1980s, which showed that while there were only twelve sf books published between 1964 and 1977—most of them in the 1960s, and none between 1971 and 1977—from 1978 to 1988 the number increased to forty-one titles published.[8] The most poignant revelation of her study is the terrible consequences that the interaction between authoritarian power and cultural production had on the island, bringing the local production of sf/f to a sudden halt after the 1971 conference.

Consequently, by the time Chaviano started writing, her local sf/f influences were related to the Communist sphere, published in Cuba by Soviet-run publishers. She also had access to the very few English-language sf authors allowed in Cuba, such as Ray Bradbury, Frederic Pohl, and C. M. Kornbluth, as well as fantasy writers like C. S. Lewis and J. R. R. Tolkien (she wrote the prologue to the 1985 Cuban edition of *The Hobbit*). In addition, Chaviano studied English philology, which gave her direct access to Saxon and Celtic legends, mythology, and the Western classics, from Shakespeare to Cervantes, and from Alejo Carpentier to Anaïs Nin.[9] Although it is difficult to assess the work of any writer based on their influences, writers are readers first, and their exposure to a cultural context gives us clues about their work. In the case of Chaviano, it is clear how fantasy, mythology, and culture from different ancient traditions inspired some of her work, such as the short stories "Niobe" (which adapts Niobe's classical story to an intergalactic encounter) and "Getsemaní" (Gethsemane, as in the biblical garden), both in *Loving Planet*; and *Fables* (where the Arthurian wizard Merlin is one of the main characters). However relevant these influences may be, it is not my intention to assert direct links between authors, traditions, and stories to justify Chaviano's work, but rather to offer an overview of her context as a reader. Among those readings is also the Cuban sf production, particularly works produced in Havana. Most Cuban authors knew each other, read each other's writing, and even published and worked together to have their literary niche be recognized.

In addition, they all had read the local authors of the 1960s who constituted a sort of Cuban "founding fathers of the genre" group: Miguel Collazo (*El libro fantástico de Oaj* [The fantastic book of Oaj; 1966] and *El viaje* [The journey; 1968]); Oscar Hurtado (*La ciudad muerta de Korad* [The dead city of Korad; 1965] and *Los papeles de Valencia el Mudo* [The papers of Valencia the Mute; posthumous and edited by Chaviano in 1982]); and Ángel Arango (*¿A dónde van los cefalomos?* [Where do the cephalhomes go?; 1964]; *The Black Planet* [El planeta negro; 1966]; *Robotomaquia* [Robotomachy; 1967]). Although only Arango published actively throughout the 1980s and 1990s,[10] it was Hurtado who really defined Chaviano's path into sf. In a 2013 interview, Chaviano called Hurtado "vital for the development of the genre in Cuba"[11] due to his writings about UFOs and alternative science and his contribution to marginal genres by editing his own collections or by creating the detective and sf/f collection *Dragón* (Dragon). Through his work, explains Chaviano, "Hurtado fostered a curious mind and a desire to break away from the scientific orthodoxy imposed by dialectical materialism. He taught us how to challenge the official order established within a closed science that excluded certain ideas. And those are some of the parameters that stimulate and push any science fiction author."[12]

Unfortunately, Hurtado died in 1977, and so his legacy was intense but brief. This intensity planted the seed of a renewed taste for sf/f in Cuba, and by the end of the 1970s another generation, not much older than Chaviano's, was equally active. This group was formed by an eclectic collective of authors and editors, including Néstor V. Román, Gerardo Chávez Espínola, Ileana Vicente, Alejandro Madruga, and Bruno Henríquez, as well as an active fandom. Henríquez in particular became a key figure when in 1978 he was recognized with a consolation award (*mención* in Spanish) for the nationally prestigious David Award for his collection *Aventura en el laboratorio* (Adventure in the laboratory). An impossible-to-prove story (an sf local legend?) claims that Henríquez's collection was "not allowed" to win the David for reasons of genre—sf was not considered good enough for a first prize, so it was given a special mention. The controversy that such a decision produced became a catalyst for the creation of an exclusive David contest for sf in 1979, whose first prize was awarded to Chaviano's collection *The Worlds I Love*, initiating her early publishing career.

The general David Award for young, unpublished writers was presented by the official Hermanos Saiz Association and was rather prestigious in Cuba before 1979. The specific David for sf followed the same pattern as the general award: official public recognition, as well as publication and distribution in print of the first-prize winner. Over the years, though, these publications became infrequent due to economic reasons. Even so, for a young writer of a traditionally marginal genre like sf, the David was an incredible opportunity to start a literary career on solid ground. *The Worlds I Love* was so well received that it soon was adapted to radio and television scripts, and even a photo-romance in 1982. Chaviano became a popular figure hosting radio and television programs related to sf/f. She soon published the novel, as well as a collection of short stories, *Loving Planet*; one of novellas, *Historias de hadas para adultos* (Fairy tales for adults; 1986); and one of mini-stories, *El abrevadero de los dinosaurios* (The dinosaurs' watering hole; 1990). She also won the Premio Nacional de Literatura Infantil y Juvenil La Edad de Oro (National Prize for Children's and Young Adults' Literature "The Golden Age") in 1989 with *Un país de dragones* (A country of dragons), a collection that was first published in Caracas in 1994.[13] Her only sf novel, *Fables*, was published in 1988 in Cuba.

Chaviano's work was created during a time in which sf regained strength in Cuba and created the right atmosphere for some of the best known Cuban sf writers. Among the David awardees of the 1980s are authors such as the late Agustín de Rojas and José Miguel Sánchez (known today as Yoss).[14] Chaviano and Yoss are perhaps the most influential names in two clear tendencies: Yoss was influenced by cyberpunk during the Cuban Special Period of the 1990s, and Chaviano by the British and American New Waves. Chaviano wrote surrounded by a group of authors who understood the generic limits of sf in a more flexible way: Gina Picart, Antonio Orlando Rodríguez, and the tandem team of Chely Lima and Alberto Serret, among a few others. This group of authors worked together, sometimes published together, and was responsible for *Nova*, the first, albeit short-lived, magazine dedicated to sf/f in Cuba. Their goal was also to distance themselves from certain sf production that was considered poorly written propaganda.[15] The new style had been publicly defended by Chaviano even before she left Cuba.[16]

That a young Cuban writer would follow this option in the 1980s should not surprise anyone, since Chaviano's new-wave style is not unusual within sf written in Spanish. Opening the boundaries between sf and fantasy and mixing them with mainstream topics and styles are techniques also present in other famous women writers who should not be confined to a single generic label, such as the Argentines Angélica Gorodischer and Silvina Ocampo, or the Spaniard Eliá Barceló—who, also identified as an sf writer, confessed in an interview that "of the 20 novels that I have published so far, only three are sf, but I love the genre."[17] We could also include other authors in this list, heavyweights like Jorge Luis Borges and Bioy Casares, who wrote many stories that are recognized as sf, whose ideas transgress generic limits, and whose writings offer good examples of a style that is well represented in Hispanic works throughout the twentieth century. Chaviano's generic (dis)continuity is thus not only part of a larger trend in Spanish sf/f production throughout the twentieth century but also one of the reasons for her success as a genre writer.

In addition, Chaviano's production of sf happened in the 1980s, a decade of relative prosperity in Cuba, which was economically supported by the USSR, and of a relative consolidation of sf. Besides the David Award, other venues supported the genre in different ways, such as the annual sf contest of the magazine *Juventud rebelde* (Rebel youth), the space that the journal *Unión* (Union) dedicated to sf on several occasions, the publishing work of small presses like *Dragón* (Dragon) and *Gente Nueva* (New people), and occasionally even the powerhouse *Letras cubanas* (Cuban letters). By the end of the decade, sf/f was more visible and respected in Cuba—mostly in Havana, but also in Santa Clara and Santiago. While the literary authorities allowed the existence of workshops dedicated to sf, like the Oscar Hurtado, created and directed by Chaviano, or the Julio Verne, authors and fandom put their efforts into small conferences. The first one took place in the eastern city of Guantánamo in 1989 and was followed by others in Havana in the 1990s that achieved international status, after Chaviano had moved to Miami. The production of sf/f in the 1980s left a very positive legacy in Cuba.[18]

The Special Period would be instrumental in the changes that occurred during the 1990s. Perhaps the most dramatic factor of change was the emigration of many authors, among them Chaviano. When she left, she was not able to take with her all of her writings. After she finally established her home in Miami, she released her only book of poems, *Confesiones eróticas y otros hechizos* (Erotic confessions and other spells), in 1994. When Chaviano started to publish narrative again, her novels were more mainstream, with topics focused on contemporary Cuba and written in a more realistic style, although not without some dose of fantasy. This new stage in her career began with *El hombre, la hembra y el hambre* (Man, woman, and hunger; 1998), a novel that was awarded first prize in the Azorín contest in Alicante, Spain, in 1998.

Despite this award, which brought Chaviano international recognition in mainstream letters for her novel and set the stage for her *La Habana oculta* (The occult side of Havana) saga, which also included *Casa de juegos* (Playhouse; 1999), *Gata encerrada* (Caged cat; 2001), and *La isla de los amores infinitos* (The island of infinite loves; 2006), we cannot forget that Chaviano was already internationally recognized before she left the island, thanks to her sf/f production. Not only was her work followed in Cuba, but outside of the island as well. Her first international recognition was the Anna Seghers Award, given for *Fables* by the Academy of Arts in Berlin in 1990, the same year she left Cuba. The same novel gained her the Premio Goliardos Internacional (International Goliardos Prize) for fantasy in Mexico in 2003. Her reputation as a genre writer opened the door for her work to appear in groundbreaking publications in English, such as the collection *Cosmos Latinos* in 2003, *Latin American Science Fiction Writers: An A-to-Z Guide* in 2004, and in an academic monograph and a doctoral thesis in the United States in 2002 by Yolanda Molina-Gavilán and Juan C. Toledano Redondo, respectively. Even before that, the Colombian writer and critic Antonio Mora Vélez had written a seminal article about *Fables* in 1989 that remains one of the best essays on Chaviano. However, Chaviano herself asked Mora Vélez not to publish it due to the political implications that his analyses and conclusions could have for her; Mora Vélez waited to publish the article until 1997. Finally, Chaviano was the first sf/f writer in Spanish to be Guest of Honor at the International Conference for the Fantastic in the Arts at their twenty-fifth conference in Fort Lauderdale, Florida, in 2004—a conference of the most important association of academic studies of sf/f in the United States, the International Association for the Fantastic in the Arts.

It is clear that the Azorín Award for *Man, Woman, and Hunger* is no more than the logical progression of an excellent and already internationally recognized writer, who had begun to explore new literary styles. And even if Chaviano has not published any new sf/f work since 1990, her work has continued to garner increasing international attention, as most of it has now been published outside of Cuba. In fact, except for *Loving Planet*, all of her literary works published before 1990 have appeared with some of the most prestigious publishers in Spanish (Alfaguara, Espasa, Océano, Minotauro), which allows us to conclude that her sf/f work is still widely read and well known.

The Continuum of Chaviano's Career

Chaviano's literary career is a continuum: we should not see it as divided by two clear stages, marked by her emigration to the United States, but rather as a progression that builds from an author deeply involved with sf beginning with 1979's *The Worlds I Love*—one who has never abandoned her style, ideas, and cosmovision. These will be key to understanding her success in the 1980s and 1990s within Cuba and throughout the world of Hispanic letters. While Robin McAllister sees in *The Worlds I Love* "many anticipations of Chaviano's classic science fiction novel *Fables of an Extraterrestrial Grandmother*,"[19] Mora Vélez claims in his analysis of *Fables* that Chaviano "has collected in this work . . . the aesthetic and philosophical principles in which she believes, and that have appeared dispersed in her previous stories."[20]

Chaviano's cosmovision is always present, and many leitmotifs are recurrent throughout her works from 1979 to 1990. Although she has an array of ideas that could be studied in this essay, I will focus only on those that reappear in most stories. Her work tells us about a universe that is understood as an interconnected totality, where all parts relate to other parts, with infinite possibilities and realities that may be similar to our own dreams and imagined worlds. Among her literary leitmotifs we find the modernization of ancient myths, the empowerment of young women and marginal beings as main characters and protagonists, and her subtle political discourse against Cuban immobilism and imposition of official discourses regarding science and openness to the outside world. All of this is written in a style that is not strictly sf or fantasy, but rather a blend of sf and fantasy.

In *Loving Planet*, we find stories with links to ancient mythology, like "Niobe," or to Christian gospels, likes "Gethsemane" and "The Annunciation," but in her first work, *The Worlds I Love*, we already see a modernization of mythology—in this case pre-Columbian—when the main character of the story that gives title to the collection travels with some aliens to the Bolivian ruins of Tiahuanaco. In addition to this modernization of well-known myths, we can also find another common element in Chaviano's production. The main character in *The Worlds I Love* is or becomes a writer by telling the story or leaving it written for future generations, just as someone once did with our present myths and legends. This recurrent idea is not only ideological (the people—anyone, not the government—control discourse) but also personal, since the author identifies with her characters' actions and experiences: Chaviano confesses that "for that reason, many magical, fantastic, mythical, or science-fiction episodes that appear in my novels are completely autobiographical."[21] In fact, when Chaviano published a new edition of *The Worlds I Love* in 2004, she added a note that explains that the story is nothing more than "the epilogue of a personal experience."[22]

The publication of *Fairy Tales for Adults* in 1986, two years before her sf/f master work, *Fables*, shows a mature writer who is able to go beyond the short-story format without abandoning her original cosmovision and literary leitmotifs. In some ways, it is a precursor of *Fables*. Of the three novellas in the collection, *La granja* (The barn), *La dama y el ciervo* (The lady and the deer), and *Un hada en el umbral de la Tierra* (A fairy at the earth's doorstep), the first two follow Chaviano's taste for mixing Christian and classical myths, together with alien intervention in human affairs. This occurs mostly in *The Lady and the Deer*, where Chaviano rewrites the biblical story of Adam and Eve and includes a deer and a woman companion, figures that appear in Celtic and Greek mythology. This story fits in with Chaviano's generic mixing, making the reader believe at the end that Vrena (Eva) and all the other characters are aliens who have been exiled on Earth and have created here a new civilization. The idea of a story that makes extraterrestrial aliens the origin of humanity, the story of which has been transformed into myth and legend, is recurrent in sf.[23] Chaviano's ability to mix sf and fantasy is quite sophisticated, and the reader only discovers after the text has been half read that some of the ideas and elements first presented as fantasy can also be explained scientifically. For instance, Vrena consults an oracle, called Apollo. However, by the end of the story, the oracle is presented in the following terms: "Yes, I activated the cyberbrain."[24] Apollo moves from a mythological oracle to a cybernetic one, making the reading generically ambivalent.

As a precursor to *Fables*, in *The Lady and the Deer* there are also other recurrent elements in Chaviano's craft: there is a grandmother,[25] and there is a debate between good and evil, or light and darkness. The main characters are presented as the "master of evil and the Shadow World,"[26] in the case of Adante; and "the dame of the Kingdom of Good,"[27] in the case of Vrena. However, as the story advances, we understand that Vrena and Adante are lovers and not real enemies. We encounter elements and tropes that are related to different traditions of the fantastic genre: there are vampires, winged horses, griffins, fairies, elves, a cabin in the middle of the forest, a river, a spinning wheel. And finally, there is *the* law,[28] a universal, supra-law that all beings on Earth must follow, no matter how magical they are. Everyone is forced to follow this law,[29] and everyone needs to obey the rules imposed by "those-we-cannot-mention."[30] These beings are Chaviano's version of God, who imposed the law on Adam and Eve as a sort of punishment for their unexplained scientific experiments that killed millions.[31] As a final consequence, in *The Lady and the Deer* the lovers face a choice between rebellion and certain death and disappearance, or acceptance of the law and a chance to become a foundational myth: "It will be beautiful to help build this planet's myths."[32] This refers, clearly, to a Christian myth, that of the expulsion from Eden, as we can confirm with Adante and Vrena's final dialogue: "'And you?'—he asked—'Would you like to become a symbol of bravery . . . or perhaps a woman who took a forbidden fruit, to then take her lover and species to their destruction?'—'Men will make us according to their image and likeness.'"[33]

As with "Niobe" or "The Annunciation," Chaviano transforms ancient myths and renews them, in this case by giving a more science-fictional explanation to those elements in the original myth that we cannot understand with logic. The merging of sf with mythology, legendary stories, and fairy tales allows Chaviano to break with generic rigidity and at the same time renew well-worn genres. Above all, it makes her writing innovative and more attractive to sf, fantasy, and even mainstream readers.

Chaviano's use of legends is also exemplified in the novella *The Barn*, where there is an early use of the sword-and-sorcery subgenre that will again be key in *Fables*. More removed from sf, *The Barn* functions as a literary archive of Arthurian elements such as characters like Merlín, Arthur, and Morgana. This story, which occurs in Galicia, Spain—a land of Celtic traditions and of Chaviano's ancestors that will reappear later in her novel *The Island of Infinite Loves*—is summarized with the phrase, "Because myths can only survive renewing their essence."[34] And that is exactly what the story does by situating these literary characters in a modern context.

Finally, if *The Lady and the Deer* follows a classic fantasy pattern that later is mixed with sf, the third and longest novella in *Fairy Tales for Adults*, *A Fairy at the Earth's Doorstep*, follows a more classically understood sf pattern that scientifically justifies the existence of fairies. These two stories mirror each other: the former ends by talking about cybernetics and aliens, presenting fantasy more like sf; while the latter is the story of space travelers, isolated on another planet, who encounter alien beings that resemble the fairies of *Peter Pan*. Both stories represent Chaviano's cosmovision of a universe that holds infinite possibilities. In *A Fairy at the Earth's Doorstep*, this idea is made explicit when Tomy, the ten-year-old main character, plays a recording made by his (supposedly) late father that defends his own goal of finding a fairy on the frozen planet Garnys who can bring his father back: "The universe is bigger than our imagination, because the latter is included in the former, and only if it exists can our imagination exist. Hence, the universe contains all that has been and that will be imagined."[35] Consequently, finding fairies on another planet is possible, even logical, and Chaviano's cosmovision thus does not exclude fairies or any other fantastic being from a sf story. Two years later, in *Fables*, the author will make this element the key argument of the plot. As we approach the end of the novel, Ana, one of the main characters, tells her friend that "fantasy is part of reality because it arises from it."[36] This idea will allow Ana herself, a Cuban teenager, to write about two other worlds and realities and simultaneously be part of them; that is, Ana creates realities in her imagination and lives them as real at the same time. And this is plausible because they exist within the infinite realm of possibilities of the universe.

Chaviano acknowledges her intention to use a modern theory that contradicts official scientific discourse: "In one way or another, I was able to violate the official scientific discourse rules of what was considered 'ideologically correct.' Those who read *Fábulas* . . . will notice this."[37] In fact, Chaviano's cosmovision resounds well within modern scientific discourse—more specifically, within quantum mechanics. In his popular bestseller *The Elegant Universe*, the theoretical physicist and string theorist Brian Greene writes about the theory of "the multiverse," affirming that "if we let our imagination run free, even the laws themselves can drastically differ from universe to universe. The range of possibilities is endless."[38] Chaviano is not alone in believing that literature can be used to experience other realities or the totality of the universe. In an interview, Angélica Gorodischer states, "And then you feel the great revelation: the big bang and family relations are equivalent. A monastery is the universe. An excursion to *Funes* . . . is an intergalactic trip, and a neighborhood is an empire more impressive than *Stars Wars*. All can be invented when you write, and nothing is invented. In some unknown place resides both, the memory of those things that never happened, and the possibility of what is considered impossible."[39] Chaviano herself acknowledges that quantum mechanics was part of her understanding of her literary world back in Cuba,[40] and, accordingly, she redefined the sf/f genres as unique: "And so, they have begun a new stage—or perhaps a new genre—that I would dare name a *cosmogonic fantasy* or *cosmo-fantasy*."[41] The novellas in *Fairy Tales for Adults* show not only Chaviano's literary progression, but also a sort of craft training that will allow her to write and develop the plot of such a complex novel as *Fables*, where different universes collide and mix.

Chaviano's sf Masterpiece

When in 1988 Chaviano published *Fables of an Extraterrestrial Grandmother* in the prestigious Editorial Letras Cubanas, she already was a famous figure in Cuba and had shown a clear literary path and style, which allowed Antonio Mora Vélez to write, "With this novel [Chaviano] poetically redescribed—symbols, images, and language—the reality of her country; she addresses science fiction in a way specifically Latin American, and places herself at the forefront of this fascinating literary form of our America."[42] No one who had followed her career doubted that this novel was sf, even if the title included the word "fables," or if the cover of one edition featured an image of a crystal ball. Following the core of her cosmovision, Chaviano wrote a novel in which science, magic, and (im)possible worlds collide and march together. In *Fables*, we witness a world that creates and modernizes myths and legends from the Zhife to Merlin, one whose main characters are either young or elderly people, humans or "monsters," depending on the perspective. This is a novel narrated by a young human who lives the plot she is creating as she writes the novel, traveling through three different parallel universes with her mind. In *Fables*, humans and aliens share a common universe and a common sense of humanity, even if some are blue, others are winged little beings with three eyes and mouths, and others are sylphs. There is also a fight between good and evil and a wonderful allegory of the Cuban authorities' inability to open up their country to the world and even to their own society.

The critical reception of the novel could have been highly problematic for Chaviano if articles and opinions such as Mora Vélez's had been published before she left Cuba. The use of an allegorical universe, with a plot that seems detached from real sociopolitical events, allowed the novel to be published, distributed, and sold in Cuba without suspicion. I also suspect that the genres used helped the novel avoid any controversy. Despite the relevance of sf/f in Cuba in comparison with other countries, I believe that the Cuban censors and authorities did not pay enough attention to their allegorical possibilities.

I do not perceive it as difficult to see what Mora Vélez analyzed in *Fables* if one knows the Cuba of the 1980s.[43] I also believe that Chaviano's readers at the time—fans or new ones—were able to understand and follow the plot and its allegories thanks to the use of new wave, fantasy, and the soft sf style used, since these make the need for scientific or technological knowledge less relevant. For instance, the twin brothers, Tiruel and Miruel, who are 308- and 299-year-old magical teenagers, describe to Arlena how they acquired their powers when their father took them to a "Center of Magic,"[44] narrating a process of irradiation that includes ambiguous sentences such as "threads that were coming out of that machine . . . stuck to Miruel's hair like golden spider webs. . . . [His father] approached the machine and his fingers hovered over the stars. . . . The colors of the lights changed."[45] Even when this explanation denotes that the twins are unaware of what we consider electricity, radiation, electrodes, and computers, the reader can easily understand the references. Using this language to talk about hard science, Chaviano allows any reader to understand the plot, even if they miss the allegories and references. In addition, the novel offers many recurrent elements of Chaviano's cosmovision and leitmotifs that make it easy for her fans to understand her ideas. The combination of all these elements certainly widened the number of readers of her novel and facilitated its popularity. With descriptions like these, Chaviano, as we have seen before in other stories, breaks with the generic conventions attached to sf and fantasy that function to separate them, mixing them with enough ambiguity to make it impossible to see them as distinct.

These and other innovations that I will discuss below were not welcome during the 1980s in Cuba. Chaviano herself states that "all this, which might seem the most innocent thing in the world, was a pretty bold issue for those who lived on the island because of the possible political consequences."[46] Combined with this merging of genres, Chaviano's novel also dared to enter into two other key debates, both related to her notion that separations are mostly artificial and harmful: the traditional Western distinction between science and magic, and her desire for a universe without borders.

In order to investigate these two topics, I first need to describe the plot in more detail, because *Fables* is not only a long novel, with 413 pages in its first edition, but also a complex one. The plot moves between three different worlds and dimensions: Rybel, Faidir, and Earth. In Rybel live the characters Arlena, the aforementioned magical twins, and Soio (a local name given to Merlinus). Faidir is the world of origin of the Zhife, but they share the world with another group of humanoids called the Jumene. Finally, Ana lives in Havana. These characters and peoples are connected in many ways. For instance,

Soio, like Ana, is from Earth, but he disappeared from Earth during Arthurian times and reappeared in Rybel, where he has been trapped—just like Arlena, who is a Jumene, but was transported from Faidir to Rybel unexpectedly and cannot return. The Jumene, a race of blue-skinned humanoids, are space travelers who were doing research in Faidir. Their spaceship was destroyed four hundred years ago, and they have been trying to communicate with the Zhife ever since. However, the Zhife believe the Jumene to be monsters who want to destroy them, and flee each time they feel their presence. The legendary Zhife Semur, in order to protect his people from the Jumene, closed and sealed the interdimensional portals that could allow all these characters to travel back to where they want to go. Finally, Ana is a teenager, attending high school in Cuba. She loves to write, and she is creating a novel about an alien grandmother who narrates to her grandchild Ijje the story of a girl called Arlena. Occasionally, the grandmother also tells the story of another alien called Ana. In the end Ana discovers, thanks to Soio/Merlinus, that Ijje, Arlena, and herself are real, live in different realities, and are destined to work together and open the sealed portals to reestablish peace in the universe. The connection between Ana and Arlena is so intense that even their names are similar (*A-rle-na*). Soio/Merlinus reveals this to us: "both are the same. One person . . . in two different universes . . . separated by the cells of parallel worlds. . . . Ana and Arlena are . . . same/different: two similar creatures in parallel worlds."[47] However, the addition of Ijje, a humanoid who looks more like a monstrous bird than a human (blue or not), makes reason and human sentiment, rather than image, universal.

This complex puzzle moves back and forth among the different worlds, connecting the plot slowly, but in no way boringly. *Fables* reads like a good YA novel, where a sword-and-sorcery world with a courtesan love story, high priests, and magic mixes with a modern Cuba and teen tensions. But the novel's allegorical readings reveal political and ideological elements that were not part of YA literature of the 1980s. The creation of three different worlds/realities, for instance, allows Chaviano to experiment with and rewrite the scientific laws of the universe as we know it. She alerts us from the beginning by citing the classical anthropological work *The Golden Bough* by James George Frazer, who writes that "if magic were to become truth and fruitful, it would not be considered magic but rather science."[48] The magical twins of Rybel call the laboratory where they were irradiated a Center of Magic. In addition, Ana believes in the existence of what she calls "genetic memory," a theory that implies that our genes carry traces of memory from the experiences of the past, from our ancestors. As Ana explains to her friend in Havana, "that's to experiment with the memory of the genes and the subconscious. If you let your mind go blank and prepare the conditions, not ten minutes will pass before the images start coming on their own. You will see people and things that have nothing to do with your current life."[49] Again Chaviano uses external sources to support her theory; and, as in the case of Frazer, this source is quoted before the novel formally begins. In this case it is by the Soviet author Vladímir Mézentsev, who wrote *Enciclopedia de las maravillas* (Encyclopedia of wonders; 1981), where he states, "It is possible that this [intuition] is the top rung of human thought, the alloy of all knowledge obtained by us in life . . . all the genetic information transmitted to the brain throughout generations."[50] The idea of genetic memory is well known in biology and psychology, but none of these fields claims that we remember actual events that occurred to other people in other lives and realities via our genes. However, Mézentev's quote is, not accidentally, positioned under Frazer's, implying that perhaps one day this fringe idea may be sanctioned as science.[51]

Like *A Fairy at the Earth's Doorstep*, where Tomy melts ancient ice to reveal the truth of the planet Garnys, Chaviano's proposals melt the established limits of literary genres and human methods of knowledge, revealing the truth that such constructs of difference have hidden over the years. By the time we finish *Fables*, our ideas about the distinctions between sf, fantasy, history, and legends are not as clear-cut as perhaps they were, and our assumptions that science cannot evolve into ideas that earlier were considered nonscientific may also be challenged. Of course, we cannot forget the context of production and publication to understand that Chaviano is fighting dogmatic ideas imposed by certain branches of Cuban sovietism.

If there is continuity between genres and between science and magic, it is easy to understand that Chaviano sees our universe also as a continuous one, and not only as containing different realities that exist separately from one another. Although quantum theory does not assert that the multiverse exists or exists as a continuum, some literary authors like Borges have proposed in their writings that the universe—even God—has the shape of a sphere, a form with no beginning and no end, eternal. In *Fables* Merlinus tells us that "The Sphere was God's shape,"[52] and Ijje dreams of it, but clarifies the concept by removing the religious component: "'*Shit*,' he whispers. '*I have no interest in the religious variant; I want an explanation*,'"[53] and focuses on its properties: "The sphere is the key to mutation: a form without angles: a perfect circle: continuous surface, without beginning or end."[54] This is important because a universe that has the shape of a sphere represents a metaphor for a space with no effective and scientific center either, and with no key elements that hold a better position than others. Rybel, Faidir, and Earth are not situated in a space more prominent one than the other, and consequently, all the characters in *Fables* are equally valuable and key to the entire plot.

To clarify the sphere metaphor, the symbolic aspect of the shape is connected to and explained through the tools that are required to reopen the sealed portals. Those tools are the Espejo (mirror) and the Piedra (stone). The first controls time and the second space: "The Stone and the Mirror symbolize the universe. If you join them together, you will have the key to open the Borders."[55] Again, Chaviano plays with our knowledge of physics. We know that space and time are the key elements physics works with in order to understand the universe, but by calling them Stone and Mirror, the reader is forced to give to these scientific concepts a more poetic and magical feeling. Chaviano again imposes blurry limits on traditional distinctions.

The novel as a whole is also presented as a circle. It ends with three epilogues, dedicated respectively to the three main characters, plus Merlinus, who connects them. The last of these epilogues, Ana's, ends with a return to Faidir: "She has not seen yet the golden bough, freshly detached from a tree, shining with soft luminescence under her desk. If she had known that Faidir was so close she would certainly have tried to find the place in her room through which, on certain nights, the light that still usually illuminates the Red Forest emerges."[56]

Notice that Frazer's golden bough, from the epigraph of the novel, reappears in the final paragraph, making a full circle and including Faidir, the world of the Zhifics imagined by Ana, in her room, under the desk, the symbolic space of creation of the writer. It is perhaps Chaviano's intent to create a *mise in abyme*, since with this ending the novel pretends to be a sphere that holds the universe, or at least the narrated universe. As in Borges's "Tlön, Uqbar, Orbis tertius," the end of *Fables* tries to join the imagined world to the real one, and to make the reader part of both.

Merlinus's epilogue also addresses a different circular issue, since Ana is revealed as a symbolic descendent of the druid, who will act as the future repository of Merlinus's history and the stories we have read about: "I will not waste space telling my own adventures out of this world; a young woman in the future will."[57] But this second epilogue, dedicated to Merlinus, also returns to the leitmotif of the superior alien race that connects us all. When Merlinus is transported back in time and space to Earth, he is mistakenly sent to a pre–homo sapiens stage of evolution instead of to the Arthurian era to which he belonged. However, this Earth is already inhabited by the "primeros brujos" (first sorcerers). The first sorcerers were also present in Rybel and Faidir in ancient times, and we learn about them as we read the novel. In both worlds there is memory of them, but not a recorded history that could confirm their existence. Like the monoliths in *2001: A Space Odyssey*, the first sorcerers have appeared in each world where civilized, intelligent races have developed, before these beings were intelligent enough to understand that they were not gods but aliens, ancient intelligent beings, older than *our* stars perhaps. Although Merlinus calls them gods, again the text reveals a second, more plausible explanation: "Now they only strive to educate the small simian flock crawling under trees from other regions: hairy creatures that hardly show the simple reactions of animals. I have seen them because I have traveled in the bright vehicles."[58] These gods are aliens who travel in spaceships but are first here on Earth educating our simian ancestors. As with Vrena and Adante in *The Lady and the Deer*, or Gabriel and María in "The Annunciation," our myths and religions are explained as mere misunderstandings of a too distant past history that we have not recorded except in legends and myths. Merlinus, a magician, a sorcerer himself, is our link to that prehistoric time. The universe may be mysterious, but it can be known through science, even if we first call it magic.

Opening the portals and the borders and diluting the limits of science and magic as well as those of science fiction and fantasy (and other subgenres) in a pro-Soviet context was, as Chaviano told us, quite daring in the Cuba of the 1980s. As Mora Vélez understood well, Chaviano's novel was a clear allegory of the asphyxiating existence of her society, in a country that had immense travel restrictions for its citizens and followed a strict imitative scientific discourse created by the Soviet Union. Chaviano's style of soft sf was key in the process of editing and publishing the novel without restrictions or censorship, since sf was mostly overlooked by the authorities.[59] However, *Fables* was very popular and sold more than twenty thousand copies, received an international award, and it is still a classic in Spanish-language sf. Chaviano reveals herself as a national and international figure in the sf/f scene written in Spanish.

Far from becoming an obsolete YA novel, I believe that *Fables*, in the present literary atmosphere of bestsellers like *Divergent* and *The Hunger Games*, could be, with some editing, a major success. Perhaps the circle is still open.

Notes

1. Chaviano, "The Annunciation," 203.
2. Molina-Gavilán, *Ciencia ficción*, 85.
3. I will write "sf/f" for "science fiction and fantasy" when mentioned together.
4. "Daína's 'pink style,' which soon enjoyed appreciation from children and especially adolescents, despite its many detractors, was characterized by focusing attention on the poetic aspect of the story as well as the psychology of her characters, in a formal and conceptual search that left aside the aspects of science and technology so appreciated

by the purists of the genre (especially the so-called hard science fiction), who in visceral reaction soon branded her style as a soft and facile way of approaching this genre" (Yoss, "Marcianos," 68). Unless otherwise noted, all translations are by the author.

5. Although there is vast information on the new man, I recommend Ana Serra's *The "New Man" in Cuba: Culture and Identity in the Revolution* (2007), and the brief but magnificent essay *On Socialist Realism* by Abram Tertz, that speaks more on the original Soviet ideas.

6. Seymour Menton wrote perhaps the seminal study, *La narrativa de la revolución cubana* [The narrative of the Cuban Revolution].

7. For a more in-depth description of this process, see Toledano Redondo, "Ángel Arango's Cuban Trilogy."

8. Chaviano "Para una bibliografía," 275.

9. In the novella *La granja* [The barn] from Chaviano's collection *Historias de hadas para adultos* [Fairy Tales for Adults], a library offers the following list of books: "*Celtic Myths and Legends: Poetry and Romance* . . . *The Evolution of the Dragon* . . . *El mito de la Atlántida* . . . *The Sun and the Serpent* . . . *Los invisibles* . . . [. . .] *Aelita* . . . *El Señor de los Anillos* . . . *El último unicornio* . . . *Las tumbas de Atuan* . . . [. . .] *El Hobbit* [. . .] *Fahrenheit 451* [. . .] *Los hechos del del rey Arturo y sus nobles caballeros*" (31).

10. See Toledano Redondo, "Ángel Arango's Cuban Trilogy."

11. Gallardo, "Los dinosaurios," 205.

12. Ibid.

13. Ibid., 199.

14. Many authors that have gone on to forge a literary career were winners or runners-up of the David, such as F. Mond, Rafael Morante, Gina Picart Baluja, and the poet Félix Lizárraga.

15. To know more about this production of poorly written Cuban sf, see Toledano Redondo, "From Socialist Realism."

16. Chaviano, "Veinte años," 128.

17. Játiva, "Eliá Barceló."

18. For instance, several publications appeared on the island. Creativity to overcome the economic debacle had no limits. Two good examples are the magazines *i+Real* and *miNatura*. *i+Real* appeared in 1993, promoted mostly by Bruno Henríquez. This was a magazine that never left the bits of the PCs that carried it and was transferred, with many viruses attached, from machine to machine (although there were very few computers around). Precisely to avoid a situation like that, Ricardo Acevedo Esplugas and Orlando J. Rodríguez created *miNatura* in 1999. *MiNatura* was published on a single sheet of paper printed on both sides, or in two folded pages, making it an eight-page magazine on two eight-by-eleven-inch sheets of paper. The magazine was supported by the *i+Real* group and the José Martí Library, and it had a longer life than any other Cuban sf/f periodical. *MiNatura* still exists, and it has become an international reference among sf magazines: it is today an e-zine put together in Spain, where Acevedo lives, but edited by an international collective that collaborates in the *Asociación Cultural miNatura Soterranía*. As

for conferences, soon the newest generation of authors and fandom claimed their own space and created new journals, magazines, and organizations. The most successful collective, the Taller de Fantasía y CF Espacio Abierto, created the annual colloquia Eventos Teóricos Espacio Abierto and the magazine *Korad*. These magazines can be read for free through Chaviano's webpage (http://blog.dainachaviano.com/).

19. McAllister, "Merlin and Stonehenge," 2.

20. Mora Vélez, "Daína Chaviano," 70.

21. Gallardo, "Los dinosaurios," 201.

22. Chaviano, *Los Mundos*, 99.

23. Mostly in film in the last decades, with samples like the television remake *Battlestar Galactica* (2004–9), the television series *Babylon 5* (1994–98), the 2000 film *Mission to Mars*, and the 2009 film *Knowing*.

24. Chaviano, *La dama y el ciervo* [The lady and the deer], in *Historias de hadas para adultos* [Fairy tales for adults], 96.

25. Ibid., 81.

26. Ibid., 78.

27. Ibid., 88.

28. Ibid., 85.

29. Ibid., 84.

30. Ibid., 86.

31. Ibid., 94.

32. Ibid., 97.

33. Ibid., 98.

34. Chaviano, *La granja* [The barn], in *Historias de hadas para adultos* [Fairy tales for adults], 59.

35. Chaviano, *Un hada en el umbral de la Tierra* [A fairy at the earth's doorstep], in *Historias de hadas para adultos* [Fairy tales for adults], 131.

36. Chaviano, *Fábulas*, 405.

37. Gallardo, "Los dinosaurios," 202.

38. Greene, *Elegant*, 367.

39. Ferrero, "Entrevista," 35.

40. Gallardo, "Los dinosaurios," 202.

41. Chaviano, "Veinte años," 121.

42. Mora Vélez, "Daína Chaviano," 70.

43. Mora Vélez had clearly seen Chaviano's allegory, and had indicated so in his essay: "Abrir las fronteras, no en Rybel sino en Cuba, es reconocer el fracaso del modelo y salir a la búsqueda de soluciones no dogmáticas" [To open the borders, not in Rybel but in Cuba, is to recognize the failure of the model and to go out in search of non-dogmatic solutions] (ibid., 70).

44. Chaviano, *Fables*, 74.

45. Ibid., 75–76.

46. Gallardo, "Los dinosaurios," 202.

47. Chaviano, *Fables*, 201–2.

48. Ibid., 5. While Frazer is a classic from the early twentieth century, other researchers followed him in the anthropological field, the most renowned being Bronislaw Malinowski and his classic *Magic, Science and Religion*.

49. Ibid., 21.

50. Ibid., 5.

51. It is important to stress that Chaviano's novel does not place religion at the same level as magic. While magic is supported as a different way to understand the universe and as a pre-science, religion is clearly attacked and reviled: "Science and magic are mutable, and purporting to act on the environment. Religion clings to its dogmas and shuns change" (ibid., 281). Clinging to a dogma in Communist Cuba is the everyday practice of its authorities. The comparison seems unavoidable.

52. Ibid., 92.

53. Ibid., 292.

54. Ibid.

55. Ibid.

56. Ibid., 413.

57. Ibid., 410.

58. Ibid., 410–11.

59. These allegories are not unique to this novel. In *El abrevadero de los dinosaurios* (The dinosaurs' watering hole), published two years later, we find the following passage: "The humans insisted: it would be a just society, the old taboos would be exiled, there would be new laws. . . . Not feeling like arguing, the dinosaurs accepted in the hope that the humans would eventually convince themselves of the uselessness of the project and of their own narrow-mindedness. The experiment would take place on an island in the Pacific" ("History Lesson" 62). Although in a different ocean, Cuba as an allegory seems rather clear.

Bibliography

Arango, Ángel. *¿Adónde van los cefalomos?* [Where do the cephalhomes go?]. Havana: Ediciones R, 1964.

———. *El planeta negro* [The black planet]. Havana: Granma, 1966.

———. *Robotomaquia* [Robotomachy]. Havana: Ediciones Unión, 1967.

Bell, Andrea L., and Yolanda Molina-Gavilán, eds. *Cosmos Latinos: An Anthology of Science Fiction from Latin America and Spain*. Middletown, Conn.: Wesleyan University Press, 2003.

Chaviano, Daína. "The Annunciation." In *Cosmos Latinos: An Anthology of Science Fiction from Latin America and Spain*. Ed. Andrea L. Bell and Yolanda Molina-Gavilán. Middletown, Conn.: Wesleyan University Press, 2003. 202–7.

———. *El abrevadero de los dinosaurios* [The dinosaurs' watering hole]. Havana: Letras Cubanas. 1990.

———. *Fábulas de una abuela extraterrestre* [Fables of an extraterrestrial grandmother]. Havana: Letras Cubanas, 1988.

————. *Historias de hadas para adultos* [Fairy tales for adults]. Havana: Letras Cubanas, 1986.

————. *Los mundos que amo* [The worlds I love]. Collection. Havana: Ediciones Unión, 1980.

————. *Los mundos que amo* [The worlds I love]. Photo-romance. Havana: Ediciones Gente Nueva, 1982.

————. "Para una bibliografía de la ciencia ficción cubana." [A bibliography of Cuban science fiction] *Letras Cubanas* 6 (1987): 273–78.

————. "Veinte años de ciencia ficción en Cuba." [Twenty years of science fiction in Cuba] *Revista Unión* 1 (1986): 119–30.

Collazo, Miguel. *El libro fantástico de Oaj* [The fantastic book of Oaj]. Havana: Unión Nacional de Escritores y Artistas de Cuba, 1966.

————. *El viaje* [The journey]. Havana: Unión Nacional de Escritores y Artistas de Cuba, 1968.

Ferrero, Adrián. "Entrevista: Angélica Gorodischer." *Hispamérica: Revista de literatura.* 43.127 (2014): 33–39.

Frazer, James George. *The Golden Bough.* 2 vols. New York: Macmillan and Co., 1890.

Gallardo, Emilio. "Los dinosaurios nunca se extinguieron: Entrevista a Daina Chaviano" [The dinosaurs never went extinct: Interview with Daina Chaviano]. *Confluencia: Revista Hispánica de Cultura y Literatura* 2 (2013): 198–208.

Greene, Brian. *The Elegant Universe: Superstrings, Hidden Dimensions, and the Quest for the Ultimate Theory.* New York: W. W. Norton, 1999.

Henríquez, Bruno. *Aventura en el laboratorio* [Adventure in the laboratory]. Santiago: Editorial Oriente, 1987.

Hurtado, Oscar. *La ciudad muerta de Korad* [The dead city of Korad]. Havana: Letras Cubanas, 1983.

————. *Los papeles de Valencia el Mudo* [The papers of Valencia the Mute]. Havana: Letras Cubanas, 1983.

Játiva, Juan M. "Elia Barceló: 'A la gente le gustaría tener poderes especiales y cortar cabezas'" [People would like to have special powers and cut off heads]. *El País, Edición Comunidad Valenciana,* August 25, 2013. Accessed July 27, 2017. http://ccaa.elpais.com/ccaa/2013/08/25/valencia/1377427068_268133.html.

Larson, Glen, and Ronald D. Moore, creators. *Battlestar Galactica.* United States: NBC/Universal Media, 2004–9.

Malinowski, Bronislaw. *Magic, Science and Religion and Other Essays.* Boston: Beacon Press, 1948.

McAllister, Robin. "Daina Chaviano's *Los Mundos Que Amo*: Megalithic Monuments and Extraterrestrial Encounters." *Femspec* 9.2 (2008): 30–36.

————. "Merlin and Stonehenge in Daina Chaviano's *Fables of an Extraterrestrial Grandmother.*" Paper presented at the Twenty-sixth International Conference on the Fantastic in the Arts, March 18 2005, Fort Lauderdale, Fla.

Menton, Seymour. *La narrativa de la revolución cubana* [The narrative of the Cuban Revolution]. Madrid: Editorial Playor, 1978.

Mézentsev, Vladímir. *Enciclopedia de las maravillas* [Encyclopedia of wonders]. Moscow: Mir, 1981.

Mission to Mars. Dir. Brian De Palma. United States: Touchstone Pictures/Spyglass Entertainment, 2000.

Molina-Gavilán, Yolanda. *Ciencia ficción en español: una mitología moderna ante el cambio* [Science fiction in Spanish: A modern mythology for change]. Lewiston, N.Y.: Edwin Mellen, 2002.

Mora Vélez, Antonio. "Daína Chaviano y el humanismo de la ciencia ficción latinoamericana" [Daína Chaviano and humanism in Latin American science fiction]. *La ciencia y el hombre* 25 (Jan.–April 1997): 65–70.

Knowing. Dir. Alex Proyas. United States: Summit Entertainment, 2009.

Serra, Ana. *The "New Man" in Cuba: Culture and Identity in the Revolution*. Gainesville: University Press of Florida, 2007.

Straczynski, J. Michael. *Babylon 5*. United States: Babylonian Productions/Warner Brothers, 1994–98.

Tertz, Abram. *On Socialist Realism*. New York: Pantheon Books, 1960.

Toledano Redondo, Juan Carlos. "Angel Arango's Cuban Trilogy: Rationalism, Revolution and Evolution." *Extrapolation* 43 (2002): 420–38.

———. "From Socialist Realism to Anarchist Capitalism: Cuban Cyberpunk." *Science Fiction Studies* 32.3 (2005): 442–66.

Yoss. "Marcianos en el platanal de Bartolo: un análisis de la historia y perspectivas de la ciencia ficción en Cuba al final del segundo milenio" [Martians in Bartolo's banana plantation: An analysis of the history and perspectives of science fiction in Cuba at the end of the second millenium]. In *La quinta dimensión de la literatura. Reflexiones sobre la ciencia ficción en Cuba y el mundo* [The fifth dimensión of literature: Reflections on science fiction in Cuba and the world]. Havana: Editorial Letras Cubanas, 2012. 61–80.

Jacek Dukaj's Science Fiction as Philosophy

PAWEŁ FRELIK

For the first 150 pages or so, almost a third of its entire volume, Jacek Dukaj's *Inne pieśni* (Other songs; 2003) seems to be a fantasy-inflected alternate history in which Alexander the Great never died at the age of thirty-three and his Hellenic empire gave rise to a separate timeline with recognizable and yet dramatically different geopolitical configurations. It is not until the midpoint in the novel that the plot is revealed, matter-of-factly, to be set in, more or less, the seventeenth century—over two thousand years since the Pythagorean sect started to evoke the "fear, hatred, scorn, jealousy, and something akin to pious awe that men subconsciously accord to What Is Occulted."[1] This temporal placement from the very beginning appears to be confirmed by the level of technological advancement, appropriately at home in what Marshall Berman calls early modernity.[2] The descriptions of aircraft, weapons, and everyday machines manifest many features that seem natural in this alternate timeline and, perhaps inevitably, tend to resonate with the aesthetics of steampunk. On page 147, however, Dukaj drops a narrative bomb when, in one of the signature, seemingly offhanded digressions that almost inadvertently expand his worlds, he notes that "Mazer ben Keshla was the first of terrestrial cartographers to openly use orbital images in drafting his maps."[3] The implication of extraterrestrial travel and satellite technology is completely unexpected and forces readers to dramatically reorient the world construction they have established. And yet this revelation is hardly exceptional in Jacek Dukaj's oeuvre. In fact, it could be said that Dukaj has made a career of such gestures, whose true significance and far-reaching philosophical ripples become apparent only after a while.

Born in 1974, Jacek Dukaj is certainly an almost complete enigma to Anglophone readership of the fantastic. Although his work has been translated into German, Italian, Russian, Czech, Slovak, Macedonian, and Hungarian, the body of his English translations is bracketed by "The Golden Galley," featured in *The Dedalus Book of Polish Fantasy* (1996),[4] hardly any measure of the author's talent, as it was his publishing debut in 1990 and was allegedly written when Dukaj was merely fourteen; and his latest e-book-only novel *Starość aksolotla* (The old axolotl; 2015), which, although beautifully crafted as a cybertext with several additional levels beyond the diegetic text, conceptually does not compare favorably to his greatest novels.[5] Outside narrowly defined literature, only marginally more recognizable internationally is his writing contribution to *The Cathedral* (2002), a short film by Tomasz Baginski, which was nominated in the Animated Short Film category for the 2002 Academy Awards, won the title of Best Animated Short at Siggraph in San Antonio in the same year, and is loosely based on the eponymous short story featured in the collection *W kraju niewiernych* (In the land of the unfaithful; 2000). Between the two English translations, Dukaj has published six novels, four long novellas, and over thirty short stories, many of considerable length. He is a ten-time nominee and six-time winner of the Janusz Zajdel Award, Poland's most important literary prize in the literatures of the fantastic, as well as a recipient of the first edition of the European Union Prize for Literature (2009) and a number of other prizes, awards, and nominations in science fiction and outside the genre. He is, finally, a regular essayist and reviewer, often taking positions dramatically different from his genre colleagues.

Dukaj may well be the single most talented science-fiction writer in Poland and a true heir to Stanisław Lem, whom he, I would propose, overshadows in terms of narrative complexity and intellectual density, however blasphemous this may sound in certain circles.[6] This position is grounded in several qualities of his writing that distinguish him from his contemporaries, both in Poland and, in as much as transnational comparisons make sense, elsewhere. Given the breadth and diversity of its themes, Dukaj's prose lends itself to a number of readings and approaches, but three aspects of his writing make him unique, both domestically and in a broader context: the genre-bending versatility of his fiction; the unusual dynamic between the practice of worldbuilding and narrative plotting; and the degree to which the author uses science fiction to engage a number of political, social, and cultural aspects of Polish society. In all three spheres, he combines cutting-edge artistry with a critical attitude towards the science fiction tradition at large and specific scientific, intellectual, and political discourses.[7] There is, naturally, much in his prose that is recognizable to experienced genre readers—inspirational debts he owes to writers and texts—but the immediate recognition of tropes and figures can be misleading as, more often than not, Dukaj, like Lem, uses the genre as a vehicle for ideas that dramatically extend beyond storytelling. Like William Gibson, China Miéville, and Kim Stanley Robinson, Dukaj often uses genre protocols and formulas as tools for thinking through philosophical and political issues, making science fiction a tool rather than an end.

Genre Bending

When it comes to questions of genre, all of Dukaj's writing, with the lone exception of the political novel *Wroniec* (The crow; 2009), which the writer himself describes as "a black national phantasmagoria masquerading as a children's tale,"[8] can be at first sight classified as science fiction. This denomination is, in fact, far from obvious—after all, such works as *Other Songs* and "Ruch generała" (The iron general; 2000) manifest steampunkish and fantasy-like features. And yet, Dukaj himself is careful to demarcate his writing from various forms of fantasy,[9] insisting on the underlying rational structures of his imagination. If one approaches science fiction not in the traditional terms of genre markers, many of which seem to be missing from a number of his texts, but in light of new genre theory, no other definition fits him better. In "On Defining SF, or Not: Genre Theory, SF, and History," John Rieder suggests that science fiction as a genre is more productively understood as a social construction within which the science-fictionality of a given text is dynamically negotiated by both historically constituted communities of practice and "differentially articulated position" in relation to other texts and bodies of texts.[10] Science fiction is thus "not a set of texts, but rather a way of using texts and drawing relationships between them,"[11] a position that was earlier expressed in Paul Kincaid's "On the Origin of Genre" and Mark Bould and Sherryl Vint's "There Is No Such Thing as Science Fiction." From this perspective, Jacek Dukaj is a quintessential science-fiction writer. At the same time, however, all his major works engage with and confound the genre's traditional protocols and conventions.

The frequency with which Polish writers of the fantastic cross generic boundaries and switch subgenres between subsequent books is probably no higher or lower than in the Anglophone world, but Dukaj's versatility seems to be invested with more consequence as well as inventiveness than most in Poland. Within a spectrum of subgenre conventions, Dukaj operates a broad palette on which certain hues nevertheless persist. A cornerstone of his early fame, first published in Poland's most important sf magazine, *Nowa Fantastyka, Irrehaare* (1995) is a cyberpunk novella set within the titular full-immersion game. At the outset of the story, the readers learn that the players have not been able to log out for months due to an unknown error and that they have to battle a rogue AI that hunts down fighters and infects entire sectors of the gameworld. While some of the story's narrative premises are reminiscent of such later texts as *Matrix* (1999), *eXistenZ* (1999), *Avalon* (2001), and the videogame *Planescape: Torment* (1999), the amnesiac protagonist's traversals of Irrehaare constitute a mere backdrop to Dukaj's musings on the nature of identity and the questions of virtuality and reality. There is certainly no fixed algorithm for authorial maturity, but given that *Irrehaare* was written when Dukaj was merely twenty, the novella's tight plotting, narrative complexity, and philosophical investment are more than impressive.

The novella's cyberpunk trappings exemplify Dukaj's broader interest in a species of science fiction that plays close to science and technology. Indeed, if there is one set of conventions to which the writer continues to return, it is certainly broadly understood hard sf, within whose scope Dukaj particularly focuses on the tropes of posthumanism and singularity as well as scientifically informed space opera. All these interests are readily apparent in *Extensa* (2002), the shortest of his standalone novels, set in a far future in which the Green Kingdom, a small community of religious holdouts, has resisted transformation into a posthuman, computronium-based mode of existence that the rest of the planet entered a long time ago. The story is narrated by a member of this community, whose insights initially seem to suggest the devilish nature of this transcendence—a scene in which the recently deceased grandfather appears to the narrator and his sister at first possesses a positive supernatural edge. However, the antivirtual prejudice turns increasingly problematic as the protagonist becomes involved in the remnants of the titular presingularity space-exploration program, which eventually leads him to the discovery of an alien anomaly that has also abandoned the material plane. By that point, readers also realize that the human enclave is not so much a solid island surrounded by a sea of virtuality; instead, it is benevolently maintained by the posthumans at enormous computational expense.

The deep time of post-singularity and the galactic scale also characterize *Perfekcyjna niedoskonałość* (Perfect imperfection; 2004), set in a twenty-ninth century in which nanotechnology reigns supreme, the barely comprehensible logic of infinite acquisition of information trumps human motivations and desires, and an entirely new metaphysics have fundamentally altered the posthuman relationship with time and space. In this world, homo sapiens are relics, and Adam Zamoyski, the novel's protagonist, revived after his death in the twenty-first century, can barely keep up with understanding the world around him, a position identical to one in which Dukaj often places his readers. Although things are often explained to Zamoyski—as well as to readers—the narrative always totters on the edge of understanding, conveying the same culture shock that the main character experiences.

The radical world without baseline humans also returns in Dukaj's latest work to date, *The Old Axolotl*, in which the last humans who survived a massive radiation flare from space that killed all organic life on earth inhabit, as deteriorating uploads, a variety of robotic waldos. A crude experimental technology when the disaster struck, the novel's cyberpunk-like uploads are humanity's twilight, and the nostalgically philosophical ruminations on the nature of humanity position the text in the genre's long last-man tradition.

Despite this commitment to hard science and singularity, which has earned Dukaj comparisons to Greg Egan, he has explored a number of other sf conventions, the most prominent of which is alternate history. Although some of his texts introduce points of divergence into more general timelines, most in this category focus on Poland and Polish history. Among the exceptions is "Serce mroku" (Heart of darkness; 1998), a short story that predictably resonates with Joseph Conrad's novel. Marlow is reimagined here as Captain Erde, a young officer of the futuristic Third Reich's AstroKorps, who is sent to the planet Darkness to capture or kill the mysterious Count Leszczyński, a Pole more commonly known as Teufel, the Devil.[12] One of Dukaj's earliest significant alternate histories using Polish history is *Xavras Wyżryn i inne fikcje narodowe* (Xavras Wyżryn and other national fictions; 1997), his novelistic debut to be discussed below in more detail. Arguably, though, Dukaj's most important contribution to the subgenre is the monumental *Lód* (Ice; 2007).

At over one thousand pages and reminiscent of Thomas Pynchon's *Against the Day* (2006), *Ice* is Dukaj's longest work to date and a veritably encyclopedic novel of an alternate-timeline world. Its point of divergence is the Tunguska event of 1908, which in addition to felling some two thousand square kilometers of taiga has also brought to Earth the Ice, a fantastic form of matter previously unknown on this planet, and "Lute," angels of frost whose mode of being eludes the terrestrial taxonomies of life. The Ice has spread across Russia and parts of Europe, freezing territories as well as history and philosophy. It has given rise to an entire new industry of cold iron (*zimnazo*) possessing extraordinary physical properties. In the world of the novel, World War I never happened, Poland remains a Russian possession, and political factions at the Tzarist court and religious sects have emerged, furiously disagreeing on the desirability of the Ice.

The novel is narrated in the rigorously Jamesian mode of the limited narrator by Benedykt Gierosławski, a Polish mathematician and gambler who is compelled by the Ministry of Winter to travel to Siberia to find his estranged father, who can allegedly communicate with Lute. Gierosławski's long journey, during which he falls in love and meets Nicola Tesla, also employed by the Tzar to harness energies of the Ice, reconfigures the geography of the heart of darkness, but also provides ample opportunity for the protagonist's extended mono- and dialogues with a gallery of characters representing conflicting views within the fictional world. Religion, philosophy, science, historiography, logic, politics, language, and identity all appear, disappear, and reappear in Gierosławski's often tortured musings and cognitive struggles, but all of them are informed by the basic premise of the alterity of this world.

Worldbuilding before Plotting

Generic fluidity is also very much apparent in *Other Songs*, which in many ways seems to be yet another alternate history. Nevertheless, in his meticulously researched study, Krzysztof M. Maj argues that the novel is an allotopia and a perfect specimen of the second aspect of Dukaj's work that makes him so worthy of serious readerly and critical attention. From the beginning of his career, Dukaj's creative process has been informed by the centrality of worldbuilding. While most stories in all genres of the fantastic have historically been, at their core, adventure stories and bildungsromans in which diegetic worlds play an important but essentially secondary role, Dukaj has always been interested in the consequences of world construction for all other aspects of narrative. This interest is most fully articulated in his two manifesto-like critical texts: "Filozofia fantasy" (Philosophy of fantasy; 1997) and "Stworzenie świata jako gałąź sztuki" (World-creation as a branch of art; 2010).[13] Although separated by over a decade, both texts manifest essentially the same creed that underlies all of Dukaj's fiction: that the author creates a world through the rigorous application of the initial assumption[14] and that worldbuilding always precedes fabulation. These two premises make Jacek Dukaj radically different from most other science-fiction writers, in Poland and elsewhere. Unlike writers who flesh out their characters and world around preconceived narrative arcs, Dukaj begins with a seed—a philosophical concept, a scientific fact, a timeline divergence—that determines the shape of the world, the characters, and their interactions but also their mental lives. This does not necessarily mean that his characters are preprogrammed in their traits and responses, but as Maj puts it, "the internal logic of the magical world requires the demonstration of principal adaptive and responsive mechanisms."[15]

Other Songs is an exemplar of this approach. While it would be easy to treat the novel as a particularly inventive alternate history in which the point of divergence is Alexander's longer life and the resultant establishment of the Hellenic timeline, Maj demonstrates that this cannot possibly account for two far more important aspects of the novel's world, "the transformation of the heliocentric model into the geocentric one and such destabilization of the table of elements that it leads to the primacy of the hylomorphic relationship of Matter and Form."[16] Dukaj's fictional ontogenesis is thus grounded in the realism of post-Hellenic principles of world operation. *Other Songs* does not only have different history; its fantastic alterity is equally centrally constructed through alternate physics and chemistry. To wit, the physics of *Other Songs* is governed by Aristotelian geocentrism: Earth is the center of the universe, and the space between it and all other celestial bodies is filled with aether, the fifth element. All matter is composed of the remaining four elements in varying proportions. There are ideal forms—features of landscape, locations, and lands—in the novel's universe, but there are also forms perverted and twisted and sick, as is the case with what in our world would be northwestern Africa. When Hieronim Berbelek, the novel's aristocratic protagonist and erstwhile brilliant strategist, and his expedition venture into such territories, the minds and bodies of some of the participants slowly yield to the malevolent influence of evil forms. But the reverse is also true: in a quasi-Hegelian manner, the human mind can influence form, too, and thus manipulate matter. Not everyone can do it, but those who can, often called "kratistos" (the Greek word for "the strongest" and "the noblest"), impose their form, whether benevolent or manipulative, onto their domains and people living in them.

Although this criminally cursory summary of the novel that runs in excess of five hundred pages sounds awfully close to fast-and-loose fantasy, Dukaj rigorously follows all consequences of such first principles in a manner characteristic of the hardest of hard science fiction. *Other Songs* is truly a tour-de-force of logic, rationality, and cause-and-effect. The only difference is that all three are dictated not by the consensual reality of our world but by Dukaj's mental construct. Everything in the novel—the characters' personalities; the world's science, technology, and philosophy; even the plot—is subordinated to the initially assumed Aristotelian parameters.

Other Songs may be the most consequential example of Dukaj's primacy of worldbuilding over action, but the author has consistently applied this method to all his writing, and the rigorous consistency is apparent in the other novels, too. The early *Czarne oceany* (Black oceans; 2001), a singularity novel that owes much to cyberpunk, is structured around scientific principles that in our world would be deemed paranormal or at best fringe science. The novel imagines the 2060s United States as an Orwellian system with near-perfect surveillance, near-complete DNA databases, and near-conscious AI and expert systems. The explorations of the human genome and telepathic abilities in some individuals have led to the emergence of monads, bodiless entities that float free and can influence—surreptitiously or by hostile takeover—people's minds. This possibility drives the novel's plot, but Dukaj extrapolates also in other spheres. The effective end of privacy has, for instance, led to the formation of the New Etiquette regulating all human relations, including those between sexual partners. In that, *Black Oceans* clearly extrapolates contemporary anxieties connected with increasing lawsuits as well as the increasingly strict hierarchies of money and power into a vision of the fictional system of social relations that resembles neofeudal governance and economic structures. The novel's fast-paced action is certainly thrilling and, by the end, turns nothing short of apocalyptic, but the detailed descriptions of thought-derived entities and the social, cultural, and political mores of the world seem to be a primary interest to Dukaj, even so early in his career, marking his flight from adventure and towards the architecture-precise blueprinting of his futures.

Dukaj's privileging of world over mind runs counter to the dominant principles of constructing science-fiction narratives and may even be seen as antithetical to the genre's commitment to social and political commentary. After all, if Dukaj's worlds are cognitive clockworks whose fascination lies in the gradually revealed causes and effects, how can they address our world's anxieties and problems? I do not necessarily think he evacuates his concerns from our world, but it certainly proves much harder to automatically apply gender or Marxist readings to Dukaj's novels. In the same way in which science-fiction texts estrange the times and spaces that produced them, *Other Songs*, *Black Oceans*, and similar stories estrange science fiction, forcing readers to reinvent reading protocols acquired over a lifetime of experience within the genre.

National Time Travel

The last distinctive feature of Jacek Dukaj's prose is his positioning in the complicated intersections of the Polish fantastic and national politics. Commenting on the state of utopia in Central and Eastern Europe, Przemysław Czapliński asserts that "post-communist societies entered the new era with a devastated utopian imagination," and the Polish fantastic is a perfect confirmation of this diagnosis.[17] While, after 1989, much nationalist and nostalgically imperial discourse has been deployed in fantasy and its slipstream cross-hatches with romance, picaresque novel, and historical fiction, the genres that have constituted the bulk of Polish fantastika,[18] science fiction has also been centrally informed by conservative mindsets.

One science-fiction convention in which these have remained conspicuously apparent has been alternate history, which, despite the presence of some earlier precedents, has truly exploded after 1989. The depth and seriousness of intersections between national politics and science fiction are exemplified by the series *Zwrotnice czasu* (Time switches), published under the auspices of Narodowe Centrum Kultury (the National Center of Culture), a proportionally smaller but equally ambitious equivalent of the Smithsonian Institution. While the series' website stresses the educational aspects of the enterprise and its commitment to the eradication of gaps in the historical knowledge of younger generations, it also openly invokes the notion of "national suffering" and suggests that the cognitive distance that such hypothetical historical scenarios give rise to "can easily aspire" to the name of "21st-century catharsis." The first year of the series saw the publication of five titles,[19] with a total of sixteen volumes in print by early 2016. Nominally, the texts are varied in their historical scope: for example, *Quietus* is set in the times of an alternate Roman Empire, in which Christianity was eradicated by Julian the Apostate and reborn as a religion of the sword in feudal Japan, and Parowski's novel takes as its point of departure the idea that a storm foiled German plans in 1939, allowing the Polish army to defeat Hitler's armies, resulting in a timeline in which *Casablanca* is never made and Ingrid Bergman costars with Marlene Dietrich in the Polish production *Escape from Warsaw '40*. Practically, however, they all deploy the thematics of Polish national exceptionalism and national identity. Such narratives are not unprecedented, and the *Time Switches* series is representative of a larger phenomenon. Other titles include Marcin Ciszewski's *www.1939.com.pl* (2008), *www.1944.waw.pl* (2009), and *Major* (2010), a series describing the adventures of a Polish special forces officer and his unit, who, en route to Afghanistan, become stranded in time and find themselves in the middle of a number of crucial World War II events. Tomasz Bukowski's *Obiekt R/W0036* (Target R/W0036; 2009) combines alternate history with fantasy in the story of an ancient basilisk awoken in the spaces under Warsaw as the city is being methodically razed by the SS in the wake of the failed uprising of 1944.

It would be a mistake, however, to treat such novels as a posthumous literary revenge on Hitler's Third Reich. Arguably, the first and now the most famous text of this kind is a 1995 short story by Konrad Lewandowski, "Noteka 2015." In it, the Polish parliament is suspended after the revelation of a secret agreement between the police and the Russian mafia (indirectly accepted by the United States). As a result, the Polish army clashes with an American expeditionary corps sent to reestablish democracy there. Applying guerrilla tactics, communication disruption, and chaos theory, Poles manage to force the retreat of the most technologically advanced army in the world. That one of the main architects of this victory is Radoslaw Tymaszewski, a journalist for the *Lecherous Dispatches* weekly dabbling in fringe science, is clearly ironic, but the unspoken premise of this and other texts mentioned earlier is, to my mind, much more serious. Superficially, "Noteka 2015" ridicules the ultrapatriotic politicians of the right and the impromptu "it'll be all right" mentality, arguably a national vice. Regardless of whether the enemies are American, German, or Russian, this particular strand of alternate-history science fictions readily invites and reflects critical examinations of the national psyche, particularly a sense of the trauma of national betrayal.[20] The vacuum left after the disappearance of an oppressive system, which for many, in one form or another, held Poland between 1795 and 1989, combined with the realization of the extent of a chasm between Poland and the world, not so much in the economic and political but, first and foremost, in the social and civic sphere, have forced to the surface a range of national anxieties and complexes. That science fiction has become a venue for staging such reckonings is not unheard of, but the persistence of certain themes and topoi is highly interesting. Almost all such narratives concern national events, almost all launch themselves from moments or events of national failure and suffering, and almost all, albeit occasionally humorously, suggest the ultimate victory of the invincible Polish spirit and resourcefulness. The same motifs recur: the haughty pride about the monolithic national identity maintained after over a century of statelessness and half a century of communism; the Manichean "us and them" perception of the world; the conflicted relationship with Catholicism; and the myth of Polish stubbornness and sacrifice in the face of great historical obstacles. More distantly, many of these texts channel what in the twenty-first century cannot be classified as anything but utterly fantastic yearnings for the long lost glory of the erstwhile empire. In many ways, this body of texts constitutes a contemporary extension of and variation on the nineteenth-century romantic ethos of national Polish exceptionalism and Slavic messianism.

Dukaj himself acknowledges this bizarre situation in his column "Wyobraźnia po prawej stronie" (Imagination on the right; 2008), in which he sketches a comprehensive panorama of Poland's fantastic genres but also soberly notes that it is impossible to offer a positive leftist vision in Poland without ridicule. More importantly, he confronts the phenomenon of the national—and nationalistic—fantastic in a number of his works, all of which challenge and problematize the dominant modes of Polishness.

Dukaj's prose offers several modalities of this engagement, the most obvious of which is the constant cycling of Polish—or, occasionally, Slavic—characters and settings. "Heart of Darkness" appropriately features the mysterious Count Leszczyński, who functions as Kurtz's equivalent, suggesting perhaps that although Poland never technically possessed colonies, there are elements of its past that are uncomfortably reminiscent of the murderous excesses of the Leopoldian Congo. In *Perfect Imperfection*, the protagonist Adam Zamoyski,[21] a twenty-first-century astronaut, is resuscitated in the twenty-ninth century into a post-singularity world of multiple modes of existence, only some of which are human in any meaningful sense of the word. Although he seems to be an important element of much larger struggles of posthuman entities, much of the novel is devoted to descriptions of his disorientation and helplessness. This, again, can be interpreted as a reference to the increasingly antiquated and unreflective veneration of the past that many conservative groups in Poland manifest in relation to modernity.[22] Finally, "Crux" (2004) is set in a future Poland, in which only about 10 percent of the population of twenty-four-million has to work, and the country is effectively governed by twelve magnate families that function as "strange attractors" for the narrow class of the educated and the rich.

Dukaj confronts the national mythologies most centrally in *Xavras Wyżryn and Other National Fictions*. Set in 1996, it is arguably the author's first major work and, in generic terms, a typical alternate-history narrative. As its point of divergence it takes the 1920 Polish-Soviet war, in which the Bolsheviks defeated Poland and reached the eastern border of Germany, a grim scenario that in itself sets Dukaj apart from other Polish practitioners of the convention. The plot is set in the European War Zone (EWZ), an area covering Central and Eastern Europe and the Balkans, which nominally belongs to the Soviet Union but is constantly ravaged by military operations. The titular character is the commander of the Polish Liberation Army, a guerilla force allegedly inspired by the reporting from the two Chechen wars. The story is told from the point of view of a journalist from the United States embedded with this anti-Soviet Polish resistance.

The text very consciously engages Poland's historical memories of guerilla warfare and grassroots resistance during various conflicts in the last two centuries, something that a number of alternate-history writers have exploited in multiple ways. For Dukaj, the alternate-history formula becomes much more than an intellectual game of "what if" and allows him to play with and deconstruct the national mythos. As Ian Smith, the journalist, travels with Wyżryn's commando through the EWZ, he witnesses wartime atrocities and the commander's recklessness and receives a semi-nihilistic lesson in the relativity of morals. Although nominally engaged in what Machiavelli would have called a just war, Wyżryn is as charismatic as he is calculating in his reliance on media and propaganda. His is a terrorist reality show culminating in a real-time live streaming of his sacrificial death during a suicidal atomic explosion at the close of the story.[23] Although by the end of the story Smith becomes utterly disenchanted by the commander, as often happens with Dukaj, no final judgment on the character is issued. At the same time, Wyżryn's presentation is a powerful challenge to the dominant national narratives of trauma and sacrifice in the name of higher causes. The divergence itself compels thinking about the contingencies of the 1920 war and how close to defeat the Poles were prior to the Battle of Warsaw in August that year. Far more radically, the protagonist's romantically defined Polishness is shown in Dukaj's text as a "form of alienness" that is "wild, oriental, and fundamentalist,"[24] which seems more at home in the cultural sphere in which most Poles wishfully deny participation.

Many of Dukaj's engagements with Polish patriotism and national identity remain in direct dialogue with the Polish romantic tradition and the mid-nineteenth-century mystical belief in Poland as a martyr of nations. A number of critics, including Marta Błaszkowska, Magdalena Mrowiec, and Kryzstof Uniłowski, have analyzed Dukaj's complex engagement with romantic tropes and myths. In fact, Uniłowski reads *Ice* as an extensive and complex dialogue with very specific texts and positions of Polish romanticism, an emotional and intellectual breeding ground of post-1918 conservative nationalism in the country. The writer has also engaged questions of faith and religion in many of his stories—almost all the stories in *In the Land of the Unfaithful* are predicated on the clash between some form of belief in confrontation with rationality and science. Few openly allude to Catholicism, whose contemporary Polish variety remains much more politically entangled and conservative than in many other countries. At the same time, from the Polish perspective, it is difficult not to read them as attempts to ruffle the complicated relationship between spirituality and materiality that has preoccupied so many science-fiction writers, from Walter M. Miller to Frank Herbert to Paolo Bacigalupi. What makes Dukaj exceptional is that there are very few contemporary science-fiction writers in Poland who have forged such undaunted and ruthless questioning of the national past.

While comparisons among writers are ultimately futile, Jacek Dukaj does differ from virtually all his Polish contemporaries. His points of divergence from science fiction and, more generally, fantastic counterparts include generic flexibility in a subculture that is often invested in categorizational purity; a subversive questioning of national mythos of history and religion that extends well beyond similar engagements; a linguistic inventiveness that demonstrates the writer's intellectual rigor; and the sheer originality of his narratives. Each of these alone would warrant attention to Dukaj's writing; when found in the work of one writer, they are a mark of a major literary figure.[25]

It is, however, the centrality of worldbuilding to his writing that really sets him apart from most other science-fiction writers in Poland and abroad. For Dukaj, the science-fiction narrative, with its fascination with science and commitment to suspenseful action and psychological characterization, is not an end but a means to one. A holder of a master's degree in philosophy from the Jagiellonian University in Kraków, Dukaj is a philosopher for whom science fiction is a tool to explore the ethical, cultural, and political ramifications of technological progress in a world undergoing future shock on a daily basis. Many of his novels operate on the same principles as Plato's dialogues—they offer parables and stories but, at their heart, extrapolate and simulate some of the most profound questions that science fiction as a genre but also the variegated post- and transhumanist groups have been preoccupied with: the nature of information, the limits of knowledge, and the evolutionary changes of the human species. His visions and answers always eschew naive optimism, never offer easy solutions, and are often as complex as the questions themselves, a mark of a major science-fiction voice in the same league as William Gibson, Kim Stanley Robinson, and China Miéville.

Notes

1. Dukaj, *Other Songs*, 235. Unless otherwise noted, all translations from Dukaj's prose are my own.

2. See Berman, *All That Is Solid*.

3. Dukaj, *Other Songs*, 147.

4. Interestingly, Dukaj is one of the two writers featured in the volume who can be identified as "science fiction" and is much younger than the other sf entrant, Marek S. Huberath.

5. According to Marta Kaźmierczak, Stanley Bill was working on the English translation of Dukaj's monumental *Lód* (2007), in English to be titled *Ice* (129). Given that the last update on the project dated back to 2011, the future of this translation is at best uncertain. In March 2017, the Head of Zeus acquired world English rights to the novel, but it is unclear at this point whether the London-based press will commission Bill to deliver the translation.

6. While the statement is my own assertion, Dukaj himself has repeatedly expressed the highest praise for Lem and has participated in several publishing projects in homage

to his writing, including an experimental essay, "Kto napisał Stanisława Lema" [Who wrote Stanisław Lem], which appeared in a 2008 edition of *A Perfect Vacuum* (1971), a Borgesian collection of fictitious criticism of nonexistent books.

7. It is, unfortunately, difficult to appreciate Dukaj's inventiveness without a good operational knowledge of Polish, and it is not clear how much of this can successfully carry into English translations—the two published translations are not really representative in this respect. *The Old Axolotl* is certainly competently translated, but it offers a rather subdued version of Dukaj's celebration (and cerebration) of language. Much of this inventiveness is attached to the inflection and, to a lesser extent, syntax of Polish, which make the language notoriously difficult. In many of his novels (e.g., in *Ice*) he also interweaves obsolete linguistic registers and the invented retro vocabulary with the highly technological jargon, whose obvious reliance on English originals renders them doubly estranging in Polish.

8. Żerański, "Wywiad Z Jackiem Dukajem."

9. Borowczyk, "Totalna Imersja," 57.

10. Rieder, "On Defining SF," 193.

11. Ibid.

12. Dukaj has explored variants of the story about a hunter or an explorer entering a territory where no clear rules apply in several other stories, including "Muchobójca" [Flykiller; 2000] and "Ziemia Chrystusa" [Christ's Earth; 2000].

13. The earlier of these essays is a systematic critique of Ewa Białołęcka's "Błękit maga" [The blue of the Magus; 1997], which Dukaj charges with lack of consequence in worldbuilding and which provides him with an opportunity to develop his own theory of the fantastic.

14. Dukaj, "Philosophy of Fantasy (1)," 67.

15. Maj, *Allotopie,* 271.

16. Ibid., 273–74.

17. Czapliński asserts that "post-communist societies entered the new era with a devastated utopian imagination" (Szczątki Utopii, 41).

18. While the word is obviously akin to the Polish "fantastika" and various regional variants, I use it here in the sense proposed by John Clute, as an umbrella term for science fiction, fantasy, and horror. Interestingly, in the early texts on fantastika, Clute fails to acknowledge the Central and Eastern European linguistic origins of the term.

19. Maciej Parowski, *Burza. Ucieczka z Warszawy '40* [The storm: Escape from Warsaw '40; 2010]; Marcin Wolski *Wallenrod* and *Jedna przegrana bitwa* [One lost battle; 2010]; Szczepan Twardoch, *Wieczny Grunwald. Powieść zza końca czasów* [Eternal Grunwald: A novel from the endtimes; 2010], and Jacek Inglot's *Quietus* (1997; rev. ed. 2010).

20. Oziewicz, "Coping with the Trauma," 7–11.

21. The name itself belongs to a British historian of Polish extraction, but more likely it is an amalgam of the first name of the famous Polish romantic poet Adam Mickiewicz and the last name of one of the old noble Polish families, the founders of the city of Zamość in the sixteenth century.

22. Given the earlier characterization of the Polish fantastic, it should not be surprising that several authors openly declare themselves as monarchists.

23. In that, Wyżryn is aided by his old comrade Konrad, whose name clearly resonates with *Konrad Wallenrod* (1828), the title of a narrative poem by Adam Mickiewicz and the name of the fictional character of pagan Lithuanian descent who rises to the position of Grand Master of the Order of Teutonic Knights only to lead them into a major military defeat. Subsequently, "Wallenrodism" has been used to describe a long-term strategy of infiltrating the enemy and becoming one of them to ultimately defeat them. In parallel, Konrad's name may allude to the middle name of Józef Konrad Korzeniowski, himself a man living between cultures, who was allegedly influenced by Mickiewicz's poem in his explorations of the conflict between publicly attested loyalty and a hidden affiliation with a national cause. Marcus, *Perilous States*, 204–5.

24. Unilowski, "Lord Dukaj," 39.

25. Dukaj's recognition beyond the world of science fiction is demonstrated by the fact that to date he remains the only writer of the fantastic apart from Lem whose entire oeuvre is made available by Wydawnictwo Literackie, a major publisher whose catalog includes books by Nobel Prize winners as well as high-literary bestsellers, Polish and international.

Bibliography

Berman, Marshall. *All That Is Solid Melts into Air: The Experience of Modernity*. New York: Penguin Books, 1982.

Błaszkowska, Marta. "Poblask Migotliwy Na Granicy Percepcji. Polska Literatura Fantastyczna Wobec Granic Symbolicznego" [Flickering afterglow at the ends of perception: Polish literature of the fantastic and the limits of the symbolic]. In *Literatura Na Granicach* [Literature at the border]. Ed. Katarzyna Kuchowicz. Kraków: AT Wydawnictwo, 2015. 7–18.

Borowczyk, Jerzy. "Totalna Imersja. Z Jackiem Dukajem Rozmawia Jerzy Borowczyk" [Total immersion: A Jacek Dukaj interview]. *Czas Kultury* 153 (June 2009): 54–60.

Bould, Mark, and Sherryl Vint. "There Is No Such Thing as Science Fiction." In *Reading Science Fiction*. Ed. James Gunn, Marleen Barr, and Matthew Candelaria. New York: Palgrave Macmillan, 2009. 43–51.

Bukowski, Tomasz. *Obiekt R/W0036* [Target R/W0036]. Warsaw: Wydawn SOL, 2009.

The Cathedral. Dir. Tomasz Baginski. Warsaw: Platige Image, 2002. Accessed July 27, 2017. http://www.platigeshorts.com/the-cathedral.html.

Ciszewski, Marcin. *Major*. Ustroń: Ender, 2010.

———. *www.1939.com.pl*. Ustroń: War Book, 2011.

———. *www.1944.waw.pl*. Warsaw: Wydawnictwo SOL, 2009.

Czapliński, Przemysław. "Szczątki Utopii. Późna Nowoczesność I Wymyślanie Przyszłości" [Remnants of utopia: Late modernity and invention of the future]. In *Nowe Dwudziestolecie (1989–2009): Rozpoznania, Hierarchie, Perspektywy* [The two decades (1989–2000): Recognitions, hierarchies, perspectives]. Ed. Hanna Gosk. Warsaw: Elipsa, 2010. 40–79.

Dukaj, Jacek. "Crux." *Król Bólu*. Kraków: Wydawnictwo Literackie, 2010. 541–94.

————. *Czarne oceany* [Black oceans]. Kraków: Wydawnictwo Literackie, 2008.

————. *Extensa*. Kraków: Wydawnictwo Literackie, 2002.

————. "Filozofia fantasy (1)" [Philosophy of fantasy (1)]. *Nowa Fantastyka* (August 1997): 66–67.

————. "Filozofia fantasy (2)" [Philosophy of Fantasy (2)]. *Nowa Fantastyka* (September 1997): 66–67.

————. "The Golden Galley." In *The Dedalus Book of Polish Fantasy*. Ed. Wiesiek Powaga. Sawtry: Dedalus, 1996. 337–62.

————. *Inne pieśni* [Other songs]. Kraków: Wydawnictwo Literackie, 2003.

————. "Irrehaare (1)." *Nowa Fantastyka* (June 1995): 25–41.

————. "Irrehaare (2)." *Nowa Fantastyka*, (July 1995): 25–42.

————. "Kto napisał Stanisława Lema" [Who wrote Stanisław Lem]. In *Próżnia doskonała* [Perfect Vacuum]. Stanisław Lem. Warszawa: Agora, 2008, 203–14.

————. *Lód* [Ice]. Kraków: Wydawnictwo Literackie, 2007.

————. *Perfekcyjna niedoskonałość* [Perfect Imperfection]. Kraków: Wydawnictwo Literackie, 2004.

————. "Ruch Generała" [The iron general]. In *W kraju niewiernych*. 2d ed. Kraków: Wydawnictwo Literackie, 2008. 5–74.

————. "Serce Mroku" [Heart of darkness]. In *Król Bólu*. Kraków: Wydawnictwo Literackie, 2010. 595–642.

————. *Starość Axolotla* [The old axolotl]. Poznań: Allegro, 2015.

————. "Stworzenie świata jako gałąź sztuki" [World-creation as an art]. *Tygodnik Powszechny* [The Catholic weekly], February 2, 2010.

————. *W kraju niewiernych* [In the land of the unfaithful; 2000]. Kraków: Wydawnictwo Literackie, 2008.

————. *Wroniec* [The crow]. Kraków: Wydawnictwo Literackie, 2009.

————. "Wyobraźnia Po Prawej Stronie" [Imagination on the right]. *WP.PL*, February 29, 2008. Accessed July 27, 2017. http://ksiazki.wp.pl/tytul,Wyobraznia-po-prawej-stronie-czesc-pierwsza,wid,11169,felieton.html?ticaid=1172db.

————. *Xavras Wyżryn i inne fikcje narodowe* [Xavras Wyżryn and other national fictions]. 2d ed. Kraków: Wydawnictwo Literackie, 2009.

Inglot, Jacek. *Quietus*. 1997; rev. ed., Warsaw: Narodowe Centrum Kultury, 2010.

Kincaid, Paul. "On the Origins of Genre." *Extrapolation* 44.4 (Winter 2003): 409–19.

Lewandowski, Konrad T. "Noteka 2015." *Nowa Fantastyka* (April 1995): 46–56.

Maj, Krzysztof M. *Allotopie. Topografia światów fikcjonalnych* [Allotopias: Topography of fictional worlds]. Kraków: Universitas, 2015.

Marcus, George E. *Perilous States: Conversations on Culture, Politics, and Nation*. Chicago: University of Chicago Press, 1993.

Mrowiec, Magdalena. "Juliusz Słowacki I Jacek Dukaj—Lodowaty Dialog Między Tekstami." *Postscriptum Polonistyczne* 2.4 (2009): 123–42.

Oziewicz, Marek C. "Coping with the Trauma of National Betrayal: Alternate Histories of Poland in Konrad T. Lewandowski's 'Noteka 2015' and Marcin Ciszewski's Major

Trilogy." In *Exploring the Benefits of the Alternate History Genre*. Ed. Marek C. Oziewicz, Justyna Deszcz-Tryhubczak, and Zdzisław Wasik. Wrocław: Philological School of Higher Education in Wrocław Publishing, 2011. 7–11.

Parowski, Maciej. *Burza. Ucieczka z Warszawy '40* [The storm: Escape from Warsaw '40]. Warsaw: Narodowe Centrum Kultury, 2009.

Planescape: Torment. Video game. Irvine, Calif.: Black Isle Studios, 1999.

Powaga, Wiesiek, ed. *The Dedalus Book of Polish Fantasy*. New York: Hippocrene, 1996.

Rieder, John. "On Defining SF, or Not: Genre Theory, SF, and History." *Science Fiction Studies* 111 (July 2010): 191–209.

Twardoch, Szczepan. *Wieczny Grunwald. Powieść zza końca czasów* [Eternal Grunwald: A novel from the endtimes]. Warsaw: Narodowe Centrum Kultury, 2010.

Uniłowski, Krzysztof. "Lord Dukaj albo fantasta wobec mainstreamu" [Lord Dukaj, or a fantasist against the mainstream]. *FA-Art* 4 (2007): 36–43.

Wolski, Marcin. *Jedna przegrana bitwa* [One lost battle]. Warsaw: Narodowe Centrum Kultury, 2010.

———. *Wallenrod*. Warsaw: Narodoew Centrum Kultury, 2009.

Żerański, Jan. "Wywiad Z Jackiem Dukajem." *Katedra.nast.pl*, July 27, 2009. Accessed July 27, 2017. http://katedra.nast.pl/art.php5?id=4239.

Jean-Claude Dunyach, Poet of the Flesh

NATACHA VAS-DEYRES

For my father

Jean-Claude Dunyach, born in 1957, belongs to the generation of French authors who began to publish during the 1980s, which includes Roland C. Wagner, Emmanuel Jouanne, Sylvie Lainé, and Jean-Marc Ligny. At a time when French science fiction was struggling to explore new ways of storytelling influenced by surrealism or the *nouveau roman*, this generation has given science fiction a new life by mixing the hard-science approach with the supernatural and the fantastic, while paying glowing tribute to authors of the golden age of Anglo-Saxon sf.

For more than thirty years, Dunyach has been one of the major authors of contemporary French science fiction, with more than a hundred published short stories (among which are two collections translated into English, *The Night Orchid: Conan Doyle in Toulouse* [2004] and *The Thieves of Silence* [2009]) and six novels, including *Etoiles mourantes* (Dying stars), cowritten with Ayerdhal in 1999.[1] He has won numerous literary prizes for his fiction, including the Grand Prix de l'Imaginaire in 1984 and 1998, the Readers Prize of the English review *Interzones* (2001), the Prix Rosny aîné Prize in both the novel (1992) and short-story categories (1992, 2008), and the Grand Prix de la Tour Eiffel (1999). And in his spare time, he is a research engineer at Airbus and a lyrics writer for local singers.

As a science-fiction writer, Dunyach was influenced by Samuel Delany, Ray Bradbury, and more particularly by J. G. Ballard. The main keywords attached to his work are *memory* and *death* (treated as opposite sides of the same coin), and his work often explores the essence of time. The specificity of Dunyach consists in making these essential concepts tangible for the reader by giving them a symbolic substance: time itself becomes as tangible as sand, stone, ashes, water; love stories can be petrified as semiprecious stones and worn as trophies—the universe itself complies as a sheet of paper or a piece of cloth and can be creased. But Dunyach's originality lies behind this realization of the metaphysical concept: once materialized, the poetic dimension of the concept is underlined and exploited through the full sensory dimension of the text and the importance granted to the feelings of the flesh. Even the more abstract concepts can be touched, smelled, and tasted.

The characters in his short stories are physically hurt or twisted, often with traumatic experiences in their past, but they still act as links between the individual and the collective. In his opinion, any kind of system—especially a political one—can be defined depending on how it deals with frontiers and marginality. Dunyach favors an individual narrative point of view for a better detection of systems' weaknesses (cities, societies, religions).

In that respect, the most distinctive and original characters in his work are the "AnimalCities"—living extraterrestrial city-shaped animals, made of flesh and cartilage, traveling through space from node to node on the web of the universe. Their symbiotic liaison with humanity gradually leads people to understand the global nature of reality. This space-opera universe gradually builds itself upon a handful of short stories and two large novels: *Etoiles mortes* (Dead stars; 2000) and *Dying Stars* (2014).

Dunyach and French Science Fiction

When Jean-Claude Dunyach started to write and publish stories at the beginning of the 1980s, the situation of science fiction in France was quite different from today: sf was part of the so-called counterculture, like rock'n'roll and tattoos, and it was an important driving force, especially among students. It was, however, neglected or even treated as garbage by anyone over thirty-five. Writers of sf had a bright future back then, and they were fighting for it. But in France, such literature was not taken seriously by the dominant media—neither TV nor mainstream newspapers were mentioning it. "It's science-fiction" was a popular way to say, "It is unrealistic, crazy, and immature." Authors and critics were mostly fans (one of the lowest life forms, in everybody's mind), and sf was the kind of nonsense everybody was supposed to abandon upon entering "real life" shortly after puberty.

At the end of the 1970s, French sf was either highly political—French society had been deeply transformed by "Mai 1968," a revolution in mentalities that took its source in a student movement—or largely inspired by the golden age of Anglo-Saxon science-fiction. Original voices were rare. Michel Jeury is the only name that comes to mind, and he was largely ignored by mainstream readers. Nevertheless, Jeury, who started his career at the end of the 1950s, is regarded today as a great French science-fiction novelist. Since the publication of *Temps incertain* (The uncertain time) in 1973, in Gérard Klein's *Ailleurs et demain* (Elsewhere and tomorrow) series, French sf exegetes perceive a metamorphosis of the representation of time travel in his work. According to this essential author of French sf of the 1970s and 1980s, time travel is not made possible through the machine, a classic science-fiction theme since 1880,[2] but through the psyche. The psyche is helped either artificially or naturally by the ingestion of a drug, chronolyse. The time traveler then occupies one or more bodies from the past or the future, incorporating their individual personality. In fact, Dunyach was influenced by Michel Jeury while he was a young writer. The author of *Uncertain Time* was one of his models, particularly to write a poeticized science fiction using visual sensations and colors.

At the beginning of the 1980s, a handful of new young writers known as "Groupe Limite" chose to develop a category of literary sf in which formal experimentation and innovative stylistic approaches were central to the project. Even if they produced only a few novels and one single collection of short stories under the name "Limite," *Malgré le monde* (Despite the world; 1987),[3] they had a certain influence on other French sf writers by partially bridging the gap between sf and the mainstream—especially by using literary techniques associated with the *nouveau roman* or surrealism—and thereby conquering some of the most important media.

In the meantime, Roland C. Wagner, Jean-Marc Ligny, and Claude Ecken were just writing classic and popular science fiction, either as short pulp-like novels for mass-market publishers such as Fleuve Noir or, more ambitiously, targeting the literary market as a whole. And then, slowly, at the end of the 1980s, the monthly magazines and anthologies that published them folded; many prestigious sf publishers disappeared or reduced their activities. Publishing something other than mass-market/pulp-like/short-and-easy novels was an almost impossible challenge.

We recall that in the 1970s and 1980s, a great number of series were created in France in the wake of the 1950s series *Rayon Fantastique*, published by Hachette, and *Présence du Futur*, published by Denoël. These include *Ailleurs et demain* (published by Robert Laffont), *Anticipation* (Fleuve Noir), *The Great Science-Fiction Anthology* (Livre de poche), *Ici et maintenant* (Kesselring), *Bibliothèque Marabout science-fiction* (J'ai lu SF editions), and *Constellation* (Seghers). This array of series and anthologies from the 1970s is due to two phenomena: utopian literature's integration of science fiction through politics, and the creation of a real culture of science fiction, in which readers and viewers are increasingly numerous, and sf arouses a growing interest in journalists as well as in the academic world. Changes in French society as a result of May 1968 account for a great diversity among sf writers, an amazing profusion that became a "carrier . . . of ideas, hopes, utopias."[4] French sf writers, induced by the changes born in those years and influenced by their major American counterparts, put their ideology and creativity to work. French sf found its singularity without isolating itself from other utopian movements of that time such as ecology, feminism, and pacifism.

In 1969, the magazine *Fiction* (the French version of the American magazine) gave pride of place to anti-establishment political fiction by publishing two short-stories: "Faith of our Fathers" by Philip K. Dick and "Final War" by Barry N. Malzberg. A few years later, *Fiction* readers discovered the English New Wave of Michael Moorcock, J. G. Ballard, and other speculative-fiction texts. It is from the French translation of those texts that a very political form of science fiction developed. Iconoclastic at first, it then tried to build utopian visions as alternatives to a Western society that it considered stifling and old-fashioned. The committed, politicized French sf of the 1970s started to decline in the early 1980s, perhaps due to the fact that many people of the counterculture believed that the dream of a utopia had come true with the election of François Mitterrand in 1981. Other reasons are put forward by the various actors of this period: for Jean-Pierre Andrevon, the economic context and the exponential development of literary series are to be blamed for this decline,[5] rather than readers' weariness with a boring, deluded, and jaded sf, as posited by Gérard Klein,[6] Roger Bozzetto, and other critics. Between 1977 and 1986, more than thirty series disappeared. Jean-Guillaume Lanuque refers to the darkness and pessimism of science-fictional visions of that time, a darkness inherited from the utopian altercation of the previous period: "Authors may well have been tempted to focus excessively on the darkest futuristic writing in a crisis context, at the expense of alternative, more inspiring perspectives, other than ecological and libertarian developments which have their limits, as we could see. As if this science fiction had not achieved its mutation process, dropping its very last traces of leftism. . . . At this point we seem to have the concretization of the disappointed hopes of '68."[7] But this movement revealed some of the talents of the next generation, such as Jean-Pierre Hubert, Joël Houssin, and Joëlle Wintrebert (among others), and "allowed the building of another science fiction on [its] very ruins."[8] The quarterly magazine *Univers*, run by Yves Frémion,[9] has made it possible to maintain the link between political sf and new authors publishing today, while integrating the "old" ones such as Michel Jeury, Michel Demuth, Philippe Curval, Pierre Pelot, Daniel Walther, and André Ruellan.

At the end of the 1980s, a handful of writers bloomed—Pierre Bordage, Ayerdhal, Laurent Genefort, Richard Canal, Serge Lehman, and Sylvie Denis—and longtime sf fans decided to create new magazines to replace the old ones. Three of them, *CyberDreams* (1994–98), *Bifrost*, and *Galaxies* (the latter two since 1996), were created almost at the same time. Jean-Claude Dunyach was one of the founders of *Galaxies*' first series and was an associate editor for more than ten years. *Bifrost* and *Galaxies* are still thriving after more than twenty years. According to Dunyach, the second half of the 1990s was a golden age for French sf, culminating in 2000: the turn of the millennium was an opportunity for writers to conquer the media—particularly TV—and to talk at length about the future. This generation of writers was unaware, however, that their readership in France was soon to turn to fantasy and paranormal romance.

Sensoriality and Poetry

Jean-Claude Dunyach offers a perfect example of what is uniquely "French" about French sf during this period; we only have to determine what the French singularity of this writer is. In an interview given at the international science-fiction festival "Utopiales" in Nantes in 2010, the French writer explains how to define the thematic specificity of French authors:

> I think that, in fact, there are some French specificities, because France is one of the countries where science fiction was born; in short, science fiction has existed in France for almost 150 years, since Jules Verne, and never stopped being here. However, we went through lots of phases. First, we inherited a lot from artistic currents like surrealism, for example, or the "nouveau roman," and as a consequence we quite often have texts which slip a little bit. Our SF can be naturally weird,[10] with no particular effort from us. . . . And there are relations to the flesh, the body, to sensuality and sensoriality—not the sexuality, I really mean sensoriality—which are probably quite different. French texts are often stuffed with smells, noises, tastes: we are people of the food, the touch, the smell. We're a country of perfumers, of cooks, and it can be seen in our literature; therefore, in our science fiction, people work on that sensoriality.[11]

The science fiction of Jean-Claude Dunyach is stimulated by form and meaning. Common notions worked out by science fiction, such as time, death, memory, relativity, mutations, and relationships with the machine or extraterrestrials, are always considered from the angle of a sensorial materiality, as if touch were the vital sense for understanding the universe and the unknown. In Dunyach's stories, time evaporates, dead love stories can be crystallized and worn as ornaments, and extraterrestrials are classified as edible or not.

Dunyach's father was a country doctor, and the writer lived his whole childhood in respect of the body, of its organic magnificence, and not in the repulsion of the flesh. As for the literary perspective, Dunyach was fascinated by poetry—he wrote poems from an early age, and to this day he still reads Japanese haiku, a form of poetry whose precision he admires. His first two influences in science fiction were the novel *Vermillion Sands* by J. G. Ballard and the short story "Time Considered as a Helix of Semi-Precious Stones" by Samuel Delany—that is to say, a poeticized American sf. Ballard fascinated Dunyach by his deconstructed process of adding meaning to the world using modern symbolism, as Baudrillard defined it in *La société de consommation. Ses mythes, ses structures* (Consumer society: Myths and structures), and by his way of slicing temporal continuity in his stories.[12]

In *Le jeu des sabliers* (The game of the hourglass; 1987), four protagonists who have embarked on a metaphysical quest are confronted by "sleepers," children that never wake up from their dreams, which alter the different dimensions of reality. Dream, pain, and poetry are closely linked:

> Dreams hit them like sharp spears. Jern, who was hit with full force, tottered. With every step, metal spearheads got deeper into his loins.... Like a scalpel, the pain ripped him open, exposed his nerves and entrails, and scratched the invisible wires that allowed him to operate. His fellow travelers advanced, bent forward to escape from pain.... All around them reality cracked, shattered into a thousand pieces.... Olym, with his face turned up, made up gorgeous dreams that he thrust out to the face of his tormentors. His poems became weapons, his lines projectiles.[13]

In the short story "Les Nageurs de sable" (The sand swimmers; 1983), the narrator is one of three test-tube children who were born on a planet of sand. As in Ray Bradbury's story "Dark They Were, and Golden-Eyed" (1949), and under the influence of the planet, he gradually turns into a creature who is able to swim in sand as easily as in water: "When I arrived at the edge of a large, gently sloping basin, I allowed myself to fall lengthwise to the ground and felt the sand embrace me. It gradually covered my legs, my torso, and my face with its fluid, burning grasp. Carried away on a flow of new sensations, I attempted to swim, but the contact with the rough silica irritated my soft skin and I was forced to get up after a few yards."[14] By means of an individual physical mutation, the flesh of the narrator becomes itself the alien planet and defeats a system of human colonization:

> The sun, at its peak, woke me. I spent a few moments savoring the relative coolness of the sand. I had swallowed a few grains during my sleep and the oxide aftertaste dried my lips. I dug a yard down and placed a handful of damp crystals in my mouth. I closed my eyes, before forcing myself to swallow them. They dulled my hunger and thirst. I got up, abandoning strips of skin behind me. . . . I hardened myself and dove through an oxide mound. The grains caressed my skin gently, without nicking it. I learned to keep my eyes closed, to guide myself by the sound of the wind on the crests of the dunes. From time to time, I swallowed a new mouthful of the desert, discovering an infinite diversity of tastes and odors. When I stopped, exhausted, I knew that the desert had accepted me.[15]

The character accepts his metamorphosis and renders useless the colonization. In fact, the planet irreparably converts people and objects to colonize them.

Dunyach substitutes the symbiosis between man and the machine in his novel *Dying Stars*, cowritten with Ayerdhal, in which the body mutates in contact with matter. In the warrior society of the Mechanists, remote descendants of humans train elite soldiers who lose their human nature by merging their body and soul into their Armor. The latter consists of a sophisticated exoskeleton that connects to the nervous system of the human body, without any possibility of return: "From its billions of pores, the Armor was breathing and sweating, constantly replacing atoms that it needed to keep the Tecamac organism alive, by the dismantled molecules it was ridding it of. For him, it processed again and again the squamae, the sweat, the urine, and the feces. Through its own functioning, it ionized its environment, generating the blue and characteristic odor of ozone."[16] In that novel, the complex exoskeleton is a symbol of the matter turning on a machine, which definitively integrates the human body. In every story, sensations are turned into metaphors and poeticized allegories, which is what gives the text its specific touch. The human body is metamorphosed; its flesh mutates and enters into symbiosis or disintegrates in time, as in the short story "Le temps en s'évaporant" (Time as it evaporates). Zorah, the heroine, lives in a village lost in a valley that is subjected to temporal distortion. As she no longer can stand her life as a humiliated and battered woman, she goes into the temporal storm and thereby allows a reestablishment of energetic forces. Here the body becomes the bond between dimensions:

> The first symptoms of time deprivation are already appearing. The diving suit she stole from her lover, after he mocked her and beat her, is losing the precious fluid through a thousand tiny cracks. The tears of time she sows splash on the earthenware tiles of the staircase and form rivulets along the steps. . . . Her thoughts no longer torment her; time, as it escapes from her, washes her clean and carries away her memories. . . . Slowly the body of Zorah cracks and breaks asunder, yielding to the unstoppable pressure from within. The first spring gushes forth, followed by a second, then by many others. The trickles of time soon become streams, then torrents, then cataracts.[17]

The perception of atoms that constitute the flesh of the body is the science-fictional ingredient of Dunyach's writing. In fact, it's necessary to distinguish the peculiarity of Dunyach as a French writer from his originality as a science-fiction author. As a French writer, he joins a tradition of literary description of perceptions of sight, touch, smell, and taste. As a science-fiction author, he integrates this tradition to create original sf: flesh is becoming a manifestation of the concepts that govern the universe.

This thematic singularity is also stylistic. In 2010, an interviewer asked him: "Do you feel that there are themes or stylistic approaches which unify French sf culturally, making it unique to an extent that would be clear in a blind 'taste test' of translated work in another language?" Dunyach answered, "People tell me that I work with artistic, impressionist, sensorial touches, where Americans would maybe give priority to the strength of the story, to the narration itself, to the adventures, and where English writers would give priority to the rigor of the experimentation."[18] His main invention, the extraterrestrial beings named "AnimalCities," are the bond between flesh and metaphysics, between science and sensations. At first sight, the AnimalCities truly belong to *sense of wonder* imagery: they are huge disks of flesh several dozen kilometers in diameter and a hundred meters deep with filaments around them that are used as antennas or tentacles, which they can retract when they land on a planet. On the top of the disk lies a flesh-and-bone city they can slowly reshape, in the middle of which stands a belfry, a sort of huge central tower-antenna turned towards the sky.

AnimalCities belong to the French urban imagination that forms the city as a gigantic living organism of the kind depicted by Émile Zola, for example, in *Le ventre de Paris* (The belly of Paris) in 1873; or in his feminized, devouring, and carnal city in *La Curée* (The kill) in 1872. Jean-Claude Dunyach's

creations—literally tentacular cities, living disk-cities surrounded by filaments—send us back to medieval urbanity, "strange miscellanies of *traboules*[19]
in city of Lyon, of Mont Saint Michel and of the catacombs of Lyon,"[20] according to Jérôme Goffette, with an architectural structure made of narrow,
winding alley lanes, short cuts, and dead-ends, without mechanized transport.
The image of catacombs is itself a *mise en abyme* of the true nature of those
baffling extraterrestrials that gets close to the reverie of Bachelar's space, the
"ultra-cellars": "the ultra-cellars reverie is a reverie of an underground space,
an internal space where entrails, stairs, corridors grow like catacombs or like
arteries and veins,"[21] no longer underscoring the mineral but the organic nature
of those beings. For Dunyach, his native city, Toulouse, is a city of flesh, "an
hermaphrodite city where the omnipresent brick is of the raw meat color. It is
invaded by anthropomorphous monuments which are visible from Garonne
riversides: several huge domes topped by a stud, a belfry (basilica Saint-Sernin
with its steeple, which is a wonderful hard-on), cobblestones that are warm in
the summer and where it is pleasant to walk barefoot, etc."[22] Dunyach's bodily
imagination stems from a medical respect of human-body functionalities, and
the contact of his characters with the AnimalCities' skin is similar to the feeling of a caress. In *Dead Stars*, the hero, Closter, travels from AnimalCities to
AnimalCities and walks barefoot on the skin of each new city that he goes into:
"Supérieure accepts with humility the criticisms pounded by my bare feet. Its
overfed flesh bounces under my feet without being bruised."[23]

   The AnimalCities are an example of what Dunyach calls the "attentive matrix," a technological environment or extraterrestrial protector, the kind of
environment sf knows how to create. Not futuristic creations that can be extrapolated from our advanced technological discoveries, but "objects of desire"
having an emotional and/or symbolic value that we would like to be real. But,
above all, they embody the ideal solution for the fear of indifference that can
haunt us. In an AnimalCity, each of us is unique and necessary. The traveler-
hero Closter from *Dead Stars* has a carnal, individualized, and unique relation
with every city he comes across: Nayrademance, Nivôse, Bayane, Supérieure,
Aigue-marine. Three labyrinthine systems intertwine in the corporal thickness
of the AnimalCities: the ultra-cellars of corridors, alcoves, and caves; a network
of pipings, gigantic interconnected circulatory systems; and the bone skeleton
that gives shape to the AnimalCity, and which allows it to build up its walls of
the flesh. A fourth network, the communication network of nerves, which is
not mentioned much in *Dying Stars* but is clearly drawn in *Dead Stars*, plays an
essential part. The reverie of the city is also a reverie of the body. AnimalCities'
body becomes a protective matrix, a sort of continued depth that adapts to the

individuality of its travelers and guides them: "In some areas, bluish mottlings contrast with the eggshell shade of the corridor. The whole is both strange and familiar, like a piece of my own body magnified millions of times. I put my hand on a fold as thick as a skull and I caress it. It vibrates, it's alive. I am overcome by a wave of tenderness. Flesh against flesh, we are communicating."[24] With the AnimalCities, occupying space consists of occupying a body, a metaphorized threshold allowing the passage between exteriority and interiority, a place where domotics would be idealized between macrocosm—the universe—and microcosm, in the privacy of one's own home.

Dunyach is also exploring this concept of attentive matrix from a more political angle in recent short stories, since he sees it as part of the transhuman mutation our society is already experiencing. The fact that our direct environment (home, cities, airports, train stations, malls) appears more and more "conscious" of who we are and is monitoring us to react to our "needs" is a fascinating—and sometimes terrifying—thought experiment.

The creation of AnimalCities is representative of the singularity of Jean-Claude Dunyach's imaginary world, shared with Ayerdhal within the space of a novel. These cities of flesh, places of passage between humanity and the universe, also present different metaphors of Dunyach's universe: halfway between a scientific iconography and a poetization of the scientific concept. Indeed, Dunyach is using scientific concepts because he's a scientist. At the same time, these concepts become allegories in his texts. They explore the complex relationship man maintains with space, infinity, and what is inconceivable. The poetization of science-fictional notions in Jean-Claude Dunyach's work expresses his singularity. If it is difficult to define what determines French contemporary science fiction, I would say that it is through the individual imaginations of writers that we are able to perceive French originality: a scientific dimension, a metaphysics expressed through a link with the flesh and with the metaphorized body for a humanist, sensorial, and earthling science fiction—maybe a sensualist form of science fiction in the philosophical sense, inherited from François Rabelais, where the Giant is a metaphor but also a gigantic realistic body, exaggerating the "organic" aspect of the human life. Dunyach wants readers to feel the sensoriality of the world: "The stories I write are not accurate scientific predictions, nor are they meant to warn the world of this or that danger, present or future. If they have a moral, it is more often than not without my deliberate intention. I only report what seems obvious to me, obvious and wonderful. And through the act of writing, I seek to share these stories with others, giving them lives of their own."[25]

Notes

1. The French science-fiction writer Marc Soulier, who used the solitary pseudonym "Ayerdhal" for his literary work, died on October 27, 2015, in Brussels.

2. The term "chronotic" refers to time travel, while "chronolyse," in Jeury's work, is the name of the drug used to travel through time. See Vas-Deyres, "Du Temps incertain."

3. *Malgré le monde* [Despite the world] is the collective work of Jacques Barbéri, Francis Berthelot, Lionel Évrard, Emmanuel Jouanne, Frédéric Serva, Jean-Pierre Vernay, and Antoine Volodine.

4. Andrevon, "Années 70," 11.

5. There are more than twenty collections from various publishers, without counting specialized magazines: among the most noteworthy are *Le Rayon Fantastique* (1951–64), *Anticipation* (1951–97), *Ailleurs et demain* (1969–), *Présence du Futur* (1954–2000), *Club du livre d'Anticipation* (1966–87), *Galaxie-bis* (1965–86), *Dimensions SF* (1973–84), *Anti-Mondes* (1972–77), *Chute libre* (1974–78), *Nébula* (1975–77), *Ici et Maintenant* (1977–79), *Presses Pocket* (1977–), and *Nouvelles Éditions Oswald* (1978–89).

6. "[The] May 1968 effect is going to be more obvious through a sort of school created by Bernard Blanc and edited by Rolf Kesselring in the series 'Ici et Maintenant,' which will express the ecological and political times, but which won't escape from the naivety unfortunately and—this is paradoxical—from conformism of ideas and form. It will lead, alas, a great part of the readers to turn away from a French sf which is unfairly mistaken with this unique trend, certainly noisy and active, but considered with some appearance of reason as sermonizing and boring." Klein, Preface. Jacques Sadoul even proposes a "true intellectual terrorism"; in other words, that science fiction in France had to be political to have value. Sadoul, *Histoire*, 455. Unless otherwise noted, all translations are my own.

7. Lanuque, "Mai 68," 148.

8. Sadoul, *Histoire*, 457.

9. Yves Frémion undertook the publication of nineteen issues, except the first and second.

10. Jean-Claude Dunyach is using this word to characterize the fact that French science fiction is weird in the Anglo-Saxon sense, but is often mixed with other literary or artistic approaches.

11. This interview can be read at https://worldsf.wordpress.com/2011/06/08/an-interview-with-jean-claude-dunyach-from-utopiales-2010/.

12. According to Jean Baudrillard, modern symbolism is a direction of objects and desires: "The logic of goods became widespread . . . all functions, all needs are objectified and treated in terms of profit, but in the deepest sense everything is made spectacle; that is to say, evoked, provoked, orchestrated in images, in signs and edible models." Baudrillard, *La société de consommation*, 308.

13. Dunyach, *Game of the Hourglass*, 221.

14. Dunyach, "Sand Swimmers," 142.

15. Ibid., 143.

16. Ayerdhal and Dunyach, *Dying Stars*, 17.

17. Dunyach, "Time as It Evaporates," 58–59.

18. Jean-Claude Dunyach, personal interview with the author, February 13, 2013.

19. A *traboule* is a narrow passage that links two streets by crossing a block of house.

20. See Goffette, "L'espace en résonance."

21. Ibid.

22. Jean-Claude Dunyach, personal interview with the author.

23. Ayerdhal and Dunyach, *Dead Stars*, 205.

24. Ibid., 89.

25. Dunyach, "Afterword," 273.

Bibliography

Andrevon, Jean-Pierre. "Années 70 . . . année 68." In *Les Enfants du mirage*, vol. 1. Paris: Éditions Naturellement, 2001. 11.

Ayerdhal, and Jean-Claude Dunyach. *Etoiles mourantes* [Dying stars]. Paris: Réédition Mnémos, 2014.

Baudrillard, Jean. *La société de consummation. Ses mythes, ses structures* [Consumer society: Its myths, its structures]. Paris: Gallimard, 2006.

Dunyach, Jean-Claude. "Afterword." In *The Night Orchid: Conan Doyle in Toulouse*. Trans. Sheryl Curtis. Encino, Calif.: Black Coat Press, 2004. 271–73.

———. *Etoiles mortes* [Dead stars]. Paris: J'ai lu SF, 2000.

———. *Le Jeu des sabliers* [The game of the hourglass]. Paris: ISF, 2003.

———. "The Sand Swimmers." In *The Night Orchid: Conan Doyle in Toulouse*. Trans. Sheryl Curtis. Encino, Calif.: Black Coat Press, 2004. 247–70.

———. *The Thieves of Silence*. Trans. Sheryl Curtis. Encino, Calif.: Black Coat Press, 2009.

———. "Time as It Evaporates." In *The Night Orchid: Conan Doyle in Toulouse*. Trans. Sheryl Curtis. Encino, Calif.: Black Coat Press, 2004. 91–112.

Goffette, Jérôme. "L'espace en résonance: corps, ville et monde dans *Etoiles mourantes* d'Ayerdhal et J. C. Dunyach" In *Poétique(s) de l'espace dans les œuvres fantastiques et de science-fiction* [Poetics of space in works of fantasy and science fiction]. Ed. Françoise Dupeyron-Lafay and Huftier Arnaud. Paris: Michel Houdiard, 2007. 33–52.

Jeury, Michel. "Le Temps incertain" [The uncertain times]. *Ailleurs et demain* 22 (1973): 264.

Klein, Gérard Klein. Preface to *L'Hexagone halluciné [The Hallucinated hexagon]*. Ed. Ellen C. Herzfeld, Gérard Klein, and Dominique Martel. Paris: Librairie générale française, 1988. 17.

Lanuque, Jean-Guillaume. "Mai 68 et la science-fiction française." In *Dissidences*, vol. 4. Paris: Le Bord de l'eau éditions, 2008. 148.

Limite [Jacques Barbéri, Francis Berthelot, Lionel Évrard, Emmanuel Jouanne, Frédéric Serva, Jean-Pierre Vernay, and Antoine Volodine]. *Malgré le monde* [Despite the world]. Collection Présence du Futur No. 452. Paris: Denoël, 1987.

Sadoul, Jacques. *Histoire de la Science-fiction moderne* [A history of modern science fiction]. Paris: Robert Laffont, 1984.

Vas-Deyres, Natacha. "Du Temps incertain au temps ralenti: variations temporelles françaises." In *L'Imaginaire du temps dans le fantastique et la science-fiction* [The imaginary of time in the fantastic and science fiction]. Ed. Natacha Vas-Deyres and Lauric Guillaud. *Eidôlon* No. 91. Pessac: Presses universitaires de Bordeaux, 2011. 57–68.

Zola, Émile. *La Curée* [The kill]. Paris: Charpentier, 1872.

———. *Le ventre de Paris* [The belly of Paris]. Paris: Charpentier, 1873.

Andreas Eschbach's Futures
and Germany's Past

VIBEKE RÜTZOU PETERSEN

In Germany, the most prestigious national prize for science fiction is named for Kurd Lasswitz, the presumed father of German science fiction. Lasswitz was a scientist, and when he wrote *Auf zwei Planeten* (Two planets) in 1897, he was hoping that speculative or fantastic narrative would be helpful in teaching science to its readers. Since science is the other—and demarcating—part of science fiction, here was an opportunity to weave science into a narrative context.[1] This kind of writing had a generation of young boys under its thrall, among them Wernher von Braun, who declared that he was much influenced by the visions in Lasswitz's novel. Von Braun went on to be one of the most brilliant and notorious rocket scientists, first employed by Nazi Germany and later by the United States. Few works of early German science-fiction writers continue to be read today, but those that are rose to popularity during the Weimar period (1919–33). Alfred Döblin, a writer of so-called serious literature well-known to his contemporaries and beyond, experimented with science fiction and wrote *Berge Meere und Giganten* (Mountains seas and giants) in 1924. Those years also gave rise to one of the first science-fiction films. Written by Thea von Harbou and directed by her husband, Fritz Lang, *Metropolis* (1927) remains the most famous film of its kind from the pre–Second World War period.

Whatever tentative tradition existed before 1933, it was interrupted by the National Socialist regime. There were, of course, science-fiction writers during the thirteen years of Nazi rule, but few survived the imposition of fascist ideological censorship. Among those who did, the best known is probably Hans Dominik. He was a proponent of the "wissenschaftlich-technische Zukunftsroman" (scientific-technological futuristic novel), and his novels—of which *Die Macht der Drei* (The power of three; 1922), *Das Erbe der Uraniden* (The legacy of the Uranides; 1928), and *Kautschuk* (Rubber; 1930), are the best known—were read avidly during the period. After the defeat of the Nazis, Dominik's works were heavily edited for the most obvious white-supremacist and imperialist notions no longer of good repute.

In 1948, an abridged edition of Kurt Lasswitz's *Two Planets* was republished, but after World War II and the division of Germany, West German science fiction took a while to reestablish itself. Among the works that appeared were some penned by authors of "highbrow" literature, like Döblin, who were trying their hands at speculative writing. Ernst Jünger, best known for his memoir of World War I, *In Stahlgewittern* (Storm of steel; 1924), published *Heliopolis* in 1949, and Walter Jens, an academic and writer, came out with *Nein: Die Welt der Angeklagten* (No: The world of the accused) in 1950. In the 1950s a small number of science-fiction narratives apppeared whose themes were influenced by the Holocaust and Hiroshima, among them Jens Rehn's *Die Kinder des Saturn* (Saturn's children; 1959). Still, most of the popular works were by Anglo-American authors.

Be that as it may, from the 1960s until the end of the 1990s, the German adventure science-fiction series *Perry Rhodan* held the place as the most popular science-fiction series ever. This meant that sf writers had to struggle with the notion that science fiction equaled "dime novels," although a number of German sf writers started out writing for the *Rhodan* series. The 1970s witnessed the appearance of *Das Königsprojekt* (The royal project; 1974) and *Der Untergang der Stadt Passau* (Flaming sword of the watcher; 1975), science-fiction works by Carl Amery, who was also known in Germany as a writer and environmental activist. By now, a handful of sf writers, editors, and small publishers, among them Herbert W. Franke, Wolfgang Jeschke, H. J. Alpers, and Horst Pukallus, had emerged, as had a small number of known publishing houses such as Heyne and Bastei-Lübbe, for example, willing to take a chance on "homegrown" science fiction. Their vigorous efforts made increasing numbers of native science-fiction works available to German readers, even though the German market for science fiction was much less developed than those in Britain or the United States. When Andreas Eschbach published his first novel, *Die Haarteppichknüpfer* (1995; translated as *The Carpet Makers* in 2005), there were still only a few bookstores that had science-fiction works on their shelves. Of those, almost all were English or American works of science fiction translated into German.[2]

The Author

Andreas Eschbach (b. 1959) studied aerospace engineering at the University of Stuttgart and worked as a software engineer for a time. He wrote from early on in his childhood. After he received a scholarship for the gifted in creative writing from the Arno-Schmitt Foundation in 1994, it took only nine months for *The Carpet Makers* to appear.[3] In a conversation about the writing of *Exponentialdrift* (Exponential drift; 2001), Eschbach explained to Frank Schirrmacher, the editor of one of the most important German newspapers, the *Frankfurter Allgemeine Zeitung*, that he doesn't write science fiction.[4] What he writes, he says, are narratives in which time travel and space ships simply "pop up" quite frequently. This vague definition of his style or refutation of genres notwithstanding, Eschbach is considered one of continental Europe's biggest science-fiction stars.[5] Every year since 1980, those professionally involved in the science-fiction industry have awarded the prestigious Kurd Lasswitz prize for the best science-fiction works (i.e novels, short stories, graphics, translations, and foreign works) to one of their own. Andreas Eschbach has been the recipient of this prize eight times in the fifteen years between 1997 and 2012. He has won for the following works: *Solarstation* (1997), *Das Jesus Video* (1998; translated as *The Jesus Video* the same year), *Kelwitts Stern* (Kelwitt's star; 2000), *Quest* (2001), *Der Letzte seiner Art* (The last of his kind; 2005), *Ausgebrannt* (Spent; 2008), *Ein König für Deutschland* (A king for Germany; 2010), and *Herr aller Dinge* (2011; translated as *Lord of All Things* in 2014).

This means that roughly every two years between 1997 and 2012 he has produced something outstanding in the genre. Said differently, of his three dozen works—thrillers, science fiction, YA novels, anthologies, nonfiction, and even a work he calls a tourist guide, *Das Buch von der Zukunft* (The book from/of/ about the future; 2004)—a quarter of them have received a prestigious prize for science fiction. *The Carpet Makers* received the Deutsche Science Fiction Preis in 1996. It is therefore safe to say that Eschbach has written and continues to write novels that rival the best in German science fiction.

He is one of the few continental science-fiction writers whose works have been translated into several languages, among them English, Norwegian, and Japanese. Of this impressive ouevre, five major science-fiction works by Eschbach have been picked for examination here: *The Carpet Makers, The Jesus Video, Quest, The Last of His Kind*, and *Lord of All Things*. All five works received the Kurd Lasswitz Prize, and each of them constitutes an exemplary Eschbach treatment of themes that are staples of the genre: faraway galaxies, space travel, time travel, cyborgs, and nanotechnology. This essay will offer comprehensive analyses of the novels, explore some major themes shared by the works, contextualize Eschbach's writing in his own cultural-historical context and point out some culturally specific tropes, and situate his novels in German and international science-fiction traditions. The overall aim of this examination is to make the case for Andreas Eschbach's importance in the larger picture of Western science fiction.

Major Works

THE CARPET MAKERS

The Carpet Makers is Eschbach's ambitious first novel. It has a complex structure and an ingenious plot consisting of seventeen loosely connected stories and an epilogue. The narrative takes place in the Gheera galaxy. Gheera is comprised of 8,374 planets, some of which support a baroque "cottage industry" exclusive to men: the knotting of hair rugs. Fathers teach their sons—only one son is allowed per family—to knot rugs of human hair, hair that comes from the heads of the men's several wives and daughters. While a rug takes a lifetime to knot, it also ravages the eyesight of the knotter. The completed rugs are sold to a traveling merchant, and the story goes that they end up covering the floors in the StarEmperor's palace.

Most of the stories have a single protagonist, but few of these reappear in later stories. In the fifth of the seventeen narratives, Nillian, a former rebel against the StarEmperor and now a space pilot with the new postrevolutionary government, is exploring the Gheera galaxy when his ship happens upon Planet G-101/2. This is the planet where readers are first introduced to the hair rugs and their makers. Nillian decides to land, despite direct orders to the contrary, and during his first hours on the planet he meets a traveling trader. In his conversations with inhabitants of this planet, left behind in the structural and economic development of the galaxy, Nillian insists upon the StarEmperor's demise. This amounts to apostasy in the eyes of the Gheerans, and consequently they take him prisoner. He is disappeared, only to reappear as a rumor throughout the rest of the novel. This motif—the whisper of Nillian's existence—is cleverly woven into the novel as a theme serving to join the two worlds, that of the government and that of the hair-rug makers.

At first, Eschbach's novel comes across as multitemporal. But upon careful reading, one realizes that the contrast between a highly developed technoscientific ruling culture and semifeudal Gheera, with its cultures closely tied to the hair-rug economy, is not so much temporal as it is one of galactic geography. Gheera has been a part of the empire for millennia, but as it turns out, it doesn't appear on any space map. It is only found through a chain of coincidences, and no one knows the reason for its "disappearance." Gheera, it seems, has been deliberately left in the dark.

The plotline that connects most of the seventeen stories is that of the quest to discover what happens to the hair rugs. The first stories familiarize readers with the rug-making process and sale. When the narratives shift to the governmental world, they introduce a handful of characters who are employed in various manners in the new governing body that is created after the fall and death of the StarEmperor at the hands of the resistance. One such character from the "ancien régime" is the imperial librarian and archivist Emparak, who, unbeknownst to anyone, possesses the key to the mystery about the fate of the hair rugs. He bitterly resents the newcomers, their lack of knowledge of the planet's history, their dismissal of him and his possible service. Consequently, he has no desire to divulge any of his knowledge. It is only when he and the beautiful state historian, Lamita, fall in love that we learn of the use for the hair rugs. He tells her the story of Pantap, king of the planet Gheera (not the galaxy), who deeply insulted the StarEmperor's predecessor by making fun of the latter's baldness. Pantap's punishment was to be connected to a life-support system for centuries, watching the extermination of his people and his kingdom as they are suffocated by hair rugs.

The narrators' many different and differing points of view suggest a structural and narrative changeability that stands in sharp contrast to the system they narrate. Multiple narrative points of view also offer the reader a kaleidoscopic view of the culture and social conditions of the Gheera galaxy, where authority, hierarchy, and blind obedience are central to life. The StarEmperor's control and command is unquestionable, and his subjects take the following vow of obedience: "We serve the Emperor whose word is law. Whose will is our will. Whose wrath is terrible. Who does not forgive but punishes. And whose vengeance is eternal."[6] Combined with the official worship of the StarEmperor as a deity, these draconian rules leave little room for resistance, and the novel describes the contagious effects of domination and authority. They express themselves, among other ways, in the rule of infanticide of male children and the absolute authority in the household of the law of the father. It is striking that Erich Fromm's observations about Weimar Germany are so applicable to Eschbach's treatment of the private lives of the carpet makers. I have in mind particularly his thesis that the powerlessness of the male subject often translates into domination of wife and children and that their obedience takes up an important compensatory function in the private sphere.[7] In the worlds of the carpet makers, the StarEmperor's authority is translated into a moral order that finds resistance to the status quo reprehensible. The rebellion and the consequent end of the StarEmperor's realm are rejected by the Gheera galaxy. Even when he is deceased, his authority is still exercised there while his army and machines cover and strangle a planet with hair rugs in a faraway galaxy. The authority and power of tradition do not dissipate quickly or easily.

The Carpet Makers may be read as a fable about how capitalism works in its simplest form; it is a reimagining of our commodity-producing society where we produce ad infinitum for someone else's benefit.

It would seem that the Gheera planetary system has been caught on paper at the historical conjunction of what Carl Freedman calls "peculiar over-determinations of the absolutist period, when classical feudalism is on the decline but fully-fledged capitalism has not yet emerged into clear view."[8] This literary snapshot depicts the material processes of capitalism that support and enable the reproduction of the existing conditions, and where the fruit of the community's labor, in this case hair rugs, are expropriated and taken off-world. The planets of Gheera are kept on a very low-tech level, where all societal structures are set up to facilitate the manufacture and shipping of the hair rugs. What we see is a paternal capitalism with fundamental class processes (the expropriation of the rugs from the weavers) as well as subsumed class processes (the purchase and transport of the rugs)—that is, distribution and reception of the expropriated surplus in the guise of banking, trade, the military, and so on.[9]

Trading (commerce) is marked as the lifeblood of small towns throughout the planetary worlds. The arrival of the hair-rug trader could have been written to Verdi's triumphal march in *Aida*: anticipated for weeks and led by a regiment of (private) foot soldiers and armed horsemen, freight wagons, private wagons, an armored hair-rug wagon drawn by eighty-two oxen, wagons for provisions and accommodations roll into town under fanfares and flag waving. The market is obviously a major event, and in effect it is coded as the most important day of the year for the community. To wit: the fruits of excruciatingly crippling and blinding labor—hair rugs—change hands at a price set by the Imperial proxy—the trader—and young women are picked as first or subordinate wives for the new hair-rug knotters (the only sons) according to hair quality and color at an open display. In fact, this day hosts the ceremonies of society's self-reproduction.

Besides the sale of the hair rugs, tax collection is marked as important work, and it interlaces the flow of money with the story of unchallengeable power wielded by the tax collector as another Imperial proxy, linking (imperial) authority and economics. The taxes collected never leave the planets but are used to buy the hair rugs from the next generation of weavers. This circular cash flow instructs us yet again about capitalism's merry-go-round: the surplus value, or goods, are in fact being bought by the surplus income extracted from the workers (not only the knotters) in the form of taxes. Said differently, the inhabitants/workers are buying the products of their own labor that were bought from them in the first place. But, in the Gheera galaxy, they still have nothing to show for taxes, wages, or labor. Instead, with time, most of them sink more deeply into poverty, since the Imperial authority invests no money in the Gheera system, which functions as a closed system not overlapping or overlapped by any other.

Apart from the gruesome use of the hair rugs themselves, their manufacture from human hair is uncannily reminiscent of the practices of Nazi Germany, where hair harvested from concentration-camp inmates was sold as a cheaper substitute for wool. This was true of Germany in general and of Auschwitz in particular, where they housed the hair of Jewish women in a storeroom next to an area with examples of uses for human skin. *The Carpet Makers* draws upon imagery that conjures up the crimes of the Holocaust, as do some of Eschbach's other narratives. The use of such imagery will be discussed later in this essay.

THE JESUS VIDEO

Although *The Jesus Video* did not become a bestseller until it was published as a paperback, it received the Kurd Lasswitz prize in 1999. In 2002, it was adapted for German TV.

The novel takes place in various locations in Israel, most importantly on the site of an archaeological excavation—presumably close to Beit Shea'rim. Here a manual for a camera and remnants of its case (but not the camera) are discovered in an archaeological stratum two thousand years old. That makes the premise of the novel time travel. While inspecting an inscription on a wall in the Bei She'arim National Park, a young man accidentally slips back into and is caught in the time of Jesus with his twentieth-century video camera. The novel hypothesizes that the youth videotapes Jesus, and the search for the camera with the tapes—ostensibly with recordings of Jesus—drives the plot of *The Jesus Video*.

Eschbach throws various players into the mix: Professor Wilford-Smith, the lower-than-top-drawer archaeologist who, as we learn along the way, actually discovered the camera paraphernalia while soldiering in Israel in the aftermath of World War II and who, up to now, has been unable to finance a way to find the camera proper; Kaun, a ruthless media magnate, and his henchmen, who initiate the search for the camera so he can use it to strengthen his media corporation; ambitious, entrepreneurial Stephen Foxx, who wants to find it on his own and who teams up with his Israeli friends to search for it; and the Catholic church's Father Scarfaro—a member of the erstwhile Inquisition—who wants to prevent the video from reaching the public at all costs. Clues as to where to look for the camera and the ambitions of the characters involved make for an exciting and fast read, with scenery shifting from Beit Shea'rim to Jerusalem's Wailing Wall to a monastery in the Negev, and the vast landscape of the Negev itself.

The character of Eisenhard adds another layer to the already ingenious plot. He is a German science-fiction writer hired by Kaun to extrapolate on discoveries of the day and consequently propose innovative ideas of what might have happened. This character is a nod to the kind of writing that Eschbach, according to his own testament, doesn't do; but in Eisenhardt, Eschbach has created a literary device that allows him to introduce discussions about how time travel, a traditionally favorite science-fiction theme, might work. Eisenhardt is certainly a comment on science fiction and the uses and functions of a science-fictional imagination both to figure things out and to expand the limits of our thought horizons and paradigms. In addition, Eisenhardt's deliberations assist Eschbach's penchant for elaborating upon any situation that may need an explanation. It is to Eschbach's credit that when he enters into theoretical discussions, he tries—and mostly succeeds—to translate scientific theorems into everyday speech. Eschbach has been praised by readers and critics alike for his ability to narrate the (fantastic) science in his science fiction with credibility and clarity.[10]

Aesthetically Eschbach's writing tends to push the limits of popular literature; at times it is even a little experimental. As we have seen above, *The Carpet Makers* consists of seventeen loosely connected stories. In *Exponential Drift*, he employs very short chapters (three to four pages each) called *Folgen* (continuations or consequences), preceded by excerpts from the daily news. In comparison, the chapters in *The Jesus Video* are of more conventional length, but they are introduced by half a dozen lines in cursive writing. These lines are purportedly commentaries from the journal of an archaeological excavation, and they describe in detail how an exploration grid is set up and how the dig proceeds from there. These separate commentaries add veracity and authenticity to the fictional narrative they introduce. They also save the writer from having to accommodate such technical details within the main narrative. Eschbach keeps sections within the chapters short and cuts them, cinematically, when the action has reached a "mini-cliffhanger" moment.

The Jesus Video has several minor characters whose raison d'etre is to function as vehicles of certain qualities or ideologogical points of view and possibly to afford the writer an opportunity to hedge his bets. An example is George Martinez, a sonogram engineer from Montana, who is also a Mexican and a Catholic. Through his faith, the novel is able to articulate another explanation for time travel. Stephen Hawking's comments on the matter are adduced—namely, that if time travel were possible, why haven't we seen or met any time travelers so far? Could it be that humanity perishes before it is possible to work out the complexities of such an endeavor?[11] But Martinez's explanation of the phenomenon is faith-based: "Surely, nothing is impossible for God, not even time travel. Maybe it was part of His unfathomable plan to give humans, specifically in a time characterized by TV, a video of their Savior in order to strengthen the Church and to lead them back to their faith."[12] Eschbach's research and realistic writing about Jerusalem, its history, religious buildings, and traditions set a credible context for George's speculation, and his notion demands no bigger a leap of faith than do those of the sf writer. Martinez's relationship to Catholic teachings illustrates an unmitigated faith similar to the one we also find in *The Carpet Makers* among the rug makers vis-à-vis the StarEmperor. Once you have that kind of faith, the texts claim, it owns you. Published in 1998, the novel's exploration of faith and historical certainties as well as doubts by means of the existence of a video of Jesus taken by a time traveler also raises the question about what is important in the 1990s, the message or the man.

The Jesus Video shares with *The Carpet Makers* an obvious nod to the Nazi past. A taxi driver at the Tel-Aviv airport—a very minor character, indeed—functions as a carrier of that past. He has displayed a little Polish flag in the cabin. When a customer comments on the taxi driver's good German, the latter answers: "Das habe ich im kz gelernt" (I learned that in the concentration camp).[13] This startling piece of information serves not only as a reminder that Israel was established and constituted largely by Holocaust survivors; it serves as another example of a subject that Eschbach returns to repeatedly in his writing.

QUEST

Eschbach has said that his motivation to write a fully fledged space opera came partly from wanting to pay tribute to his science-fiction readers who "adopted" him early on in his career.[14] In *Quest*, we are back in the Gheera galaxy, the universe of the StarEmperor, although the novel is situated in a time before that of *The Carpet Makers*. In this space opera, the novel's protagonist, legendary commander Quest of the reconnaissance starship Megatoa, is fatally ill and on his last journey through the universe. He is obsessively focused on the search for the origin of life. The commander is driven to find the mythical planet where life began; he is convinced that this is also where he can argue with God—God, who let Commander Quest's planet be annihilated (presumably by StarImperial troops), leaving him with the impossible burden and guilt of survival.

This is a trope that resonates in the narratives of Holocaust survivors, but Eschbach does not leave Nazi atrocities with the commander's anguish. He makes another reference: *Quest* features a group of human beings from another galaxy, the Tigans, who are classified as "lower" beings. They have spotted skin, and in certain parts of the universe they are hunted for their highly desirable skin that in turn is used for bags and other commodities.

The journey takes Quest and his crew through unexplored areas of the universe, and they visit planets whose inhabitants are true aliens (i.e. nonhumanoid), some of whom help them to the next stage of the journey. On the way, the crew rescues Smeeth, a survivor of a wrecked spaceship. Despite the humans' distrust of him, his knowledge of the universe is indespensable to Quest's journey. Eschbach transliterates the name Smith to Smeeth (based on the German pronunciation of the name?), and through this character he introduces the Common Man into space narratives, creating an agent for a dwindling sense of confidence in the future—which may be shared by the author. History is part of Eschbach's world, and his stories often point to distastrous consequences if we forget our pasts. In *Quest,* Smeeth turns out to be one of twelve immortals from a well-known legend, and as such he is the repository of human history, most of which has been lost. Consequently he worries about the future, and he cannot hide his disappointment at what he sees onboard the Megatoa—namely, humanity's political regression from democracy to autocracy.

The novel consists of an overture, ten portraits, and a coda. Each of the portraits contains its own "adventure," but the quest for God and the planet of origin runs through them all. Framed by the overarching search, the characters are also searching—for love, the meaning of life, and power, respectively—at a time when their worlds are being conquered one by one by the forces of the StarEmperor. It is a journey that, despite its obvious search for the past, is just as intensely looking for a future.

THE LAST OF HIS KIND

The Last of His Kind represents Eschbach's first excursion into cybernetics and cyborg science fiction. Duane Fitzgerald is a prototype of a cybernetic warrior produced by an unsuccessful U.S. Army experiment. He and his few surviving fellow Steel Men have been put out to pasture. Secretly supervised by the army, they are forbidden from having any contact with each other. Duane has chosen to settle in a small Irish village, Dingle, from whence his ancestors came.

The novel's opening sentence, "Saturday, I awoke blind and paralyzed on one side," indicates that the narrator is deliberating upon an extraordinary bodily experience.[15] The section that follows guides the reader through various collapsing body functions toward a gradual awareness that the protagonist is no ordinary human, but one augmented by technoscience.

Eschbach's prose allows glimpses into the cyborg's past (whoever thought of cyborgs having a childhood?) while humanizing his protagonist by juxtaposing the pinnacle of military technoscience—the cyborg—with trivial, practical, knowledge: "I have learned that you should only use cold water if you want to wash blood out," the first-person narrator observes.[16] Comments such as these also serve to destabilize a popular injunction vis-à-vis cyborgs: the need for them to be "special," particularly tough, fierce, and aggressive wo/men of action.

There is, of course, no clear reason that cyborgs shouldn't possess mundane knowledge. Even though he is a cyborg filled with special metals and implants, Fitzgerald's thoughts focus mostly on traditional topics such as hunger, thirst, and companionship. He frequently talks to himself about his metal structural parts rusting away as part of his aging process.[17] This once military wonder contains much to which the reader, occupying a less techno-scientifically marked body, can relate. In this manner, Eschbach lays the first bricks in a path towards de-exoticizing the ordinarily superlative being, the cyborg.

The village doctor, O'Shea, is the only one in whom Fitzgerald has confided, and O'Shea, fascinated by the American's technologically enhanced body, operates on and fixes the organic cybernetic interfaces as they show increasing signs of wear and tear. Fitzgerald realizes that his days as a cyborg are numbered, and he agrees to travel to a medical conference with the doctor to tell his story. Soon after that conversation, the doctor is found murdered, and Fitzgerald's previous cyborg colleagues begin to disappear one by one. Fitzgerald gradually comes to realize that his military bosses are planning to create a new series of cyborgs without any of the old, unsuccessful samples around to remind the taxpayer of the failure. He is contacted by some previous IRA sympathizers, among them Bridget, the object of his unrequited love, with a plan to expose the U.S. Army's Steelman experiment. All the while, the cyborg's system, without Dr. O'Shea's care, quickly deteriorates. But before his cybernetic system fails completely, Fitzgerald prints out a downloaded journal he has kept about his life as a cyborg. Whatever his fate, he does not want his story to be lost. Yet again, Eschbach reminds us of the importance of history.

The United States' military research deems it prudent to scrap earlier models of the cyborg and move on to genetically modified warriors exhibiting a lack of what Elaine L. Graham has called "responsibility of human knowledge released from theological prohibition."[18] The development of Fitzgerald's cyborg model was facilitated by past technological and medical economies, and it has thus outlived its usefulness. The narrative emphasis on Fitzgerald's disintegrating cyborg body reads as a contradiction to the disembodiment that has characterized many posthuman theories. Fitzgerald is very embodied. The narrative marks each of the cyborg's failing circuits and translates them into human angst and pain.

The Last of His Kind uses a first-person narrator, and Eschbach makes good use of it to voice humor, even sarcasm. This voice is paired with quotations from the stoic philosopher Seneca, which precede each chapter. The prose is conversational, as if Fitzgerald is shrugging the whole narrative off, refuting what he feels, observes, and experiences, such as his terror of life as an aging cyborg who is beginning to disintegrate. "If anyone disbelieves immortality, it is I," says Fitzgerald, and at that point he actively engages Seneca in the text as he explores the philosopher's notion that if one does not embrace one's frailties, one falls into danger of squandering one's life.[19] The strong sense of mortality from Fitzgerald and Seneca flies in the face of the fantasies of eternal youth that have followed much of the transformation of flesh into data in scientific as well as in science-fictional narratives. Fitzgerald very much wants to be considered a human, with all its trappings.

Seneca is perhaps an unlikely guide for a cyborg warrior, but it works in this case because the Roman philosopher's reasoning about life—and death in particular—informs Fitzgerald's striving to stay calm in the face of his own fate. Among Seneca's notions are those that life is finite, that all life contains the seeds of its death, and that life lived diligently prepares us for death.[20] In his acceptance of the Stoic philosopher's teachings on mortality, the cyborg seems to prepare for his own built-in obsolescence and death. This is his future, and, although he doesn't say so, he is resigning himself to his lack of usefulness and the consequently inexorable road toward his end, as a cyborg and a man. True to Seneca, Fitzgerald does not wax poetic about what he once was, but unlike Donna Haraway's cyborg, he does harbor nostalgia for his origins.[21] While the cyborg does not want to live in the past—although this past was one of power and brotherhood—he wants to live as a human, in and with his current conditions. Any other way of living is unrewarding.[22]

Like the other stories discussed in this essay, *The Last of His Kind* was an award-winning novel, and in it Eschbach puts forward his arguments vis-à-vis cyborgs and posthumanism. The novel can be read as a response to the cyber-punk movement (waning at this time in Anglo-American science fiction) and to terrorism, which in the story is enacted by the IRA and the U.S. military. Still, Eschbach—with the help of Seneca—seems particularly eager to lay to rest myths about immortality tied to technology and virtual reality—hence his unrelenting focus on Fitzgerald's clearly deteriorating material reality. But the novel wouldn't be complete without a Holocaust reference, and in *The Last of His Kind*, a very minor character, a taxidermist, wants perfect specimens for his "art." To this end, he builds a gas chamber where he can kill the animals without marking them.

LORD OF ALL THINGS

Lord of All Things represents another Eschbach foray into the realm of techno-science, in this case nanotechnology. Hiroshi Kato and Charlotte Leroux meet as children in Japan. Charlotte becomes Kato's love interest, and, although her character could have been better developed, she represents one of the stronger female protagonists in Eschbach's science-fiction works. Kato dreams of making everyone in the world rich, which for him means alleviating people's daily toil. His own work leads him to develop a prototype of a nano- or swarm intelligence that can replicate everything it is programmed to, even itself. However, the program isn't refined enough, and when it crashes, Kato withdraws from the public eye. Charlotte becomes a paleoanthropologist whose vague thesis about a human race predating our own having inhabited the earth serves as the foil for her travels. One of her trips leads her to an arctic Russian island, where her expedition runs afoul of an inexplicable and menacing nanotechno-logical activity. Due to its advanced and sophisticated nature, the expeditional members presume the technology to be alien. Kato is called in as an expert and does indeed pronounce the phenomenon alien. He steals samples of it, explores it, and learns to read it. He consequently arrives at the conclusion that an earlier civilization developed this technology to eradicate life in the universe. He downloads the alien program into his brain and is now indeed Lord of All Things. The U.S. government fears the power of the technology and hunts Kato down. A spectacular flight, greatly aided by his enhanced system, demonstrates the ability of the alien technology.

In the narrative, ecology constitutes a tertiary and dark topic that Eschbach does not take the opportunity to elaborate: Kato's aunt lives with his grandparents in the Bay of Minamata (Japan) and is a victim of the mercury poisoning that afflicted that community in the 1950s. It is up to the reader to make the tenuous connection between capitalism, Kato's interest in a sustainable, green technology, and industrial waste—mercury—dumped in the Bay of Minamata.

Eschbach has great fun imagining the awesome power of swarm intelligence and nanotechnology. *Lord of All Things* aptly generates traditional science-fiction excitement. It provides us with utopian notions based on a "scientific rationality" that is related to the effects of nanotechnology, its limitations, and the possible dangers such technology poses. What would a future world of nanotechnology be like, and how would we function and perform in it? The novel has no clear answer, and Eschbach hedges his bets when in an interview with the sf.fan.de website, he says with a moderate scientific optimism: "I do not worry about technology; I worry about people."[23]

Parallel to the theme of technoscience runs an economic discussion about the increasing gap between rich and poor, labor and capital, and the reliance of the latter on human work for its viability. In *Lord of All Things*, Kato attempts to dismantle capitalism, although this is not stated in so many words. The protagonist comes from straitened circumstances, and in his adulthood, he translates his boyhood dream of universal riches into a robotic complex that can be programmed into making anything anyone needs, as well as re-producing itself. There will be an unlimited supply of robotic workers and raw materials reclaimed from constant 100 percent recycling—just as nature does it, says Eschbach. And as for foodstuffs, smaller garden plots will take the place of industrial agriculture with its vast fields of monoculture crops. As people's needs are covered through the process, the demand for work disappears, and people will do with their time what they want.

This, of course, spells the demise of ownership of the means of production, wage labor, and profit, supporting Marx's claim that capitalism is a historically specific mode of production. Interestingly, in *Lord of All Things*, it is not the working classes that bring about this revolution but bourgeois research and benevolent corporate investment. Moreover, the novel plays with introducing a new "working class" in the form of nanoworkers.

Although Eschbach's ouevre plays out a number of economic systems, it doesn't suggest systemic changes from capitalism to socialism but seems quite content to work inside capitalist parameters and its consequences. Still, Eschbach posits, not all kinds of capitalism work equally well—or at all—for everybody.

Eschbach's knowledge about and enthusiasm for technoscience informs many of the plots in his novels, but there are other themes at work in his science-fiction oeuvre. Some of them have their roots in Germany's national history, and others are grouped within overarching Western tropes. According to Paul Kincaid, religion as a world issue, global terrorism, climate change, and ecology are major factors in our world.[24] It is through such themes that Eschbach converses with national and international science fictions. *The Carpet Makers* deals with the terrible consequences that result when a planet is deprived of sun and air.[25] *The Jesus Video* grapples, among other things, with the ineffability of the power of Jesus's message to humanity.

In his essay "Final Frontiers," Peter Mühlbauer examines the role of science fiction in the development of libertarian ideology, and he observes that it is found above all in American science fiction. German science fiction belongs to an authoritarian tradition evidenced by notions of the "übermensch" and racial supremacy scattered throughout German speculative fiction.[26] Eschbach's past is the German past, and this national-historical context makes itself felt in particular tropes or cultural "quotes" that recur in many of his novels. The omnipresent reference to the Nazi reign and its terrors is a feature of Eschbach's writing that is recognizable and that surfaces in his narratives whether they concern cyborgs, time travel, space, adventures in space, or carpet makers in loosely connected stories. Elsewhere I have written extensively about the use of the Holocaust in German science fiction in general, and by Andreas Eschbach in particular.[27]

This essay is not trying to answer the question of why those references are there. Instead, it posits that the presence of Holocaust metaphors in popular fiction has several consequences. One of them is keeping the event alive in popular memory, as the last generation of survivors is dying off. Another effect is that the Holocaust itself is being rewritten; there are also the issues of representing that which is darkly ineffable as well as the ethics of such representations. Together, these gruesome images suggest that the German present is standing on the shoulders of the Nazi past and that this past acts as a source of or referent to something *unheimlich*, sinister, and something that keeps creating/having meaning.[28] It is a past that Eschbach acknowledges fully in many of its horrors throughout his works.

Another theme pervasive in Eschbach's work is authority. Jan Fuhse writes that the emphasis given to action in popular novels comes across as a challenge to take responsibility for one's life; in other words, not to have it decided by the powers that be but to problematize those existing sociocultural limits set for actions.[29] Storytelling is, in itself, an exercise in authority—the mapping of a plot, its limits, its aesthetics, and so on. In every narrative, there is an unspoken claim to a truth that bestows authority upon the narrative realm. A character in a science-fiction novel by Herbert W. Franke—a contemporary of Eschbach's—thinks, "Somewhere in a corner of my brain I still hang on to a spark of critical sense. We probably inherited it when we were born as human beings. A spark of skeptical consciousness, which enables us to escape a blind knee-jerk modus vivendi."[30] Authority and the resistance to it appear to be hardwired into the human brain.

The Jesus Video argues that the church, an institution based on the authority of faith, appropriates the power of faith and translates it into zealousness: the Vatican exercises the ultimate authority of inquisitional violence through the character of Monsignore Scarfaro. Similarly, in *Quest*, obeying the word of the commander, however much the sanity of the orders is doubted, is what makes the space journey succesful in reaching its faraway goals. Again, unquestioned authority, as demonstrated in *The Carpet Makers*, is a theme that looms large, and the echoes from Germany's own twentieth-century national history, in which Eschbach is embedded, are loud.

In addition to the way authority is treated as a narrative theme, one has to mention the authority of the genre itself. Science fiction in Germany has long suffered from the imposition of a literary hierarchy that placed—and in some critics' minds still places—science fiction at the low end of the literary ladder, alongside pulp fiction. That is different from the United States, where science-fiction writers such as Heinlein, Dick, Asimov, Le Guin, and others are often regarded as popular-culture prophets, thus lending credibility and authority to the genre. In Germany, the struggle to be accepted into the literary realm is still an uphill journey for science-fiction writers. Works of this type were (and many still are) published as utopian or futuristic rather than science fiction.[31]

Andreas Eschbach's oeuvre has a broad wingspan. He insists that European science fiction has its own distinct voice, and, as we have seen, he taps into his own cultural context. Still, no cultural context these days is only national; rather, it consists of an international, interwoven textum. In this way, he is connected to the German as well as the Anglo-American science-fiction communities, where many of his peers are affected by or embedded in similar cultural conversations.

Eschbach's narratives are not in-depth examinations of issues current at the time of their writing. His writing does not first and foremost comprise inquiries into urgent societal and cultural questions, nor does it overtly insert any ideological assumptions, neither of its cultural context nor of the genre (utopia or dystopia, for example). Rather, Eschbach's stories are driven by plots and characters, and sometimes a discussion among characters that touches upon "current" problems may bubble up to the surface, at times very subtly or even sparsely. It is the intrigue, danger, improbable scenarios, and, infrequently, the romance that drive the narratives.

Eschbach's faithful following is a testament to his readers' long-lasting loyalty to what the British critic Bernard Bergonzi called "characters, story, atmosphere."[32] But I would even narrow Eschbach's narratives down to story and atmosphere. His characters are not always developed past the two-dimensional stage, and we seldom gain insight into their psychological or spiritual journeys. Dwayne Fitzgerald in *The Last of His Kind* is an exception to the rule. In that novel, we have an in-depth look into the existential struggles of a cyborg warrior as he and his cybernetic body break down. The character is made all the more intriguing when we realize that he is attempting to understand various writings by the Roman philosopher Seneca the Younger as a guide to living the rest of his life accordingly.

Is there worldbuilding? Not the way we know it from Ursula K. Le Guin, Kim Stanley Robinson, or even William Gibson. There is no Ekumen or Red Mars. The closest to a new and unknown world is that of the *Carpet Makers* in the Gheera galaxy. Eschbach's readers can identify with the world in most of his novels, as it is their world with a few adjustments, be these aliens or cyborgs.

"Keeping the SF novel *novel* . . . means finding new premises, new technology, as well as new textual forms and strategies."[33] Eschbach's *The Carpet Makers* and *The Jesus Video* offer new premises, and both of them evidence a fertile imagination with obvious links to contemporary circulating discourses concerning ecology and faith. Eschbach's past as a computer engineer gives him the requisite credibility when he describes technology in his narratives, but his technology seldom constitutes radically new developments. Instead, his protagonists' electronic gadgets are only "ahead" of our time—we recognize them as a credible continuation of what we currently have.

Eschbach's narratives are a mix of science-ficton, thriller, and detective novels, and according to the German scholar Karen Harasser, they are examples of a "newer" science fiction that has taken over from the once traditionally "hard" science fiction or space opera styles.[34] It is easy to agree with that suggestion if one defines "newer" as a hybridization of subgenres. This would explain the writer's assertion that he doesn't write science fiction. Is Eschbach's science fiction living up to Suvin's demand that it be "wiser than the world it speaks to?"[35] Not really, but then few science-fiction narratives can make that claim. Eschbach's narratives operate within and accommodate with relative ease capitalism's hegemonic discourse, albeit with some suggestion of minor changes. It is therefore fair to say that none of his stories suggest radical change, without suggesting that Andreas Eschbach is a cheerleader for the status quo. Taking his oeuvre as a whole, one detects a gentle prodding toward making the world a better place. The worlds he builds are ours, and we recognize them without estrangement.

Notes

1. Harrasser, "Science Fiction," 17.

2. A symposium held in Berlin in 1997 titled "Loving the Alien: Science Fiction, Diaspora, Multikultur," did not include a single German science-fiction novel or film from that era (ibid., 22 n. 57).

3. See http://andreaseschbach.de/vita/vita.html for details about Eschbach's publications (accessed July 28, 2017).

4. Eschbach, *Exponentialdrift*, 220.

5. In his own way, Eschbach participates in the current genre discussion when he notes that the moment an sf novel is considered good, it is removed from the sf category and "claimed" to belong with the more highbrow works of literature. It is a notion that the American writer Lev Grossman, author of *The Magicians*, shares. Grossman suspects that otherwise the "carefully constructed (literary) hierarchies" might collapse "in the presence of such a taxonomical anomaly." Qtd. in Gavaler, "Genre Apocalypse."

6. Eschbach, *Carpet Makers*, 231.

7. Fromm, *Working Class*, 163.

8. Freedman, "Science Fiction and Utopia," 95.

9. See also Resnich and Wolff, *New Departures*.

10. Bettermann, "Andreas Eschbach."

11. Eschbach, *Jesus Video*, 166–67.

12. Ibid., 237. All translations from the German are mine unless otherwise indicated.

13. Ibid., 36.

14. Breitsamer, "*Quest*."

15. Eschbach, *Last of His Kind*, 5.

16. Ibid., 16.

17. Ibid., 12, 18.

18. Graham, *Representation of the Post/Human*, 14.

19. Eschbach, *Last of His Kind*, 31.

20. Vogt, "Seneca."

21. Haraway, "Manifesto for Cyborgs," 150.

22. Eschbach, *Last of His Kind*, 128.

23. Breitsamer, "*Herr aller Dinge*."

24. Kincaid, "Fiction since 1992," 174.

25. See also Sonja Fritzsche's reading of that novel as well as *Ausgebrannt*. Fritzsche, "Andreas Eschbach," 67–87.

26. Mühlbauer, "Final Frontiers," 2.

27. See Petersen, "German Science Fiction," 31–48; and Petersen, "Holocaust," 221–39.

28. Petersen, "Holocaust," 239.

29. Fuhse, "Einleitung," 8.
30. Franke, *Kälte des Weltraums*, 123.
31. Gottwald, *Science Fiction*, 11.
32. Qtd.in Roberts, *History of Science Fiction*, 297.
33. Roberts, *History of Science Fiction*, 303.
34. Harrasser, "Science Fiction," 18.
35. Qtd. in Williams, "Recognizing Cognition," 36.

Bibliography

Amery, Carl. *Das Königsprojekt* [The royal project]. Munich: Piper, 1974.

———. *Der Untergang der Stadt Passau* [Flaming sword of the watcher]. Munich: Heyne, 1975.

Bettermann, Ulrich. "Andreas Eschbach—*Jesus Video.*" SF-Fan.de. https://sf-fan.de. Search Quest. Acessed August 30, 2017

Breitsamer, Florian. "*Herr aller Dinge*—Science-Fiction-Autor Andreas Eschbach im Interview" [Lord of All Things—An Interview with SF Author Andreas Eschbach]. SF-Fan.de. September 15, 2011. Accessed July 28, 2017. https://sf-fan.de . Search Herr aller Dinge. Accessed August 31 2017

———. "*Quest*: Ein Interview mit Andreas Eschbach" [Quest: An interview with Andreas Eschbach]. SF-Fan.de. https:/sf-fan.de. Search Quest. Accessed August 30, 2017.

Döblin, Alfred. *Berge Meere und Giganten* [Mountains seas and giants]. Berlin: S. Fischer, 1924.

Dominik, Hans. *Das Erbe der Uraniden* [The legacy of the Uranides]. Berlin: Scherl-Verlag, 1928.

———. *Kautschuk* [Rubber]. Berlin: Scherl-Verlag, 1930.

———. *Die Macht der Drei* [The power of three]. Berlin: Scherl-Verlag, 1922.

Eschbach, Andreas. *Ausgebrannt* [Spent]. Bergisch Gladbach: Lübbe, 2008.

———. *Das Buch von der Zukunft* [The book from/of/about the future]. Berlin: Rowohlt, 2004.

———. *The Carpet Makers*. Trans. Doryl Jensen. New York: Tor Books, 2005

———. *Exponentialdrift* [Exponential drift]. Bergisch Gladbach: Lübbe, 2003.

———. *Herr aller Dinge* [Lord of all things]. Köln: Lübbe, 2011.

———. *Das Jesus Video* [The Jesus video]. München: Schneekluth, 1998.

———. *Kelwitts Stern* [Kelwitt's star]. Munich: Schneekluth, 2000.

———. *Ein König für Deutschland* [A king for Germany]. Bergisch Gladbach: Lübbe, 2010.

———. *Der Letzte seiner Art* [The last of his kind]. Bergish Gladbach: Lübbe, 2005.

———. *Quest*. Munich: Heyne, 2001.

———. *Solarstation*. Munich: Schneekluth, 1997.

Franke, Herbert W. *Die Kälte des Weltraums* . Phantastische Bibliothek, No. 121. Frankfurt am Main: Suhrkamp, 1984. 123.

Freedman, Carl. "Science Fiction and Utopia: A Historico-Philosophical Overview." In *Learning from Other Worlds: Strangement, Cognition, and the Politics of Science Fiction.* Ed. Patrick Parrinder. Durham, N.C.: Duke University Press, 2001. 72–98.

Fritzsche, Sonja. "Andreas Eschbach." In *Detectives, Dystopia, and Poplit: Studies in Modern German Genre Fiction.* Ed. Bruce Campbell, Alison Guenther-Pal, and Vibeke Rützou Petersen. Rochester, N.Y.: Camden House, 2014. 67–87.

Fromm, Erich. *The Working Class in Weimar Germany: A Psychological and Sociological Study.* Trans. Barbara Weinberger. 1929; reprint, Cambridge, Mass.: Harvard University Press, 1984.

Fuhse, Jan. "Einleitung: Science Fiction als ästhetisches Versuchslabor der Gesellschaft." In *Technik und Gesellschaft in der Science Fiction.* Ed. Jan Fuhse. Berlin: LIT Verlag, 2008. 6–18.

Gavaler, Chris. "Genre Apocalypse." *Chronicle of Higher Education,* January 27, 2015. Accessed July 28, 2017. http://chronicle.com/article/Genre-apocalypse/151327.

Gottwald, Ulrike. *Science Fiction als Literatur in der Bundesrepublik der siebziger und achtziger Jahre.* Frankfurt am Main: Peter Lang, 1990.

Graham, Elaine L. *Representation of the Post/Human: Monsters, Aliens, and Others in Popular Culture.* New Brunswick, N.J.: Rutgers University Press, 2002.

Haraway, Donna. "A Manifesto for Cyborgs: Science, Technology, and Socialist Feminism in the 1980s." In *Simians, Cyborgs, and Women: The Reinvention of Nature.* New York: Routledge, 1991. 149–81.

Harrasser, Karen. "Science Fiction in Deutschland. Erkundigungsgänge in einem literarischen Grenzgebiet." *Quarber Merkur* 93/94 (2002): 17.

Jens, Walter. *Nein: Die Welt der Angeklagten* [No: The world of the accused]. Hamburg: Rowohlt, 1950.

Jünger, Ernst. *Heliopolis.* Tübingen: Klett-Cotta, 1949.

———. *In Stahlgewittern* [Storm of steel]. London: Chatto and Windus, 1924.

Kincaid, Paul. "Fiction since 1992." In *The Routledge Companion to Science Fiction.* Ed. Mark Bould, Andrew M. Butler, Adam Roberts, and Sherryl Vint. London: Routledge, 2009. 174–82.

Lasswitz, Kurd. *Auf zwei Planeten* (*Two Planets*). Berlin: Felber, 1897.

Mühlbauer, Peter. "Final Frontiers Teil 3: Die Rolle der Science Fiction in der Entwicklung libertärer Ideologie" [Final frontiers part 3: The role of science fiction in the development of libertarian philosophy]. *Telepolis.* January 1, 2001. Accessed August 31, 2017. https://heise.de.

Petersen, Vibeke Rützou. "German Science Fiction: Its Formative Works and Its Postwar Uses of the Holocaust." In *Detectives, Dystopia and Poplit: Studies in Modern German Genre Fiction.* Ed. Bruce Campbell, Alison Guenther-Pal, and Vibeke Rützou Petersen. Rochester, N.Y.: Camden House, 2014. 31–38.

———. "What Is the Holocaust Doing in German Science Fiction?" *Extrapolation* 55.2 (Summer 2014): 221–39.

Rehn, Jens. *Die Kinder des Saturn* (*Saturn's Children*). Darmstadt: Hermann Luchter-hand, 1959.

Resnich, Stephen, and Richard Wolff. *New Departures in Marxian Theory.* New York: Routledge, 2006.

Roberts, Adam. *The History of Science Fiction.* Houndsmills: Palgrave Macmillan, 2005.

Vogt, Katja. "Seneca." In *The Stanford Encyclopedia of Philosophy.* Accessed August 31, 2017. https://plato.stanford.edu/entries/seneca/.

Williams, Rhys. "Recognizing Cognition: On Suvin, Miéville, and the Utopian Impulse in the Contemporary Fantastic." *Science Fiction Studies* 41.3 (November 2014): 617–33.

Angélica Gorodischer

Only a Storyteller

YOLANDA MOLINA-GAVILÁN

Although Jorge Luis Borges, Adolfo Bioy Casares, Julio Cortázar, and even Gabriel García Márquez are the major authors that come to mind when one thinks of Argentine fantasy and science fiction, to that list we must add Angélica Gorodischer (1928–), the refreshingly down-to-earth author from the city of Rosario who insists on describing herself simply with the phrase: "I am only a storyteller." While her fiction is now recognized in the Spanish-speaking world to be of the same measure and caliber as that of the aforementioned world-famous writers, Gorodischer still remains relatively unknown in the Anglophone literary world. This is not surprising, since relatively few of her works have been translated into English, and there are even fewer English-language scholarly articles examining them. In spite of this limitation, in the international arena Gorodischer's fantasy and science-fiction oeuvre has been compared to that of Italo Calvino, Franz Kafka, Umberto Eco, Philip K. Dick, and Ursula K. Le Guin. Perhaps prompted by the fact that Le Guin herself translated Gorodischer's *Kalpa Imperial* (1983) into English in 2003 as *Kalpa Imperial: The Greatest Empire that Never Was,* some have made a strong connection between the two women writers. In fact, being contemporaries—Gorodischer was born a year before Le Guin—these two authors have greatly influenced fantasy and science fiction by infusing an enduring feminist sensibility into the genre. Analogously, and notwithstanding their fifty-year age gap, Gorodischer has also been associated with Virginia Woolf in that both writers consider androgyny as central to feminist politics, while the Argentine writer focuses especially on those who are powerless or at the margins.

The English-speaking science-fiction reader had a first glimpse of Gorodischer's style in 1992 through Mary G. Berg's translation of "Bajo las jubeas en flor" ("Under the Flowering Juleps"), a short story first published in 1973. Linda Britt's 1998 translation of the 1977 story "Casta luna electronica" ("By the Light of the Chaste Electronic Moon") came out six years later, in 1998. This second story introduces one of Gorodischer's most memorable characters: Trafalgar Medrano, a traveling salesman who happily hops from galaxy to galaxy peddling his wares but always returns to the Burgundy café in his native city of Rosario for a coffee and a bit of gossip with his friends about his intergalactic adventures. Amalia Gladhart's translation of *Trafalgar*, recounting all the voyages of the adventurous salesman, appeared in 2013. Fortunately, the list of Gorodischer's texts available in English has grown lately, and some previously translated stories have even been reanthologized. Such has been the lucky fate of "Los embriones del violeta" ("The Violet's Embryos"), a short story translated by Sara Irausquin that first appeared in the anthology *Cosmos Latinos: An Anthology of Science Fiction from Latin America and Spain,* which I coedited with Andrea Bell in 2003, and which was included a year later in David G. Hartwell and Kathryn Cramer's *Year's Best SF9.*

This new interest in Gorodischer's writing by American science-fiction and fantasy scholars and publishers was possibly triggered by Le Guin's translation of *Kalpa Imperial.* Jo Walton articulates this idea best when she candidly states: "Gorodischer is one of Argentina's leading writers. I'd never heard of her until Le Guin began publishing this translation."[1] The original *Kalpa imperial* appeared in 1983 and 1984 as a two-volume short-story collection and was later published as a single volume in 2000. Although somewhat misleadingly marketed as Gorodischer's "first *novel* translated into English," Le Guin's excellent rendition of the original Spanish text will probably become the most renowned English translations of Gorodischer's works. This essay aims to provide a general introduction to the writer as a personality, to her science-fiction and fantasy production, and to her position within the genre. In addition, because of the wider readership that Le Guin's translation of *Kalpa Imperial* will surely provide, and since the work captures the main characteristics that constitute Gorodisher's take on the genre, this essay will take a closer look at *Kalpa* as an illustration of the Argentinian author's style.

Angélica Gorodischer (*née* Arcal) is recognized in Spanish-speaking literary and scholarly circles as "the queen of Argentine science fiction"[2] and is often described as a "grande dame" of the genre.[3] She has been branded "the female Borges,"[4] as well as the greatest Argentine and the greatest Latin American practitioner of the genre.[5] And yet whoever reads her interviews, listens to her speak in public, or meets her in person is always struck by the writer's seemingly unassuming persona and ease of manner. She has used several registers in her writing, from a highly polished literary style to conversational prose, but she always chooses to use informal language when speaking in public. And this choice, as she explains, is calculated: "My affinity for colloquial expression is present when I give lectures and speeches. Rather than express myself with academic terminology, I purposely use language that is conversational and colloquial, and this has the effect of surprising and amusing the audience and has served me well in my public speaking as well as in my writing."[6] Another peculiarity one immediately associates with the writer is her use of wit. The humor in her writing and in her speech often takes the form of puns and language games. Gorodischer's direct, informal approach is completely at odds with the typical character traits one would apportion a so-called grande dame but would assign instead to an assertive, kind, and wise lady one would gladly hear chat about literature for hours.

A website currently managed by the Argentinian Ministry of Culture and dedicated to introducing major contemporary Argentinian writers has the following phrase next to Angélica Gorodischer's name: *Soy una escritora como tantas,* which may translate into: "I am a writer among many," or even "I am nothing special as a writer."[7] One could interpret that sentence in a number of ways, but after reading a few of the many interviews she has given over the years or watching "Obra en construcción" (Work in progress), an interview videotaped in 2011 as part of the cultural project mentioned above, the real meaning behind that sentence is revealed: Gorodischer considers herself to be the equal of other writers, their colleague. Moreover, being a fiction writer is all that she considers herself to be, no more and no less. In her distinctively charming, direct manner, she declares that when asked to provide a resumé, the only words she writes are: "Angélica Gorodischer, Storyteller."

Gwendolyn Díaz also notes that Gorodischer is known for her playful wit and dry humor, an example of which is the following autobiographical caption that the writer composed for her personal bibliography, translated here by Díaz herself:

> She has published a bunch of books, all of them narratives. She affirms with certain petulance that she never wrote plays nor poetry, not even when she was sixteen, the age when everyone writes poems, particularly about unrequited love. She studied in Rosario in the Escuela Normal Número Dos (Teacher's School Number Two) and in the School of Philosophy and Letters

of the Universidad Nacional del Litoral (the Littoral National University). She received no title at all. She is not a professor, not a Licentiate, not an academic, not a Ph.D., not anything. During her fourth year of studies she remembered she wanted to write, not teach, and she abandoned the classroom. She is a narrator.[8]

And yet, the writer's family background did not spare her from being exposed to the elitist attitudes inherent to upper-class status. Gorodischer's ancestors had an aristocratic European pedigree. Her mother's French family immigrated to Argentina in the early 1900s and intermarried with a local family who could trace their genealogy back to the founders of Buenos Aires and to Spanish royalty. Her father's family hailed from Spain and soon amassed a fortune in their new country. With her blue-blooded and wealthy family background, the title of grande dame could well have been applicable to the writer. Still, Gorodischer never considered her privileged background really to be relevant to her life.[9] On the contrary, the author declares to be informal by conviction and describes herself as a disobedient child who dared to defy her family by marrying a Jewish man. She is proud to have fought the patriarchy in her own humble way and states that she has been, somehow, an anarchist.[10]

In her childhood memoir *Historia de mi madre* (My mother's story; 2004),[11] the author provides clues as to her mother's influence in her early development. Angélica de Arcal, a painter and a writer in her own right, was a sort of cultural socialite with progressive attitudes, especially in regard to the arts. To her Rosario home were invited all the significant artists, musicians, and writers of the time, and her house was filled with books, so the young Angélica was exposed to a literary and artistic environment from childhood. Gorodischer also recounts how her mother was her first model as a storyteller, one who would make up fairy tales with untraditional plots featuring both good and evil princesses as protagonists. During her video interview for the Writer's Audiovisual Library, the author reports that she was a lonely child whose first toys were books; that she started reading at five, and after two years of reading anything that would fall into her hands she made a conscious decision to become a fiction writer. As she recounts, she was seven years old and reading Sir H. Rider Haggard's *King Solomon's Mines* when she said to herself: "I want to write this myself!" From her personal library Gorodischer lovingly picks up the books that marked her life: two traditional children's storybooks,[12] the *Complete Works* of "the Master" (Borges); Honoré de Balzac's *Illusions perdues* (Lost illusions, serialized between 1837 and 1843), and, finally, Michio Kaku's *Hyperspace* (1994). What she says about the American physicist's work reveals Gorodischer's primary attraction to science fiction:

This book was written by one of those physicists who is completely mad and speaks of things that science-fiction writers already invented a long time ago because—some attribute this to Einstein and others to Freud—someone told scientists that it didn't matter what they discovered or designed because those who wrote poems and stories would always have been there before them. That's true. About forty or fifty years ago science-fiction writers invented hyperspace as a way to travel to the stars, and now physicists are trying to discover hyperspace. Don't tell me this world isn't wonderful! How could I not write?[13]

Early Work

In spite of her precocious penchant for writing, Gorodischer had a relatively late start as a professional writer. Her first published work was "En verano, la siesta y con Martina" (In summer, napping, and with Martina), a short story that won a detective-fiction contest in a local magazine in 1964 when she was thirty-six years old. A year later, her first short-story collection, *Cuentos con soldados* (Stories with soldiers), came out, and the next two years saw a total of seven short stories published in several local newspapers and magazines. Angela Dellepiane notes that most of these early stories lack the sardonic humor and flights into fantasy that characterize Gorodischer's subsequent production.[14] The year 1967 marked a definite change of direction when she published her first science-fiction novel *Opus Dos* (Opus two), a piece that would launch her writing into the fantasy mode that has afforded her fame. The novel, set in the geographical site where Buenos Aires used to be located, presents a post-holocaust scenario where a previously oppressed black population rules over formerly dominant white people. *Opus Two* underlines the cyclical nature of human history and the recurrent pattern whereby those who were previously oppressed become oppressors in their turn. Gorodischer will pick up this motif of the cyclical aspect of human nature and develop it further in *Kalpa*. Yet, this first science-fiction novel already exhibits key features of her use of the genre: a highly literate style using narrative fragmentation to depict a metaphysically unfounded, chaotic universe, and a thematic focus on philosophical and psychological issues rather than on technological artifacts or scientific details. During the following decade Gorodischer would continue writing in a style that has been named "soft" as opposed to the "hard" science fiction that aims for scientific plausibility.

Two science-fiction short-story volumes she originally wrote during the 1970s were *Under the Flowering Juleps* and *Chaste Electronic Moon*. The aforementioned stories "Under the Flowering Juleps" and "The Violet's Embryos," now available in English, were included in the former collection, whereas "By the Light of the Chaste Electronic Moon" originally appeared in the latter. Both works are generally seen as marking the beginning of Gorodischer's mature phase as a fantasy and science-fiction writer. Indeed, the stories included in these two volumes further develop her particular style—one that is informed by Anglo-American 1960s feminist science fiction and eschews hard science in favor of philosophical ideas that have a sociopolitical reach. An example of this is "The Violet's Embryos," a story that presents an alternate reality where military men are sent to a distant planet on a mission to rescue possible survivors of an earlier expedition. The men find violet circles that mysteriously allow them to act like gods and reproduce anything they wish, provided they are able to "feel" the object. Yet the violet circles' powers are not explained in scientific terms, since Gorodischer's fiction prefers to avoid detailed technological descriptions typical of "hard" science fiction. Circumstances will ultimately force the military men to resort to feminization to fulfill their sexual needs because they will prove unable to create any women. In this story Gorodischer speculates in general on the nature of desire and happiness but also asks us to reconsider the traditional Argentinian equation between military power and masculinity. By problematizing sexual desire and its relationship to political and social power, the story draws attention to patriarchal patterns of thought, ultimately inviting the reader to question them.[15]

Her highly literate style and use of fantasy with a metaphysical core in stories like "The Violet's Embryos" and "Under the Flowering Juleps" soon caused Gorodischer to be labeled as a female Borges and instantly linked to the type of Argentinian fantasy whose major exponent is the world-famous male author. Indeed, Borges had greatly influenced fantasy and science fiction in Argentina, starting in the 1940s by permeating the genre with an idealistic and ironic quality and by incorporating elements of magic as well as science. The Belgian critic Bernard Goorden identifies an Argentinian school of the genre characterized by its emphasis on issues related to humanity rather than technology, whereas the Argentinian critic Pablo Capanna points to its connection to European fantasy, as opposed to other Latin American traditions more influenced by magical realism.[16] Enrique Luis Revol, in turn, designates this particular Argentinian variety as the "fantastical-metaphysical" and identifies Kafka as a major inspiration.[17] In any case, Gorodischer's approach to fantasy and science fiction means that inexplicable phenomena do not drive the narrative and may even at times be absent.

Following the two short-story collections that earned Gorodischer a seat on a figurative Mount Olympus next to Borges, *Trafalgar* came out in 1979.

As previously mentioned, the nine short stories included in this book are all integrated around Trafalgar Medrano, a character Gorodischer had created two years earlier. In her typically informal way of speaking when interviewed, Gorodischer describes Trafalgar as: "a crafty fellow from Rosario, slightly chauvinistic but still okay, a smoker, a consumer of coffee by the gallon, a tango dancer, metaphysical and wary."[18] The salesman from Rosario seems to leap off the page, and the author herself has acknowledged him to be "so powerful that I may run into him on the street at any moment, or he may come to ring my doorbell and invite me out for a cup of coffee."[19] It is because of *Trafalgar* that, in the words of Darrell B. Lockhart, "both the protagonist's and Gorodischer's place in science fiction are sealed."[20]

Some critics have noticed how openly Gorodischer references other writers she considers her colleagues. In *Trafalgar*, for example, she pays homage to Borges, Victor Hugo, and Cortázar right from the start. Gorodischer recalls Borges when she introduces her protagonist as one of the most distinguished members of the community by means of an apocryphal citation in the *Who's Who* of Rosario. The imprint of that bogus publication pompously reads: "Edited by the Public Relations Subcommittee of the Association of Friends of the City of Rosario." In the best Borgesian tradition, the imprint of the journal obviously mocks the snobbish attitudes of the people who may read that sort of publication. And in a metafictional move that Cervantes and Borges would favor, Trafalgar Medrano refers to the Argentinian master as his personal friend, Jorge. Gorodischer pays her respects to another literary master via the epigraph: a quartet from Victor Hugo's poem "Voeu" (The lover's wish) that encourages the reader to let his or her imagination fly: "On the pinions of air I would fly, I would rush / Thro' the glens and the valleys to quiver; / Past the mountain ravine, past the grove's dreamy hush, / And the murmuring fall of the river."[21] And, in a playful wink to Cortázar's instructions to the reader in *Hopscotch*, Gorodischer amusingly warns her reader not to rush to the table of contents to find the shortest story and to read the stories as presented rather than skip around.[22]

The charismatic millionaire salesman Trafalgar Medrano has deservedly become probably the most famous character in Argentine science fiction. A similar distinction has been won by Veroboar, the world ruled by a thousand beautiful aristocratic women that the famous salesman visits during his intergalactic travels in "By the Light of the Chaste Electronic Moon." In Veroboar, as Trafalgar will tell his friends back in Rosario, there were no men to be found because their women had substituted them with machines that provide them with love fantasies and orgasms. As Melissa Fitch observes, in spite of the fact that Gorodischer has admitted to deploring modern advances like electric appliances and fast cars, the use of technology to reconfigure sex, gender, and sexuality is of paramount importance in this story.[23] And yet, in *Trafalgar*, universal philosophical concerns such as the selfish nature of human beings or the meaning of human evolution inform Gorodischer's use of the genre.

The genre in Argentina would flourish in the 1980s with the return of democracy in 1983. Even though there had been an earlier explosion of fantasy and science-fiction production in the country during the late 1960s, which coincided with the so-called Latin American literary boom, the 1980s saw much greater activity in specialized magazines, publishing houses, criticism, writing, and fandom. Indeed, more Argentinian science-fiction works were published between 1983 and 1989 than in the whole of the previous period.[24] During the early 1980s Gorodischer wrote the two-volume work at which we will take a closer look later: *Kalpa imperial. Libro I: La casa del poder* (Imperial Kalpa, Book I: The house of power; 1983) and *Kalpa imperial. Libro II: El imperio más vasto* (Imperial Kalpa, Book II: The grandest empire, 1984). During the second part of the decade, despite the thriving of the science-fiction and fantasy community, Gorodischer started to use the genres more sparingly or turned to different modes of writing used at the service of a more straightforward feminist sensibility.

To this new phase belong the decidedly feminist short-story collection *Mala noche y parir hembra* (Bad night and birthing a female; 1984) and the two novels *Floreros de alabastro, alfombras de Bokhara* (Alabaster flower vases, Bokhara carpets; 1985) and *Jugo de mango* (Mango juice; 1988). These three texts center on social criticism and use parody to undermine patriarchal discourses.[25]

And yet, Gorodischer never completely abandoned the fantasy and science-fiction genres. One of the stories in *Bad Night*—available in English as "The Perfect Married Woman,"—uses the time-travel trope and a fantastical premise to drive the plot. The perfect housewife of the title is, in Jane Donawerth's words, "a woman in her forties with grown children [who] goes about her daily housewife's tasks, except that occasionally, when she opens a door, there is an unexpected place or time on the other side, offering her its secrets. The woman eventually interferes with political events behind the doors; she assassinates leaders, hides the weapons of armies, and opens escape routes to people trapped in a riot."[26] As the reader soon realizes, the adventures the protagonist undertakes during breaks from her work as a modern housewife are sometimes linked to famous historical murders by women. Like Charlotte Corday did with Jean-Paul Marat, she beheads a man in a bathtub, and, just as the Old Testament Judith did with Holofernes, Gorodischer's "perfect wife" decapitates a bearded man in a tent. Since these horrific events are connected with the housewife's use of modern technological appliances, Donawerth's reading of this story links the body parts of the slain men to modern science's imprisonment of middle-class housewives turned servants. The figure of the silent, repressed housewife is combined with the mythical female avenger, and Gorodischer ultimately asks the reader to regard the figure of the ordinary housewife in a new light: what if she were to obtain power and use it to torture and dismember?[27] But the writer's feminist hand is never too heavy or devoid of humor. The story's title in Spanish, "La perfecta casada," must be a direct ironic reference to the work the Augustinian friar Luis de León wrote in 1583 and dedicated to a female friend who was about to marry. De León's *La perfecta casada* is an instruction manual and guide for young women spelling out rules of proper behavior and defining their subordinate place in Spanish Renaissance society. *The Perfect Wife* remained a popular gift for young high-society women in the Hispanic world throughout the centuries as well as part of the literary canon, so Gorodischer's parodic use of the title must have been obvious to a majority of her readers.

Bad Night is generally considered a feminist, even militant book. Rosana López Rodriguez points out that Gorodischer's feminist texts do not depict working-class or socially minded women but rather center on isolated middle-class ladies who manage to escape from their oppression as individuals.[28] And yet, as do many of Gorodischer's works, *Bad Night* centers on women's lives and responds to a central theme in her fiction: a passion to find justice for the oppressed. Beatriz Urraca notes that Gorodischer's works break several stereotypes of feminist science fiction in the sense that in them we do not find the all-female utopias or the sympathetic, powerful female role models typical of the golden age of British and American feminist science fiction of the 1970s, but instead Gorodischer "dares to imagine a world like ours, in which a few crucial changes make it possible for us to see what encumbers us."[29]

After the short break from the genres mentioned above, in 1991 Gorodischer returned to writing overtly in the fantastic and science-fictional modes with the five-story collection *Las Repúblicas* (The republics). *The Republics* introduces environmental concerns as a new subject in her writings but retains the use of informal language and dry humor as well as the feminist vein of the three previous works. An example of how Gorodischer's writings aim to subvert gender stereotypes and challenge gender roles in this volume is the short story "Al Champaquí" (To Mount Champaquí), which may be seen as a meditation about human sexuality and gender construction. The main character is first presented as a woman, but the reader soon learns that she has a double sexual identity since s/he is able to remain young and change sex at will by means of a technological device inserted in her or his left arm. A rite of passage involving physical violence and rape will eventually lead the protagonist to maintain that there is absolutely no difference between males and females. "To Mount Champaquí" re-creates the transgendering Greek myth of Kaineus, a warrior who is said to have changed sex and become invincible by divine sanction from a beautiful woman named Kainis. In some versions of the story, Kaineus is actually a woman who has been given superhuman powers.[30] In Gorodischer's hands, the divinely ordained or biologically imposed gender becomes a matter of will and of available technology—in other words, an invitation to consider human sexual identity not as a biological destiny but as fluid and variable.

A New Mythology: Kalpa Imperial

Although she uses other genres, Gorodischer never abandons the fantasy and science-fictional modes completely. As is the case for most Latin American and Spanish practitioners of the genre, her science-fiction production may be categorized as "soft," since it is informed by the social and political sciences and the humanities rather than by the "hard" sciences.[31] When asked specifically what spurred her interest in science fiction, Gorodischer immediately mentions Arthur C. Clarke's *Childhood's End* (1953) and Isaac Asimov's *The End of Eternity* (1955). These two texts made her realize the creative freedom the genre could add to her own fiction, the lack of restrictions that the fantastic allows the literary imagination. Other American science-fiction writers Gorodischer acknowledges as having made an impact on her are Robert Silverberg, Cordwainer Smith, and especially Ursula K. Le Guin, with whom she shares a strong affinity.[32] In her typical conversational style unencumbered by punctuation, Gorodischer explains what it is about the genre that attracts her:

> I don't care one bit about what happens to a spaceship on its way to an unknown galaxy, how it works or how big it is; but I do care about a story like J. G. Ballard's (a writer I don't care for) "Fourteen to Centaur" [*sic*] where the anguish of the void runs rampant. And I am interested about guys who are headed towards the absurd, the monstrous, the wondrous, and the mythical, such as Lafferty, like Ursula Le Guin, like Natalie Henneberg, like Philip Dick, people who work within the great frameworks that humans use as pretext to keep the fighting for life, such as Zelazny. Campbell's kind of science fiction I'm not interested in, it bores me to tears.[33]

Within the framework of the Anglo-American science-fiction tradition, critics have connected Gorodischer mostly to Le Guin, in part because of gender identity politics, but also because both writers share a similar fictional style.

For instance, *Kalpa* has been associated with Le Guin's *Tehanu* (1990) and *Always Coming Home* (1985) because of their focus on ordinary people's effect on History, with a capital "H," and the use of large-scale events, the focus on the grand scheme of things. When interviewing Gorodischer, Adrián Ferrero refers to her and Le Guin as twin sisters, one from the North and the other from the South. Gorodischer agrees by revealing that she had been a long-time admirer of Le Guin's fiction, especially *The Left Hand of Darkness* (1969) and *The Dispossessed* (1974). Gorodischer adds that when she met Le Guin in Portland in 1988 she felt a great affinity: they share the same likes and dislikes, even the same lifestyle. Le Guin and Gorodischer corresponded for years, and it was because of this personal connection that Le Guin asked her permission to translate *Kalpa,* and Gorodischer granted it to her.[34]

The connection between them was even more obvious when the celebrated writer from Oregon translated one of Gorodischer's better-known works into English. Twenty years after its publication in Argentina and three years after its publication in Spain, Le Guin's impeccable translation was presented to the English-speaking reader in 2003 as *Kalpa Imperial: The Greatest Empire that Never Was.* Puzzlingly, the editors chose to leave out Gorodischer's original acknowledgment page citing her literary sources of inspiration for the book: Hans Christian Andersen, J. R. R. Tolkien, and Italo Calvino. Including those authors' names would have made the work's debt to Andersen's oral narrative tradition, to Tolkien's pseudo-medieval heroic fantasy setting, and to Calvino's stylish prose, postmodern bent, and philosophical insights even more transparent.

The term "kalpa" in the title is a Sanskrit word meaning an eon, the vast period of time that a universe lasts. In Hindu cosmology the word describes the time in which a universe experiences a cycle of creation and destruction. Appropriately, in *Kalpa* a series of stories are told by a nameless narrator who records the vast cyclical history of an imaginary empire's many rises and falls over an immense span of time.[35] This empire is divided into a North, which holds power and would like to conquer the South, and a South that has never been completely subjugated. *Kalpa* holds at its core the literary cachet of the storytelling tradition, the power of the fable to ignite the reader's memories of early childhood tales. In a manner similar to that of Salman Rushdie, Gorodischer's modern fantasy work bestows on the narrator the function of constantly renewing the old tales of the past. *Kalpa* is, in this sense, a celebration of the power of storytelling itself. As John W. Fail puts it: "Gorodischer never gets bogged down in the trappings of fantasy writing. Her imagination conjures mysterious alchemists, generals and beggars who trade places, and princes who think that they are ferrets. While some of this imagery may be familiar to fantasy readers, Gorodischer avoids tepid dramatic tendencies and cookie-cutter plots."[36]

By introducing surprising details such as modern firearms that are out of place in its Tolkienesque, vaguely medieval atmosphere, *Kalpa* creates a new sort of mythology out of familiar archetypal figures like kings and queens, peasants, empresses, soldiers, and poets. This effect is perhaps most noticeable in the last story included in the work, "The Old Incense Road," where a caravan master retells Greek myths and legends by substituting the familiar character names with oddly spelled ones:[37] Helen of Troy's new name is Marillín, her husband is Yeimsdín, and the Trojan prince Paris is now called Kirdaglass. The legendary thousand ships have new names as well, such as Marlenditrij, Betedeivis, Martincarol, Maripícfor, Avagarner, Tedabara, Loretaiún, Briyibardó, and Jedilamar. And, as told by the caravan master in Le Guin's masterful translation, an Odysseus whose new name recalls another Hollywood star will have adventures with amusingly named entities:

> The wily Clargueibl was returning like the others to the house called *saloon* when he heard sweet voices singing that drew him irresistibly. They were the ringostars, beautiful, evil, voracious beings who used their magic voices who attract all who heard them and attack passing sailors. Clargueibl and his crew stopped to listen and so were captured by the ringostars. One of these beings was a powerful witch called Monalisa whose smile turned men into pigs. This is what happened to Clargueibl and his men, and the ringostars shut them up in a pigsty and fattened them up until they started eating them one by one. But Clargueibl, who even as a pig kept his cunning wits, persuaded one of the pig keepers, the giant Gualdisnei, to let him live just a few days longer.[38]

These references to Western cultural icons and historical or pop-culture figures of the late twentieth century catch the reader by surprise. They point to a later historical period that is close to our own era and obviously out of place in the mythical realm of classical fantasy or Greek legend. Therefore, if those familiar figures have now themselves become legendary characters, the caravan master's world must be located in his distant future. This temporal dislocation adds to the perception that Vélez García notes: the world in *Kalpa* is located *in illo tempore,* and it stands for all empires and for no particular empire at the same time.[39]

Although *Kalpa,* like many fantasy worlds, is set in an undetermined past or future time, Gorodischer, being true to her unconventional take on the genre, does not present history through the eyes of heroes or kings, nor as a series of cause-and-effect events. Similarly to Calvino´s *Cosmicomics*, the loosely associated tales in *Kalpa* may be classified as postmodern literature because of their somewhat absurd premises and the inclusion of countless names of characters and places that have the potential of frustrating the reader. Also, like *Cosmicomics*, the plot lines offer dramatic tension and elements of romance that keep the reader engaged. *Kalpa* does not present great epic events, geographical specifics, genealogies, or timelines but offers instead tales of how "small 'h' histories"—including women's—influence great events in what is ultimately a reflection on power in all its forms and manifestations. As Fail notices in his review of Le Guin's translation: "There's a very modern undercurrent to the Kalpa empire, with tales focusing on power in a political sense rather than generic moral lessons."[40]

Other American reviewers have also noticed *Kalpa*'s focus on power and its political denotations. Karen Burnham, for example, highlights the political current informing the text as it pertains to matters of governance and power relationships but does not see the stories as political "in the sense of bearing on contemporary politics."[41] And Jo Walton is even more candid when she states that *Kalpa* "doesn't open any windows on Argentinian culture" for her since she lacks "the context the book was written in" and thus she may be missing several levels of meaning.[42] Knowledge of Argentina's recent history would indeed enrich the reader's understanding of the text since, as Gorodischer herself has stated, she meant to write a Western *Thousand and One Nights* and ended up writing a cruel parable of Argentina's dictatorship instead.[43] When asked if her country's political situation influences her writing as far as choosing her themes, Gorodischer answered: "Of course it does. Unless one is totally crazy or autistic, it influences you. Here, in Argentina, politics infiltrates everything because the situation is so unstable, so tragic that politics infiltrate everything. Look, I wrote *Kalpa Imperial* convinced that I was writing traditional stories in the fashion of *A Thousand and One Nights*. I was convinced of that and I treated the text as such, and when it was published I realized that I had written about the Process."[44] The Process, as the National Reorganization Process is commonly known,[45] was the name of the dictatorship that ruled Argentina starting with a military coup in 1976 and ending in 1983, after the ruling junta relinquished power following the loss of the Falklands War. In 1983, Leopoldo Galtieri, senior member of the junta and commander-in-chief of the army, was tried in a military court for human-rights violations. Not surprisingly, the publication of *Kalpa Imperial* (1983–84) coincides with the return of democracy to the country, but Gorodischer had conceived her stories during the dictatorship, a time of cultural and political repression when power was concentrated in the hands of a few. At its core, *Kalpa Imperial* is a reflection on the concept of power itself, which, as the narrator says in the first story, "Portrait of the Emperor," is "as dangerous as an animal not fully tamed, dangerous as acid, sweet and fatal as poisoned honey."[46]

The thread linking the separate stories in *Kalpa Imperial* is the ascension to power of the different rulers in the empire and their particular way of using authority. As Patricia Mosier notices, each ruler represents a different way to wield power, and the process of rise and fall of emperors and empresses and their empires provides "a view of politics as real as the politics of any place or time."[47] As Walton has observed, specific allusions to Argentine politics or political figures during the Process period are not easily found in the text. The rule of good government present in *Kalpa*, however, is a universally applicable one: personal ambition is not to be placed above the welfare of the people. And yet, the fact that Kalpa's imperial center of power is located in a cold northern area that often tries but fails to conquer an often rebellious warm southern region, coupled with the other characteristics in both societies, have inspired critics to identify allegorical references. The last story, "The Old Incense Road," gives the clearest clues in this respect because it finally describes the southern part of the empire. In contrast with the cold climate, big cities, great palaces, political intrigue, commerce, culture, and patriarchal social structure of the North, the South is hot and fertile and has small towns where people live in more egalitarian, less technological society with a slower pace of life and more humanistic values. As Burnham notes, the North and South stand in a similar relation to the empire as the kind South America and the United States have historically had.[48] *Kalpa Imperial*'s North has never been able to conquer the South, and it never understands the challenges of operating in the area, nor does it grasp their cultural differences. Writing in 2008, Burnham notes that this allegory "may strike a little closer to home" and exhorts the reader to remember that "various Western superpowers have been meddling in places they fail to understand long before our current misadventures in the Middle East. And certain South American countries still bear the scars of some of that meddling."[49]

Despite the explicit allegorical reading described above, *Kalpa Imperial* explores the general concept of power, its universal quality, and its connections not only to politics but also to the role of writers and to gender inequality. For instance, the need for historians and journalists to be free from political censorship and not to bow to authority is central to the tale "Portrait of the Empress." When asked by the Empress to go to her palace every day and tell her the history of the empire, the storyteller responds that he must go in secret so as not to lose credibility with the people:

And I told her that no storyteller ever bows down to power and I would not. If she, the empress, knew nothing about the empire, I could teach her, and it was my duty to do so, serving not the throne but the people who upheld the throne; but nobody else should know about it. . . . I didn't want people saying that I hadn't been paid anything . . . for the same stories I told in the streets and squares. Other people . . . can enter the palace without risk because they have nothing to lose. And a poet can, if he's the real thing, because being beyond power he can't lose. But a storyteller is no more than a free man, and being a free man is a dangerous business.[50]

As Patricia Mosier explains in her fittingly titled "Women in Power in Gorodischer's *Kalpa Imperial*," the text presents a lyrical vision of the South, whose virtues are epitomized in their women, whereas in the male-dominated North women must adapt to patriarchal values and use different stratagems to survive and even to thrive.[51] In fact, Gorodischer has stated her belief that power is at the core of gender inequality and is central to one's ideological position in regards to the status of women. The writer's own belief is that power should be shared equally between the genders, although women—given their current position in the social structure—must proactively seek an equitable power balance. Gorodischer's fiction focuses on exploring the trajectory of a character from weakness to power or vice versa. She is interested in exploring the impulse that causes someone to seize a position of power.[52]

It is in this sense that Gorodischer has been related to Virginia Woolf. Both writers mistrust any value imposed by the patriarchy and believe in the feminist concept of the androgynous spirit: the idea that under the same conditions, both genders are able to develop equally. Also, both writers propose the exercise of writing itself as an alternative to patriarchal power, believing that feminists must take special care not to fall into the trap of authoritarianism.[53] Because her brand of feminism does not discriminate the genders according to biological or cultural essences, Gorodischer creates the cruelest, most evil and destructive empresses as well as the most enlightened, benevolent ones. As Mosier notes, the difference in human behavior between *Kalpa Imperial*'s North and South is dictated by the different social and political structures present in both societies.[54] In the hierarchical North, power may be obtained from the outside, and only exceptional individuals would use it to benefit the common people; whereas in the more open, equalitarian society of the South power comes from people's inner strength and is therefore impossible to usurp. Just as the northern values of ambition and dominance are not the exclusive purview of male characters, the southern virtues of intuition, empathy, and closer contact with Nature are not, in Gorodischer's fiction, limited to female characters.

Women are still in the minority among fantasy and science-fiction writers in Latin America, and yet Gorodischer's positive effect in correcting the gender imbalance is undeniable. Her stories show alternate worlds where the weak can become powerful, where fully fledged female protagonists are at the center of the action. Not all of Gorodischer's literary production—especially those works published in the 2000s—belong to the fantasy and science-fiction genres. Nevertheless, the Argentine author's impact on the field is indisputable, and her style is all her own. Her science fiction and fantasy are at times used in a hybrid way that has been described by María Esther Vázquez as playful in the manner of her Colombian and Spanish counterparts García Márquez and Álvaro Cunqueiro who, like Gorodischer, enjoy pushing the limits of genre and taking their characters into unusual situations without losing sight of their true nature.[55] Many readers see reflections of Borges and Le Guin in Gorodischer's style and yet praise the author's individual imprint, a tell-tale sign of having encountered a case of good Literature, with a capital L. Such is Jo Walton's impression after reading *Kalpa Imperial*: "It isn't like anything else. Well, a little like Borges, perhaps, but much more approachable. And it's a little like Le Guin's own *Changing Planes*, but much better. I occasionally come across something where I read a page and then immediately read it again, more slowly, or even aloud, just out of sheer pleasure at the way the words go together."[56]

Gorodischer is indeed a writer of national and increasingly international stature, a distinct voice in Latin American fantasy and science fiction; and yet she likes to describe herself as a narrator, no more, no less. When asked to provide a resumé, she simply writes: "Angélica Gorodischer: Storyteller." When asked in 2011 how she would be remembered in the future, the "grande dame" replies: "Who knows? They'll say: Okay, she was an interesting girl who wrote a lot (because the truth is I wrote a lot, about thirty books by now), some weren't bad. She was a fun and optimistic chick. Who knows? And she had wonderful kids."[57] Yet, regardless of how modest and unpretentious a persona she portrays, the Argentinian writer's oeuvre has been widely recognized. Gorodischer has received numerous literary prizes, honors, and awards; she has been invited to participate in over 350 conferences, both national and international; she has been awarded two academic Fulbright scholarships to participate in writing workshops and teach in the United States; and her works have been translated into Czech, English, French, German, Italian, Russian, and Swedish. Among the most significant literary awards Gorodischer has received for her fantasy and science-fiction works are the Mas Allá Prize and the Poblet Prize for *Kalpa Imperial* in 1984, the Sigfrido Radaelli Prize for the best short story of 1985, the Gilgamesh Prize for the best fantastic story published in Spain in 1986 and again in 1990, the Konex Award in 1984, and the Konex Platinum Award in 1994. More recently, Gorodischer has been honored with the World Fantasy Award in 2011 and with the Konex Literary Achievement Award in 2014.[58]

In her late eighties now, Gorodischer has authored a steady stream of novels, short-story collections, magazine and newspaper essays, biographies, literary criticism, and film scripts. True to her craft, she says that she writes every day, edits her writing obsessively, and considers each book to be a new challenge, each new genre a territory to be conquered.[59] Trying to place Gorodischer's entire literary output into a single category would be impossible, since she has availed herself of several writing modes, such as the detective and mystery genres, as well as realist and nonfiction modes of writing, incursions into experimental and gothic literatures, and even what could be called "narrative poetry." Yet the author's early works, especially those written in the 1970s and 1980s, belong squarely within fantasy and science fiction and have afforded her a definite association with the genres ever since. There is no question that the quality and quantity of Gorodischer's fantasy and science-fiction production makes her one of the most prominent representatives of the genre in Argentina and the Hispanic world. Today the Argentinian author continues to enjoy a steady popularity among a growing readership and undoubtedly merits the term "grande dame" in the best sense of the expression.

Notes

1. Walton, *What Makes*, 95.
2. Garzón, "Angélica Gorodischer."
3. Vélez García, *Angélica Gorodischer*, 63.
4. Dellepiane, "Mester de fantasia," 634.
5. Urraca, "Angélica Gorodischer's Voyages," 85.
6. Díaz, *Women and Power*, 48.
7. The "Audiovideoteca de Escritores" (Writers' Audiovisual Library) project aims to interview major contemporary Argentinian writers as well as preserve historical archives. See "Audiovideoteca de Escritores: Archivo visual sobre literatura argentina," http://audiovideotecaba.com/.
8. Díaz, *Women and Power*, 43.
9. Ibid.
10. Ferrero, "En busca de un lenguaje," 197.
11. All translations of titles and texts are mine unless otherwise noted.
12. "El capullo rojo" (The red cocoon), from the short-story collection *Cuentos de Calleja* (Calleja stories) and Lesbazeilles's *Colosos antiguos y modernos* (Colossuses ancient and modern).
13. The original reads: "Este es un libro que para mí también fue muy importante. Es de uno de esos físicos que está totalmente loco y que habla de cosas que inventaron los autores de ciencia ficción hace mucho tiempo porque, alguien se lo atribuye a Einstein y

otros a Freud que dice a los hombres de ciencia que no importa lo que nosotros descubramos o inventemos, siempre habrán pasado por aquí antes los que escribieron poemas y cuentos. Es cierto. Los escritores de ciencia ficción inventaron hace 40 o 50 años el hiperespacio como una manera de viajar a las estrellas y ahora los físicos están tratando de descubrir el hiperespacio. ¡No me digas que no es maravilloso este mundo! ¿Cómo no va a escribir una?" From the "Obra en Construcción" interview.

14. Dellepiani, "Mester de fantasia," 628.

15. For an in-depth analysis of this aspect of "The Violet's Embryos" see Molina-Gavilán, "Alternate Realities."

16. Cited in ibid., 401.

17. Revol, "Tradición," 426.

18. The original text is, "un rosarino socarrón, levemente machista pero buen tipo, fumador, tomador de litros de café, tanguero, metafísico y desconfiado." Gorodischer, "Poca paciencia y muchas pulgas," 14.

19. In the original: "es tan poderoso que me voy a topar con él en cualquier momento en la calle, o va a venir a tocar el timbre de casa y me va a invitar a tomar un café." In Vázquez, "Angélica Gorodischer," 574.

20. Lockhart, *Latin American Science Fiction Writers,* 95.

21. English translation from the Project Gutenberg eBook of Poems, by Victor Hugo, http://www.gutenberg.org/files/8775/8775-h/8775-h.htm#link2H_4_0036.

22. Dellepiane, "Mester de fantasia," 635–36.

23. Fitch, *Side Dishes,* 64.

24. Molina-Gavilán et al., "Chronology," 385.

25. These humorous feminist texts introduced a stereotype-breaking, late-middle-aged, selfish, and ambitious Argentinian female detective.

26. Donawerth, "Body Parts," 477.

27. Ibid., 478.

28. López Rodriguez, "La mujer ausente."

29. Urraca, "Angélica Gorodischer's Voyages," 99.

30. D'Angou, *The Greeks,* 74.

31. Molina-Gavilán, *Ciencia ficción,* 192.

32. Ferrero, "En busca de un lenguaje," 191.

33. The original text is as follows: "No me importa un pito lo que le pasa a la nave que va a la galaxia desconocida, ni cómo funciona ni de qué tamaño es, pero sí me importa (y eso que es un autor que no me interesa) un cuento como 'Catorce a Centauro' [de J. G. Ballard], donde corre la angustia de la nada. . . . Y me interesan los tipos que se dirigen a lo absurdo, a lo monstruoso, al sueño, al mito como Lafferty, como Ursula Le Guin, como Natalie Henneberg, como Philip Dick, la gente que trabaja con los grandes frisos que le sirven de pretexto al hombre para seguir peleando por vivir, como, por ejemplo, Zelazny. . . . Toda la ciencia ficción de tipo Campbell, a mí no me interesa . . . me aburre soberanamente." Qtd. in Dellepiane, "Mester de fantasia," 630.

34. Ferrero, "En busca de un lenguaje," 191–92.

35. Some readers conceive of the narrator as separate entities, but I will consider the storyteller(s) as a single voice.

36. Fail, Rev. of *Kalpa Imperial.*

37. For the benefit of the reader who may not be familiar with Spanish phonetics and spelling, I list the original names that Gorodischer playfully spells anew here: Marilyn [Monroe], James Dean, Kirk Douglas, Marlene Dietrich, Bette Davis, Martine Carol, Mary Pickford, Ava Gardner, Theda Bara, Loretta Young, Brigitte Bardot, Hedy Lamarr, Clark Gable, Ringo Star, the Mona Lisa, and Walt Disney.

38. Gorodischer, *Kalpa Imperial,* 232.

39. Vélez García, *Angélica Gorodischer,* 75.

40. Fail, Rev. of *Kalpa Imperial.*

41. Burnham, Rev. of *Kalpa Imperial.*

42. Walton, *What Makes,* 95.

43. Santiago and López Rodríguez, "Presentación," 7.

44. Qtd. in Fares and Cazaubon Hermann, *Contemporary Argentinean Women Writers,* 62–63.

45. The Process (in Spanish, El Proceso de Reorganización Nacional) is a period also known as "la última junta militar" (the last military junta) or "la última dictadura" (the last dictatorship).

46. Gorodischer, *Kalpa Imperial,* 15.

47. Mosier, "Women in Power," 153.

48. Burnham, Rev. of *Kalpa Imperial.*

49. Ibid.

50. Gorodischer, *Kalpa Imperial,* 111–12.

51. Mosier, "Women in Power," 155.

52. Díaz, *Women and Power,* 49–50.

53. López Rodríguez, "Del feminismo," 58.

54. Mosier, "Women in Power," 158, 160

55. Vázquez, "Angélica Gorodischer," 572–73.

56. Walton, *What Makes,* 95.

57. The original text reads: "Qué sé yo. Dirán: 'bueno, era una mina interesante que escribió mucho—Porque la verdad que escribí mucho, llevo como 30 libros—. Algunos no eran malos. Era una tipa divertida y muy optimista—Qué sé yo—. Y tuvo unos hijos maravillosos." In "Obra en Construcción."

58. Her other literary prizes include the Vea y Lea Prize in 1964, the Club del Orden Prize in 1965, the Emecé Prize in 1984–85, the Silvina Bullrich Prize in 1998, the Esteban Echeverría Prize in 2000, and the ILCH (Instituto de Literatura y Cultura Hispánica) Prize in 2007. Her work to advance women's rights has been recognized with the Dignity Award granted by the Permanent Assembly for Human Rights in 1996. The city of Rosario honored her as an Illustrious Citizen in 2007, and the City of Buenos Aires named her a Prominent Cultural Figure in 2012.

59. Garzón, "Angélica Gorodischer."

Bibliography

Asimov, Isaac. *The End of Eternity*. Garden City, N.Y.: Doubleday, 1955.

Balzac, Honoré de. *Illusions perdues* [Lost illusions]. Paris: Werdet, 1837–43.

Bell, Andrea, and Yolanda Molina-Gavilán, eds. *Cosmos Latinos: An Anthology of Science Fiction from Latin America and Spain*. Middletown, Conn.: Wesleyan University Press, 2003.

Burnham, Karen. Rev. of *Kalpa Imperial* by Angélica Gorodischer. *Spiral Galaxy Reviews* 17 (October 2008). Accessed July 29, 2017. http://spiralgalaxyreviews.blogspot .com/2008/10/kalpa-imperial-by-anglica-gorodischer.html.

Cano, Luis. "Angélica Gorodischer y Jorge Luis Borges: La ciencia ficción como parodia del canon" [Angélica Gorodischer and Jorge Luis Borges: Science fiction as parody of the canon]. *Hispania* 87.3 (2004): 453–63.

Clarke, Arthur C. *Childhood's End*. New York: Ballantine Books, 1953.

D'Angou, Armand. *The Greeks and the New: Novelty in Ancient Greek Imagination and Experience*. New York: Cambridge University Press, 2011.

Dellepiane, A. B. "Mester de fantasía o la narrativa de Angélica Gorodischer" [The tradecraft of fantasy or the narrative of Angélica Gorodischer]. *Revista Iberoamericana* 51.132–33 (1985): 627–40.

Díaz, Gwendolyn, ed. *Women and Power in Argentine Literature: Stories, Interviews, and Critical Essays*. Austin: University of Texas Press, 2007.

Donawerth, Jane. "Body Parts: Twentieth-Century Science Fiction Short Stories by Women." *Publications of the Modern Language Association of America* 119.3 (2004): 474–81.

Fail, John W. Rev. of *Kalpa Imperial: The Greatest Empire that Never Was*, by Angélica Gorodischer. *Review of Contemporary Fiction* 24.1 (2004): 147.

Fares, Gustavo, and Eliana Cazaubon Hermann, eds., *Contemporary Argentinean Women Writers: A Critical Anthology*. Gainesville: University Press of Florida, 1998.

Ferrero, Adrián. "En busca de un lenguaje no amputado. Entrevista a Angélica Gorodischer. Rosario 2004" [In search of a non-amputated language: An interview of Angélica Gorodischer. Rosario 2004]. *Confluencia* (2005): 190–202.

Fitch, Melissa. *Side Dishes: Latina American Women, Sex, and Cultural Production*. New Brunswick, N.J.: Rutgers University Press, 2009.

Garzón, Raquel. "Angélica Gorodischer: La muerte y otras sorpresas [Angélica Gorodischer: Death and other surprises]." *Clarín.com*, January 14, 2001. Accessed July 29, 2017. http://edant.clarin.com/suplementos/cultura/2001/01/14/u-00311.htm.

Gorodischer, Angélica. "By the Light of the Chaste Electronic Moon." Trans. Linda Britt. In *Contemporary Argentinean Women Writers: A Critical Anthology*. Ed. Gustavo Fares and Eliana Cazaubon Hermann. Gainesville: University Press of Florida, 1998. 65–78.

———. *Historia de mi madre* [My mother's story]. Buenos Aires: Emecé, 2004.

———. *Kalpa Imperial: The Greatest Empire that Never Was*. Trans. Ursula Le Guin. Northampton, Mass.: Small Beer Press, 2003.

————. "The Perfect Married Woman." Trans. Lorraine Elena Roses. In *Secret Weavers: Stories of the Fantastic by Women of Argentina and Chile.* Ed. Marjorie Agosín. Fredonia, N.Y.: White Pine Press, 1992. 243–47.

————. "Poca paciencia y muchas pulgas" [Little patience and many fleas]. In *Boca de dama: La narrativa de Angelica Gorodischer* [Lady's mouth: The narrative of Angélica Gorodischer]. Ed. Balboa Echeverría, Miriam Balboa Echeverria, and Ester Gimbernat González. Feminaria Editora, 1995. 11–16.

————. *Las repúblicas* [The republics]. Buenos Aires: De la Flor, 1991.

————. *Trafalgar.* Trans. Amalia Gladhart. Northampton, Mass.: Small Beer Press, 2013.

————. "Under the Flowering Juleps." Trans. Mary G. Berg. In *Secret Weavers: Stories of the Fantastic by Women of Argentina and Chile.* Ed. Marjorie Agosín. Fredonia, N.Y.: White Pine Press, 1992. 259–80.

Hartwell, David G., and Kathryn Cramer, eds. *Year's Best SF9.* New York: Harper Collins, 2004.

Kaku, Michio. *Hyperspace.* Oxford: Oxford University Press, 1994.

LeGuin, Ursula K. *Always Coming Home.* New York: Harper and Row, 1985.

————. *The Dispossessed: An Ambiguous Utopia.* New York: Harper and Row, 1974.

————. *The Left Hand of Darkness.* New York: Ace Books, 1969.

————. *Tehanu: The Last Book of Earthsea.* New York: Aetheneum Books, 1990.

Lockhart, Darrell B., ed. *Latin American Science Fiction Writers: An A-to-Z Guide.* Westport, Conn.: Greenwood, 2004.

López Rodríguez, Rosana. "Del feminismo liberal al deconstructivismo de género: la narrativa de Angélica Gorodischer en los '80 y los '90 [From liberal feminism to the deconstruction of gender: The narrative of Angélica Gorodischer in the '80s and '90s]." *Cuadernos del CILHA* 10.11 (2009): 54–67.

————. "La mujer ausente. La construcción de género en *Mala noche y parir hembra* de Angélica Gorodischer." [The absent woman: The construction of gender in *Bad Night and Birthing a Female* by Angélica Gorodischer]. *Temas de Mujeres* 6.6 (2010).

Molina-Gavilán, Yolanda. "Alternate Realities from Argentina: Angélica Gorodischer's 'Los embriones del violeta.'" *Science Fiction Studies* 79.2 (July 1999): 401–11.

————. *Ciencia ficción en español: Una mitología moderna ante el cambio.* Lewiston, N.Y.: Edwin Mellen Press, 2002.

————, Andrea Bell, Miguel Ángel Fernández-Delgado, M. Elizabeth Ginway, Luis Pestarini, and Juan Carlos Toledano Redondo. "Chronology of Latin American SF, 1775–2005." *Science Fiction Studies* 103.34 (2007): 369–431.

Mosier, Patricia. "Women in Power in Gorodischer's Kalpa Imperial." In *Spectrum of the Fantastic: Selected Essays from the Sixth International Conference of the Fantastic in the Arts.* Ed. Donald Palumbo. Westport, Conn.: Greenwood, 1988. 153–61.

Murphy, Jeanie. "That Isn't All: Angélica Gorodischer and the Anti–Fairy Tale." *Journal of the Midwest Modern Language Association* 42.1 (2009): 105–16.

"Obra en Construcción: Angélica Gorodischer 1/2" [Under construction: Angélica Gorodischer 1/2]. *Audiovideoteca de Escritores.* March 2006. Accessed July 29, 2017. https://www.youtube.com/watch?v=tDC-ISCJyyw.

Revol, Enrique Luis. "La tradición fantástica en la literatura argentina" [The fantastic tradition in Argentine literature]. *Cuadernos hispanoamericanos* 233 (1969): 426–27.

Santiago, Juanma, and Rosana López Rodríguez. "Presentación." In *Kalpa Imperial*, by Angélica Gorodischer. Barcelona: Gigamesh, 2000. 7–8.

Urraca, Beatriz. "Angélica Gorodischer's Voyages of Discovery: Sexuality and Historical Allegory in Science Fiction's Cross Cultural Encounters." *Latin American Literary Review* 23.45 (1995): 85–102.

Vázquez, María Esther. "Angélica Gorodischer: una escritora latinoamericana de ciencia ficción" [Angélica Gorodischer: A woman, Latin American writer of science fiction]. *Revista iberoamericana* 49.123–24 (1983): 571–76.

Vélez García, Juan Ramón. *Angélica Gorodischer: fantasía y metafísica* [Angélica Gorodischer: Fantasy and metaphysics]. Seville: Consejo Superior de Investigaciones Científicas, 2007.

Walton, Jo. *What Makes This Book So Great*. New York: Tor, 2014.

Sakyo Komatsu's Planetary Imagination

Reading Virus and The Day of Resurrection

Whoever sees Kinji Fukasaku's film *Virus* (1980) for the first time will undoubtedly be amazed by its conceptual affinity with the Robert Wise–directed film *The Andromeda Strain* (1971): both films share the idea of discovery of a strain of virus in outer space, and both offer not only a mysterious epidemic but also the nightmare of full-scale nuclear war. Of course, since the former was produced nearly a decade after the latter, you might consider this affinity as reflecting the natural influence of Anglo-American science fiction upon the Japanese imagination. However, if you pay attention to the publication years of the original novels, your shock will be doubled: Sakyo Komatsu's novel *Fukkatsu no hi* (The day of resurrection), the inspiration for *Virus*, was published in 1964 (hereafter I will call the film version *Virus* and the original novel *The Day of Resurrection*, although the English edition of the latter is titled *Virus: The Day of Resurrection*).[1] Michael Crichton's novel *The Andromeda Strain* was conceived by the author in 1966 and published in 1969. The Japanese author's idea preceded the American author's. Neither film is radically different from the original novel. It is also possible for us to reconsider these novels, for the time being, as literary works deeply and similarly influenced by the Cuban Missile Crisis in October 1962, which caused the rise of the apocalyptic imagination all over the world. Without this crisis, we would not have seen Kurt Vonnegut's novel *Cat's Cradle* (1963), Stanley Kubrick's film *Dr. Strangelove or: How*

I Learned to Stop Worrying and Love the Bomb (1964), or Sidney Lumet's film *Fail Safe* (1964). To further investigate this problem might be the best way for us to speculate upon the distinct nature of postwar Japanese science fiction, with Sakyo Komatsu as one of its founding fathers.

Sakyo Komatsu
and the Postwar Japanese Imagination

One of the "Three Greats" of the first generation of postwar Japanese science fiction (together with Hoshi Shin'ichi and Tsutsui Yasutaka), Komatsu Sakyô (pen name for Komatsu Minoru) was born in Osaka, Japan, on January 28, 1931. His father studied pharmacy at Meiji Pharmacy University in Tokyo but opened an electrical appliance store in Osaka and later started running a metalworking factory in the neighborhood of Amagasaki, Hyogo Prefecture. This family background was undoubtedly the incubator for his science-fictional imagination.

Komatsu attended Kyoto University, where he majored in Italian literature and wrote his B.A. thesis on Pirandello. He was an avid reader of avant-garde Japanese literature by such figures as Hanada Kiyoteru (1909–74) and Abe Kôbô (1924–93). Around 1950, inspired by the early work of the manga artist Osamu Tezuka (1928–89), Komatsu began publishing such feature-length manga as "Andromeda, Terror of the Cosmos" under the pseudonym Mori Minoru. After graduating in 1954, he worked at a variety of jobs that included factory manager, reporter for the financial magazine *Atom*, and radio comedy writer. Finally it was in science fiction, the "Great Literature of Tomorrow," rather than the left-wing dominated *jun bungaku*, or "pure literature" (serious fiction), that Komatsu felt he had discovered the possibility of rebuilding the lost values of a defeated, postwar Japan. Komatsu entered a writer's competition, the Hayakawa SF Contest, announced in the early issues of *Hayakawa's SF Magazine*, which inaugurated publication in 1959. In 1961 his story "Chi ni wa heiwa o" (Pacem in Terris) received honorable mention, and in 1962, he debuted in the same publication with "Ekisentôriki" (Memoirs of an eccentric time traveler), thus beginning his career as a science-fiction writer. In 1963, "Pacem in Terris" and "Ochazuke no aji" (The taste of green tea over rice) were shortlisted for the fiftieth Naoki Prize, one of Japan's most prestigious literary awards for emerging authors.

In 1964, Komatsu's first full-length novel, *Nihon Apache zoku* (The Japanese Apache), a Swiftian and Čapekian fable narrating the advent and hegemony of metallivorous superhuman beings in postwar Japan, sold seventy-five thousand copies, an exceptional feat for a new author. In the same year, he published *The Day of Resurrection*, a hard science-fiction novel describing the end of the world caused by biological and nuclear weapons of mass destruction, later made into a successful 1980 film directed by Fukasaku Kinji, released as *Virus* in the United States in 1981. In 1966 he wrote what is still regarded as his most important work and what Brian Aldis would have called a "widescreen baroque," *Hateshi naki nagare no hate ni* (At the end of an endless stream), a work that consistently tops Japanese surveys of the best science fiction of all time. His 1970 pre-cyberpunkish novel featuring Homo Electricus, *Tsugu no wa dare ka?* (Who will inherit?), won the second Japanese Seiun Award (established in 1970 as the Japanese equivalent of the Hugo, although the name translates as "nebula") in the Japanese long-fiction category. In 1973 Komatsu published the best-selling *Nihon chinbotsu* (Japan sinks), which garnered the twenty-seventh Japanese Mystery Authors Association Prize and the fifth Seiun Award, and which was translated into English in an abridged version in 1976. This novel about the destruction of Japan in a giant earthquake has recently been hailed by quite a few journalists as a forerunner of today's Tom Clanceyesque "simulation" novels. It sold over four million copies and was later made into a film and manga, becoming a milestone in postwar publishing.

In 1982, Komatsu started working as a film director and was also awarded the fourteenth Seiun Prize for his novel *Sayonara Jupitaa* (Bye-Bye Jupiter)—conceived in 1977–79, published in 1983, and made into a movie by Koji Hashimoto and Sakyo Komatsu himself in 1984. Note that Komatsu's concept of transforming Jupiter into another sun coincides with *2010: A Space Odyssey* (1982), written by his friend Arthur C. Clarke and later made into a movie by Peter Hyams as *2010: The Year We Make Contact* (1984), a sequel to Clarke and Kubrick's *2001: A Space Odyssey* (1968). His other important works include *Esupai* (Espy; 1965) and the unfinished *Kyomu Kairô* (Corridors of emptiness; 1987–). These highlights emphasize Komatsu's novels, but he has also produced many short and medium-length works, including "Kesshô seidan" (Crystal cluster; 1972), "Vomiisa" (Vomisa; 1975), and "Gorudiasu no musubime" (Gordian knot; 1976), which won the fourth, seventh, and ninth Japanese Seiun Prizes for short fiction, respectively.

In addition to his fiction, Komatsu has energetically pursued other writing outlets, including nonfiction reportage based on his travels in Japan and around the world, essays considering the relationship between the Earth and human culture, and interviews with scientists in many fields. He worked passionately on the planning and production of the 1970 World Expo in Osaka and the

International Garden and Greenery Exposition in 1990. Komatsu served as chair of the Executive Committee of the International Science Fiction Symposium (ISFS1), held from August 29 through September 3, 1970, in Japan, one of the major sponsors of which was the Science Fiction and Fantasy Writers of Japan (SFWJ).[2] The symposium invited approximately a dozen of the world's premier science-fiction writers as distinguished guests. They immediately accepted the offer, as most of them were eager to see the first-ever World Expo in Asia. Therefore, it is through Komatsu and his SFWJ colleagues' production of ISFS1 that science-fiction writers from the West such as Brian Aldiss, Arthur C. Clarke, Frederick Pohl, and Judith Merril met their colleagues from the Eastern Bloc and Japan for the first time. Reviving the spirit of Komatsu and ISFS1, SFWJ produced ISFS2 in 2013 in honor of its fiftieth anniversary. This second symposium took a new look at global negotiations between Western science fiction and Japanese science fiction.

From 1980 to 1983, Komatsu was the third president of the SFWJ, and in 1980 he and the fourth president, Tsutsui Yasutaka, helped to establish the Japanese equivalent of the Nebula Award, the Nihon SF Taishô (Japan SF Grand Prize). Komatsu's own novel *Shuto shôshitsu* (The capital vanishes) won the sixth Japan SF Grand Prize in 1985. Although he wrote few original stories in the 1990s and the 2000s, Just System published the five-volume series of the Komatsu Sakyo Collection in 1995, just after the Great Hanshin Earthquake on January 17 of that year. What is more, *Japan Sinks: Part 2*, his collaboration with Koshu Tani published in 2006, won the thirty-eighth Seiun Award given at Nippon 2007, the first-ever World Science Fiction Convention in Asia, which featured Komatsu as Guest of Honor. In 2006 Josai International University Press started publishing the Collected Works of Sakyo Komatsu (as yet incomplete). His last article is the preface to *The Future of 3.11 Eastern Japan Earthquake*, coedited by Kasai Kiyoshi and Tatsumi Takayuki, a collection of essays on the impacts of the earthquake, tsunami, and multiple aftershocks (the most famous result of which was the meltdown of nuclear reactors at the Fukushima Daiichi Nuclear Power Station and the subsequent release of large quantities of radioactive contaminants) published by Sakuhinsha in the summer of 2011. Sakyo Komatsu passed away on July 26, 2011, without seeing the completion of *The Future of 3.11 Eastern Japan Earthquake*.

Not Exactly a Diptych but Approximately Twins

As I noted in my 2006 book *Full Metal Apache*, Komatsu's first official science-fiction novel, *The Japanese Apache*, published by Kobunsha in March 1964, sold seventy-five thousand copies and was followed by *The Day of Resurrection* from Hayakawa Publishers in August of the same year. Here we also have to be aware of the complex situation of the publication of these books: although having promised Fukushima Masami, the editor-in-chief of *Hayakawa's SF Magazine*, to publish his first hardcore science fiction, *The Day of Resurrection*, with Hayakawa, the publication of *The Japanese Apache* by a different and larger publisher preceded it chronologically. Feeling as if he were devastatingly and irrationally betrayed by one of his most faithful disciples, one whom he helped to make his debut as a professional writer, Fukushima made every effort to re-press and control the storm of furious and resentful emotions he experienced.[3] However, he ended up concluding that it was good for Japanese science fiction to have started with the bestseller *The Japanese Apache*, a kind of literary fable appealing to a much wider literary audience, and not with the hard science-fiction novel *The Day of Resurrection*, an exclusive gift for science-fiction fans. According to the author himself, while Fukushima asked him to write the first hardcore science-fiction novel in 1963, the manuscript of *The Japanese Apache* had already been completed and sold to Kobunsha; the manuscript was origi-nally written in the late 1950s when he and his wife were financially poor without any means of entertainment. It was through the elder brother of a classmate at Kyoto University working at Kobunsha that Komatsu signed the contract with that publisher. Nonetheless, since both of the novels deal with the end of the world—that is, the end of postwar Japan and the end of the planet itself, respectively—I would like to reconsider *The Japanese Apache* and *The Day of Resurrection* as literary twins.

Now let me take the opportunity to focus on *The Day of Resurrection*. It is noteworthy that while Kubrick's *Dr. Strangelove* centers around the fear of full-scale nuclear war, Komatsu's story gives a keen insight into the possible coincidences between natural and artificial disaster, which we were to witness nearly fifty years later than the original publication of the novel; that is, in the multiple disasters in eastern Japan on March 11, 2011.

The Day of Resurrection starts in the 1960s, when a shady transfer is happen-ing in England between an East German scientist, Professor Gregor Karlsky, and a group of secret agents. It is revealed that a deadly virus, MM-88, based on microbes collected by satellites in outer space in 1963 and 1964, is created accidentally by an American geneticist. The virus amplifies the potency of any other virus or bacteria with which it comes into contact. Stolen from Fort Detrick's laboratory in Maryland and transferred to Porton Down's Center of Applied Microbiology and Research in the United Kingdom, MM-88, it is later renamed "Linskey nucleic acid bacteria" and nicknamed "WA5PS." The virus passes into the possession of Professor Karlsky, who meets with the secret agents on the condition that they hand a sample directly to Dr. Leisener of the B.C. Weapons Research Center in Pilsen, as he is the only scientist in the world capable of developing pharmaceuticals to resist MM-88. However, the secret agents, interested only in recovering the virus as a bioweapon, betray him. Like Adolf Eichmann, all they can do is to receive a request, send back an estimate, draw up a plan, and make the deal. This betrayal leads Professor Karlsky to commit suicide at his sister-in-law's house in Brighton. Meanwhile, while escaping an attack by East German soldiers, the spies crash their plane in the Alps, and the virus is released, creating a worldwide epidemic initially known as the "Tibetan Flu" ("Italian Flu" in the film version). Within seven months, the world's entire population has died off except for 863 scientists and support personnel wintering in Antarctica. The virus becomes active at ten degrees below zero Celsius, and the polar winter has spared the ten thousand men and sixteen women stationed on the southern continent.

Enter the protagonist Yoshizumi, a seismologist on board the American nuclear submarine *Nereid*, on patrol at the time the epidemic begins. *Nereid* joins the scientists after joining forces with Soviet sub T-232 to sink the American submarine *Sea Serpent*, whose infected crew attempt to make landfall near Palmer Station on Antarctica as another utopia. Note that this surprise attack is disguised as a suicide: "Colonel McCloud, however, the captain of Nereid, insisted that Sea Serpent had, in reality, chosen its fate when it made its report."[4] However, just as the group begins to repopulate their new home in Antarctica, it is revealed that an earthquake near Alaska will set off the U.S. nuclear arsenal, since Joint Chiefs of Staff chairman General Garland had activated the Automated Reaction System (ARS) before his death, believing that the Soviet Union would use the confusion caused by the pandemic to launch an attack on North America. It is worth mentioning that this novel conceived the post-JFK vision of Pax Americana, for it was written from 1963 through 1964—that is, from the critical moment of the assassination of President Kennedy on November 22, 1963, into the Lyndon Johnson presidency. At a meeting of the Supreme Council of the Antarctic Federation, Major Carter explains that ARS was created in the post-JFK years by then-President Silverland and Lieutenant General Garland, who at the time was said to be a capable man at Joint Chiefs of Staff headquarters. The peaceful path Kennedy chose is the one that Silverland reversed by force, planning to crush the Soviet Union. The whole system of ARS is powered by an un-manned, underground nuclear power station. All the president has to do is throw a hidden switch in the White House's special underground chamber, "and the whole command system is taken out of the defense personnel and put under ARS control—and ARS doesn't even have any hands."[5] Yoshizumi assumes that "observable, abnormally intense changes"[6] have taken place in

Alaska, an area with frequent earthquakes, and predicts that there will be a huge earthquake of 8.6 to 9 magnitude, whereas Major Carter magnificently links the possible disaster of earthquake in Alaska with the possible tragedy of ARS: "The geographical point you showed us—it's relatively near the Distant Early Warning line. If the U.S. radar stations in Alaska are destroyed by a major earthquake, the ARS Command Center will transmit a six-minute warning, and if the base doesn't answer, intercontinental ballistic missiles tipped with nuclear warheads will be automatically fired at the Soviet Union."[7] The Soviets have their own version of the ARS and will fire off their weapons when the American missiles hit their targets. This is what we call the system of MAD (Mutual Assured Destruction), conceived in the 1960s as another name for deterrence. MAD rationalized the strategy of destroying incoming missiles as a means of national self-defense, which was to be the inspiration for SDI (Strategic Defense Initiative) in the 1980s, nicknamed the Star Wars program. Moreover, Captain Nevski reveals that there is a high probability that "several of the Soviet missiles are *aimed at* Antarctica."[8] This crisis causes Yoshizumi and Carter to visit the White House in Washington, D.C., in order to stop the total nuclear war. The visit is in vain; it's too late. This is the way technology out of control causes the second end of the world.

The epilogue portrays Yoshizumi dressed in rags after miraculously surviving the total apocalypse, walking all the way from Washington, D.C., to Rio Gallegos, Argentina, the southernmost tip of South America. His survival, however, is not a gift of God's grace but the ironic effect of total nuclear war. The story closes with Dr. Henri Louis de la Tour's letter explaining what happened to Yozushimi and the world. According to him, the neutron bombs launched by both sides saved humankind from the plague of Linskey nucleic acids. Dr. de la Tour already knew that in order to make mutants of the host bacteria WA5PS themselves, it would be necessary to irradiate them with enough high-energy neutrons to destroy every living thing on Earth. Thus, being the inventor of the antivirus named "the de la Tour vaccine," Dr. de la Tour clarifies that WA5PS was eradicated via "neutron irradiation due to thousands of neutron bomb detonations on the continents of both the Old and the New World, where human beings had already died out," and that with the irradiation of the WA5PS, a large number of de la Tour variants were created, "unleashing viruses that would consume and destroy the WA5PS."[9] Here lies the utmost irony of the novel: "It's a common thing for mutants to be stronger than their progenitors."[10] Thus, he concludes the letter bravely: "Tomorrow morning, we head north. We have to breathe life back into the country of the dead. The road north runs far into the distance, and our Resurrection Day is even farther. And the tale of that day does not belong to our generation."[11]

This outline will reconfirm that in 1964 Komatsu already predicted the total apocalypse to be caused by a coincidence between a natural disaster such
as a tremendous earthquake and artificial disaster as represented by full-scale
nuclear war. When Kubrick's *Dr. Strangelove* was first shown in 1964, the logic
of MAD or total nuclear war must have been scarcely comprehensible; what
impressed the audience most deeply was the film's sense of black humor. However, Komatsu's *Day of Resurrection* brilliantly convinced readers of the logical
way the system of MAD leads to a full-scale nuclear war and abolishes all of
humankind. Indeed, technology is the fruit of the civilization that human beings created, but it is also highly plausible that technology gets so out of control
as to wipe out its creator, inheriting and reperforming the negative tradition of
human beings.

At this point, let me note that this novel features a character going by the
handle of "Ahab" over Australia's Mawson Station in Antarctica,[12] which is located next door to Showa Station. It is obvious that Komatsu is conscious of
Herman Melville's *Moby-Dick* (1851) and its mad protagonist Captain Ahab.
Although this Australian man's personality has nothing in common with Captain Ahab's, we could well note the analogy between the antebellum American
encyclopedic fiction and the postwar Japanese hard science fiction. As *Moby-
Dick* dramatizes the apocalyptic shipwreck of the whaler Pequod, whose name
recalls the genocide of the native American Pequot tribe in 1637, so *The Day of
Resurrection* reveals the logic of total apocalypse leading to the genocide of the
whole of humankind. What matters here is that even though no country on
Earth is habitable, something else inherits humanity's dynasty. Admiral Con-
way states: "Even if the North American continent is uninhabited, something
there *still lives*. . . . Humanity's hatred. . . . The germ of hatred has survived the
destruction of humanity in an uninhabited land, and it is what is tying together
Antarctica and this great earthquake in Alaska."[13] He here refers to ARS (Automated Reaction System) itself as a symptom of humanity's hatred that will
survive even the total apocalypse. Major Carter attributes this aspect of ARS
to the character of President Silverland himself, who had hunted Reds and
spies with several times the intensity of Senator McCarthy, stating, "Even if
I am killed, the arrow of vengeance will fly from my cold, dead hands."[14] This
vengeance cannot help but recall Captain Ahab, who says, "I'd strike the sun
if it insulted me."[15] While Antebellum America produced President Abraham
Lincoln, another paranoiac who compared himself to a whaler by saying, "We
are like whalers who have been long on chase: we have at last got the harpoon
into the monster, but we must now look how we steer, or with one 'flop' of his
tail he will send us all into eternity,"[16] President Silverland became paranoid
enough to out-Ahab Ahab in establishing an eternal chain of revenge on the

planet. Although Komatsu seems partly aware of H. G. Wells's science-fiction classic *The War of the Worlds* (1898), in which Martians ironically wind up being slaughtered by Earthly germs, reinventing the Orientalist image of the other in the heyday of the Yellow Peril, Komatsu's *Day of Resurrection*, written sixty-six years later in a postwar East Asian country, could well be reconsidered not only in terms of disaster science fiction but also in the context of post-Melvillean world literary history.

Going South, Coming from the South

After its publication in 1964, *The Day of Resurrection* was supposed to be made into a film in Hollywood. Although the screenplay was completed in English, a number of financial problems caused the failure of the completion of the film. It is rumored that Michael Crichton, a best-selling novelist who was to be well-known for *Jurassic Park* and *Rising Sun*, had a chance to read the screenplay of *Virus*, the film version of *The Day of Resurrection*, as he was working in Hollywood, and came up with the idea for his novel *Andromeda Strain*, published in 1969. Crichton's novel also depicts coincidences between fatal bacteria from outer space and nuclear war. The truth remains hidden from sight. Therefore, I am not in a position to accuse Crichton of plagiarism. And yet, it is widely known that in his 2002 autobiography *Travels* Crichton humorously confessed that as an undergraduate student in English at Harvard University in the early 1960s he once retyped George Orwell's 1946 essay "Politics vs. Literature: An Examination of *Gulliver's Travels*" and submitted it as his own, ending up by getting a B-.[17] Although Crichton explained that he plagiarized Orwell to outwit his instructor, who had kept giving him poor grades, this episode does prove his case history of literary plagiarism. Nonetheless, I would entrust a further exploration on this topic to the younger critics of science fiction or scholars of comparative literature in the near future. What I would like to emphasize now for the English-speaking audience is that Sakyo Komatsu's postwar planetary imagination exhibited in *The Day of Resurrection* preceded Crichton's panic novel *The Andromeda Strain*, not vice versa, and that without witnessing the atomic bomb's impacts upon Japan at the end of World War II as a junior high student, Komatsu could not have provided the sharp insights into the coincidence between tremendous earthquakes and nuclear technology out of control that miraculously predicted the multiple disasters in March 2011 in eastern Japan.

Let me conclude by taking notice of a novel by one of today's most cutting-edge Latino American writers, Junot Díaz's *The Brief Wondrous Life of Oscar Wao* (2007), the winner of the 2008 Pulitzer Prize for Fiction and the National Book Critics Circle Award for the Best Novel of 2007. Born in 1968 in the

Dominican Republic and reared in New Jersey since he was four years old, this highly talented author has paid attention to the hybridity of global pop culture, including Japanese science fiction. The protagonist Oscar Wao, a young nerd ("Otaku" in Japanese) nicknamed after the slightly overweight figure of Oscar Wilde, enumerates his favorite films:

> At night, unable to sleep, he watched a lot of bad TV, became obsessed with two movies in particular: *Zardoz* (which he'd seen with his uncle before they put him away for the second time) and *Virus* (the Japanese end-of-the-world movie with the hot chick from Romeo and Juliet). *Virus* especially he could not watch to the end without crying, the Japanese hero arriving at the South Pole base, having walked from Washington, D.C., down the whole spine of the Andes, for the woman of his dreams.[18]

Readers of *The Day of Resurrection* will immediately figure out that the film *Virus* does not include the hero's romance with "the woman of his dreams" in the last sequence. However, as I have explained above, it is true that the protagonist Yoshizumi walks from Washington, D.C., down the whole spine of the Andes to a southernmost village, if not the South Pole base as Díaz describes it. It is interesting to note that while Komatsu, a big fan of William Faulkner, showed deep interest in going south back in the 1960s not only in *The Day of Resurrection* but also in *Who Will Inherit?* (1970)—starting with a fabulous campus life in Virginia and locating the origin of Homo Electricus in Bolivia—it is a young Latino American writer who has since the 1980s been deeply moved by the film *Virus* and its reflection of the spirit of Sakyo Komatsu. At this point, allow me to recollect an incredible coincidence. A Japanese newspaper asked me to write a review of the Japanese edition of *Oscar Wao*, just out from Shinchosha Publishers the previous month—on February 25, 2011. I was therefore reading with deep interest Díaz's high tribute to Komatsu/Fukasaku's *Virus* during my series of lectures at the University of Oslo, Norway, in the middle of March 2011—exactly in the wake of multiple disasters in eastern Japan. Reading the work in this transnational apocalyptic context could not help but induce me to meditate upon the dramatic convergence in Fukushima between natural and artificial disasters, accurately predicted by Komatsu's original novel *The Day of Resurrection* nearly half a century ago. Junot Díaz's emotional allusion to Komatsu's work in the twenty-first century in his highly praised novel might be preparing for the resurrection day of Sakyo Komatsu himself as a prophet not only of transnational literary history but also of planetary nuclear crisis.

Notes

1. Translated by Daniel Huddleston, it was published by Haikasoru in San Francisco in 2012—approximately half a century later than the original edition.

2. See the SFWJ's website at http://www.sfwj.or.jp.

3. Fukushima, *Mito no Jidai*.

4. Komatsu, *Day of Resurrection*, 238.

5. Ibid., 269.

6. Ibid., 259.

7. Ibid., 269.

8. Ibid., 271.

9. Ibid., 309.

10. Ibid.

11. Ibid., 312.

12. Ibid., 191.

13. Ibid., 263.

14. Ibid., 268.

15. Melville, *Moby-Dick*, 140.

16. Qtd. in Goodwin, *Team of Rivals*, 688.

17. See Coleman, "George Orwell Got a B- at Harvard.".

18. Díaz, *Brief Wondrous Life*, 33.

Bibliography

2001: A Space Odyssey. Dir. Stanley Kubrick. United States: MGM, 1968.

2010: The Year We Make Contact. Dir. Peter Hyams. United States: MGM, 1984.

The Andromeda Strain. Dir. Robert Wise. United States: Universal, 1971.

Clarke, Arthur C. *2001: A Space Odyssey*. London: Hutchinson, 1968.

———. *2010: Odyssey Two*. London: Granada Publishing, 1982.

Coleman, Dan. "George Orwell Got a B- at Harvard, When Michael Crichton Submitted an Orwell Essay as His Own." *Open Culture*, January 1, 2014. Accessed July 31, 2017. http://www.openculture.com/2014/01/george-orwell-got-a-b-at-harvard.html.

Crichton, Michael. *The Andromeda Strain*. 1969; reprint, New York: Harper, 2008.

———. *Jurassic Park*. New York: Alfred A. Knopf, 1990.

———. *Rising Sun*. New York: Alfred A. Knopf, 1992.

———. *Travels*. 2002; reprint, New York: Vintage, 2014.

Díaz, Junot. *The Brief Wondrous Life of Oscar Wao*. London: Faber and Faber, 2008.

Dr. Strangelove or: How I Stopped Worrying and Learned to Love the Bomb. Dir. Stanley Kubrick. United States: Columbia Pictures, 1964.

Fail Safe. Dir. Sidney Lumet. United States: Columbia Pictures, 1964.

Fukushima, Masami. *Mito no Jidai* [Science Fiction as a Literary Frontier: A Memoir]. Tokyo: Hayakawa Publishers, 1976.

Goodwin, Doris Kearns. *Team of Rivals: The Political Genius of Abraham Lincoln.* 2005; reprint, New York: Simon and Schuster, 2012.

Hashimoto, Koji, and Sakyo Komatsu. *Sayonara Jupitaa* [Bye-bye Jupiter]. Japan: Toho Co. Ltd., 1984.

Kasai, Kiyoshi, and Tatsumi Takayuki, eds. *3.11 no Mirai* [The future of 3.11 eastern Japan earthquake]. Tokyo: Sakuhinsha, 2011.

Komatsu, Sakyo. "Andromeda, Terror of the Cosmos" [ca. 1949]. In *The Collected Manga Works of Sakyo Komatsu/Minoru Mori.* Vol.1. Tokyo: Shogakkan, 2002. 93–189.

———. "Chi ni wa heiwa wo" [Pacem in Terris]. *Uchujin* [Cosmic dust] 7.63 (January 1963): 78–111.

———. "Ekisentôriki" [Memoirs of an eccentric time traveler]. *Hayakawa's SF Magazine* 3.35 (October 1962): 74–91.

———. "Gorudiasu no musubime" [Gordian knot]. *Yasei-Jidai* [Kadokawa's wild age] 3 (January 1976): 162–89.

———. *Hateshi naki nagare no hate ni* [At the end of an endless stream]. Tokyo: Hayakawa Shobo, 1966.

———. "Kesshô seidan" [Crystal cluster]. *Hayakawa's SF Magazine* 13.164 (September 1972): 18–83.

———. *Komatsu Sakyo Jiden: Jitsuzon wo motomete* [Autobiography of Sakyo Komatsu: In search of existence]. Tokyo: Nihon Keizai Shinbunsha, 2008.

———. *Kyomu Kairô* [Corridors of emptiness]. Tokyo: Tokuma Shoten, 1987– .

———. *Nihon Apache Zoku* [The Japanese Apache]. Tokyo: Kobunsha, 1964.

———. *Nihon Chimbotsu* [Japan sinks]. Tokyo: Kobunsha, 1973.

———. "Ochazuke no aji" [The taste of green tea over rice]. *Hayakawa's SF Magazine* 4.38 (January 1963): 139–85.

———. *Sayonara Jupitaa* [Bye-bye Jupiter]. Tokyo: Sankei Publishers, 1982.

———. *Shuto shôshitsu* [The capital vanishes]. Tokyo: Tokuma Shoten, 1985.

———. *Tsugu no wa dare ka?* [Who will inherit?]. Tokyo: Hayakawa Shobo, 1970.

———. *Virus: The Day of Resurrection.* Trans. Daniel Huddleston. San Francisco: Haikasoru, 2012. Originally published as *Fukkatsu no Hi* (Tokyo: Hayakawa Publishers, 1964).

———. "Vomiisa" [Vomisa]. *Hayakawa's SF Magazine* 16.200 (July 1975): 17–39.

Melville, Herman. *Moby-Dick; or, the Whale.* Ed. Hershel Parker and Harrison Hayford. New York: Norton, 2002.

Napier, Susan, Tatsumi Takayuki, Kotani Mari, and Otobe Junko. "An Interview with Komatsu Sakyo." *Science Fiction Studies* 29.3 (November 2002): 323–39.

Sayonara Jupitaa [Bye-bye jupiter]. Dir. Koji Hashimoto and Sakyo Komatsu. Japan: Kabushika Kaisha, 1984.

Tatsumi Takayuki. *Full Metal Apache: Transactions between Cyberpunk Japan and Avant-Pop America.* Durham, N.C.: Duke University Press, 2006.

Virus. Dir. Kinji Fukasaku. Japan: Kadokawa, 1980.

Vonnegut, Kurt. *Cat's Cradle.* New York: Holt, Rinehart and Winston, 1963.

Liu Cixin's Three-Body Trilogy

*Between the Sublime Cosmos
and the Micro Era*

MINGWEI SONG

A popular belief among Chinese science-fiction readers is that Liu Cixin (b. 1963) has "single-handedly lifted Chinese science fiction to a world-class level."[1] A genre first promoted by Chinese cultural reformers at the beginning of the twentieth century, science fiction experienced a boom in the late Qing period (1644–1911) and then again in the early post-Mao reform period (1978–89).[2] Early sf authors often wrote in the form of political utopianism combined with a strong "obsession with China."[3] Liu Cixin emerged as a different type of sf writer, one who belongs to a new wave that has signaled the arrival of the third boom of Chinese science fiction. The new wave began at the turn of the twenty-first century and has appropriated and parodied those earlier themes in a changing context of globalization and fast-paced technological changes.[4]

Winning the 2015 Hugo Award for his novel *Santi* (The three-body problem; 2006), a milestone in the history of not only Chinese science fiction but also of world science fiction, may have qualified Liu Cixin as "rising to a world-class level." The first non-English novel to win the Hugo Award for Best Novel, it has stayed on the top of Amazon's bestselling list in the category of Chinese literature for almost a year. Ken Liu, a Chinese-American sf writer who himself is a Hugo Award winner, has fine-tuned Liu Cixin's novel with a smooth combination of the original Chinese text's dynamism and the stylish accuracy and neatness of American sf. Tor released *The Three-Body Problem* to critical acclaim in November 2014, followed by its sequel, *The Dark Forest* (translated by Joel Martinsen), in August 2015, with the final volume of the trilogy, *Death's End* (translated by Ken Liu), released in August 2016.

Before *The Three-Body Problem* "touched down" in the United States (words borrowed from the title of a report in the *Wall Street Journal*),[5] the trilogy had already been a national sensation in China; and before it was published in China between 2006 and 2010,[6] a new wave of Chinese science fiction had already emerged at the turn of the twenty-first century. The success of the trilogy in the American book market is a small echo of its record-breaking popularity among Chinese readers. In the meantime, Liu Cixin's success should also be contextualized by looking at it as one facet of the revival of the genre in China over the past fifteen years, which was made possible by various cultural and social elements ranging from the free platform for new authors on the internet to the nation's collective yearning for social changes or anxieties about the lack of change. In a peculiar way, Chinese science fiction has simultaneously entered its golden age and generated a "new wave" subversion of the genre. This new wave has been generally marked by a dystopian vision of China's future, ambiguous moral dilemmas, and a sophisticated representation of the power of technology or the technology of power. The poetics of the new wave point to the illumination of the invisible, the unknown, and the fantastic, which energize the genre as an imaginary realm opening up to infinite new possibilities. Dozens of writers, belonging to different generations born between the 1940s and 1980s, gained fame for writing science fiction at the same time. In 2012, a special issue of *Renditions* introduced eight authors of this new wave to English readers, including Liu Cixin, Han Song, Wang Jinkang, Zhao Haihong, La La, Chi Hui, Fei Dao, and Xia Jia.[7]

Liu Cixin stands out as the most successful science-fiction writer of his generation. While he has quoted American and British space-opera writers like Isaac Asimov and Arthur C. Clarke as major influences on his own writings,[8] his fans consider *The Three-Body Problem* winning the Hugo as a game-changing event that has pushed Chinese science fiction into the limelight for Anglo-American audiences. Called "Da Liu" (Big Liu) by his fans, Liu Cixin is celebrated as the national pride of China's cyberspace. The phenomenal success of Liu's trilogy, domestically and internationally, also corresponds to the Chinese government's promotion of the "Chinese dream," which mirrors, twists, and speaks back to its American counterpart. Although I have elsewhere pointed out the darker, subversive side of the new wave, which presents a nightmarish mutation of the "Chinese dream,"[9] *The Three-Body Trilogy* is a more complex text that combines the sublime and the uncanny, mingles cosmopolitanism and nationalism, and undermines scientific certainty with the agency of human variability. Its complexity also indicates in general the significance and dynamics of Chinese science fiction that reflects on the uncertainty and probabilities China confronts when entering a new world order.

This essay consists of four parts: an introduction to the new wave of Chinese science fiction through analysis of Liu Cixin's unpublished political cyberpunk novel, *Zhongguo 2185* (China 2185; 1989); an evaluation of the aesthetics and politics represented in Liu Cixin's major works; an analysis of his magnum opus *The Three-Body Trilogy*; and finally a questioning of Liu Cixin's ambiguity in representing a posthuman future in his novella *Weijiyuan* (Micro era; 1999).

Liu Cixin and the New Wave

The new wave of Chinese science fiction is both popular and subversive. It mingles utopianism with dystopian anomalies, challenges conventional ideas of humanity through posthuman imaginaries, and questions some of the key concepts of Chinese modernity, such as progress, development, nationalism, and scientism. Compared with fantasy fiction, the new wave of science fiction has engaged more seriously with social, political, and philosophical themes. The world systems created by authors like Liu Cixin are both sublime and provocative, characterized by wild imagination beyond the mundane as well as the uncanny estrangement of the familiar.

I identify 1989 as the year when a new paradigm of science-fictional imagination began to complicate the utopianism that had dominated Chinese politics and intellectual culture for more than a century. What served as the larger political/cultural backdrop for the changes in Chinese science fiction (and in perhaps all of Chinese literature) are the collapse of idealism and optimism as well as a pervasive disillusionment with a political utopianism instituted by the state after the tragic end of the 1989 democratic movement in Tiananmen Square.[10] One unique science-fiction novel, the first of its kind, was written in the spring of 1989, and it signaled the arrival of a new wave in Chinese science fiction, which is more sophisticated, reflective, and subversive in terms of mixed representations of hope and despair, utopianism and its dystopian reflection, and political dictatorship and (cybernetic) popular uprising.

Liu Cixin, then a young computer engineer, began to write *China 2185* in February 1989, and it has later only been circulated on the internet and never published in book form.[11] Without any straightforward reference to the student movement, the novel nevertheless begins with a scene in Tiananmen Square: a young computer engineer crosses the deserted square on a dark night and approaches the Mao Mausoleum, which still exists in 2185. He manages to scan

Mao's dead brain cells and turns the simulated consciousness of the great man into a cybernetic existence.

Combining political fantasy with science fiction, *China 2185* describes the resurrection of Mao and five other dead old men's consciousness in cyberspace, which triggers a cybernetic popular uprising that paralyzes the authorities in the real world. The government of China in 2185 has no other way out but shutting down the entire internet, so the cyber-republic, called "Huaxia Republic," quickly sees its own demise. It turns out that Mao's cybernetic existence is not, as one would have thought, the cause of the revolution, which has actually been launched by an ordinary old man's consciousness that replicates itself millions of times and quickly builds a utopian society that lasts for 850 years—in virtual reality, which is equivalent to only two hours in reality. After the republic is wiped out, when all the democratic outcries in the cybernetic uprising die out, the novel ends with a conversation between Mao's cybernetic specter and the young female leader of the Chinese government: Mao's "ghost" honestly tells his future successor that any attempt for immortality is futile, for "immortality is mortality"; he appears to be at ease with his own eventual farewell to revolution. In this novel, Liu Cixin does not seem either to glorify the cybernetic uprising or discredit Mao's political legacy, but instead he concentrates on experiments of conceiving "alterity" for the "post-Mao" as well as "posthuman" new age, which is crystalized in the effects of cybernetic democracy and technologized governance.

China 2185 creates a dynamic utopian/dystopian variation reflecting on democracy, governance, and revolution in new terms informed by cybernetic technology. Its distance from utopianism is obvious, but it is not a dystopian novel, which, as defined by the genre's Western classics such as *1984*, presents a pervasive criticism of totalitarianism. Liu's novel does not portray an ideal society, and the future society it depicts is actually split into two conflicting parts: the "real" world and the "virtual" nation. The novel holds social criticism at bay and questions the technological constructs of political consciousness, cybernetic subjectivities, and revolutionary ethics through the depiction of the rise and fall of the Huaxia Republic as a virtual community of intercybernetic subjectivities.

China 2185 is the first political cyberpunk novel written in Chinese. Although largely unknown until Liu Cixin became a bestselling author much later, it predicted a radically different, less idealistic and optimistic future for Chinese science fiction. A dark version of science fiction—a new wave—gradually came into existence in the decades after 1989. *China 2185* can be identified as the first work of the new wave of Chinese sf that contains a self-conscious effort to energize the utopian/dystopian variations rather than a simple denial of uto-pianism or a total embrace of the dystopian disillusionment. Utopianism and its dystopian variety have rather been presented in a complex entanglement in the new wave, an entanglement that opens up to new possibilities for restoring imagination in the cultural politics of contemporary China.

The Invisible Dimensions of the Sublime Cosmos

Compared with other new wave writers, Liu Cixin appears to be the least in-fluenced by Chinese politics in his works written after *China 2185*. With a clear advocacy of "hard" science fiction, combining scientific speculation and liter-ary imagination, Liu focuses some of his most ambitious works on speculative changes in the fundamental principles of the physical world, which he proposes as the foundations for creating alterity.[12] After publishing his first stories in 1999, Liu quickly established his fame as China's most devoted "hard sf" writer, and over the past decade he has been widely recognized as the most popular Chi-nese science-fiction author. He had published dozens of short stories and two novels before he began to serialize *The Three-Body Problem*, the first volume of his trilogy.

The sublime cosmos that Liu Cixin envisions largely through a scientific ap-proach testifies to the ideal of a "utopia of science and technology"[13] as a central motif in Chinese science fiction. This echoes the Chinese government's call for advancing the scientific and technological modernization that has particularly guided Chinese educational policies since 1978. It is deeply rooted in a belief in scientific certainty that counteracts China's constantly changing political cli-mate, particularly during Mao's chairmanship. The popularization of the vision of a scientific utopia provides ground for Liu Cixin's advocacy of hard science fiction, which is based on a faith in the power of science and technology instead of moral consciousness, as clearly expressed by Liu in a 2008 interview.[14]

In Liu Cixin's fictional world, human society is often treated as a minor problem against the extravagant and grandiose backdrop of a universe mea-sured in light years. Human survival is made possible merely by the mercy of a supreme alien species, and human extinction does not have much impact on the universe. Experimenting with ideas of changing the physical reality, he creates entire new universes or depicts them—"like God."[15] His master plot is man's encounter with the unknown dimensions of the universe, a place that remains largely alien to human understanding. Populated by grandiose superhuman, transhuman, or posthuman figures or visions, Liu's fictional world is fiercely lofty, sublime, and awe-inspiring.

This vision appears in "Xiangcun jiaoshi" ("The Village Schoolteacher"; 2001, translated in 2012), one of Liu Cixin's earliest-published, most well-received short stories. It combines realistic depictions of the bleak state of education in rural China with the wondrous imagination of an intergalactic war that extends over the entire Milky Way. The former appears as a nuanced detail in the unfolding of the latter's divine drama, though it proves crucial for human survival. When one side of the space war aims to create a five-hundred-light-year-wide buffer zone in the first arm of our galaxy by destroying all stars in this enormous space, it conducts a life scan to make sure that no advanced intelligent species is eliminated in the military operation. Many stars are wiped out after the creatures inhabiting their planets fail to respond intelligently to questions concerning the basic laws of the universe. Singled out as examples of the life forms on the third planet of the solar system, eighteen Chinese children happen to have just learned Newton's three laws from their teacher, who passed away after giving them the last lecture. Their recital of the correct answers in unison saves the Earth from destruction. The story can be read as a touching testimony of human agency, particularly when it is manifested in children, but it also more clearly points to the vulnerability of humanity even as it bases human survival solidly on mastery of scientific knowledge. Human life is rendered as a contingent existence in the universe, while the laws of the physical world remain constant. Liu Cixin writes into the seemingly sentimental story of a selfless, devoted teacher and his students a cosmic determinism that overwhelms human agency.

In another story, "Shiyun" ("The Poetry Cloud"; 2003, translated in 2012), another alien species that is not as benign as the one portrayed in "The Village Schoolteacher" descends on Earth. This highly acclaimed story depicts the apocalyptic end of humanity when an immensely intelligent creature destroys the solar system. Presenting itself as a perfect sphere in front of humans, it shows cold contempt toward the so-called human civilization. However, this godlike creature is captivated by traditional Chinese poetry. It has all-embracing technologies that enable it to explore the eleventh dimension of the universe, but it has yet to learn how to write Chinese poetry. So it keeps one Chinese poet alive and uses up all the energies of the solar system to create a "poetry cloud" that can produce and store all the poems that can ever be written. At the end of the story, the alien creature assumes the identity of the greatest Chinese poet of the Tang Dynasty, Li Bo (701–62).

In this story, Liu presents an ambivalent negotiation between poetry and technology and, envisioned on a larger scope, between humanity and the universe. But the tricky part of Liu's narrative is his final solution of the problematic of poetry and technology through programming the poetry cloud to encompass all possible poetic creations. Although the godlike alien intelligence still cannot identify real poetry, all possible poems have theoretically been created and stored in his enormous "computer." The poetry cloud symbolizes the possibility of the eventual success of technology, and the last part of the story—a seemingly utopian description of the two Chinese poets' happy life (one of them is the alien) after the total extinction of the solar system—can best be read as a simulacrum, a virtual reality fabricated by the technologized mimesis of the poetic vision after its creators have been wiped out. In this way, Liu Cixin sticks to the belief in scientific certainty, in contrast with the uncertainty and contingency of the human vision, thus turning the utopia of science and technology into a potential dystopia for humanity.

For Liu Cixin, writing science fiction is, first of all, like a scientific experiment. The possible changes in physical laws motivate the plot development, and his task is to concretize these possibilities to make them appear plausible. For example, in his novella *Shan* (Mountain), Liu imagines a bubble world at the center of a rocky planet, in which some metallic intelligent creatures evolve into a civilization. Their "sky" is solid rock, and their world is an enclosed space. What if there were a Copernicus living among them who dared to propose that the bubble they inhabit is not, in fact, the center of the universe? What if their Columbus dared to sail to the other side of the solid sky? Liu Cixin presents an epic story about this alien civilization, which overcomes all sorts of difficulties and eventually comes to the surface of its planet to see the infinite sky full of stars.

"Mountain" illustrates how Liu makes visible a world that closes itself within an invisible planetary core. His speculations focus on the strenuous effort to bring the invisible to the surface—a process that turns imaginative possibilities into scientifically plausible reality. For Liu Cixin, such a story is not intended to be an allegory of a national experience, and it can even be said that there is a touch of political apathy in most of his works, which show tendencies of transcending China's contemporary political reality and looking beyond the horizon of our own time toward a technological utopia of the future of humankind or posthumanity. Although *China 2185* is full of political references, Liu also invests its narrative with a strong scientism that experiments with cybernetic constructions of governance and also points to a posthuman future decided by technological progress.

The creation of world systems can take place on both macro and micro levels. "The Village Schoolteacher" connects the fate of some Chinese students in a poverty-stricken rural area to an intergalactic war that has been raging for twenty millennia, and in the novella *Micro Era*, humanity has evolved into microbe-like creatures adapted to the deteriorating environment of an Earth torched by an explosive sun. The common characteristic of these two worlds is their invisibility, as the advanced beings engaging in the intergalactic war are never depicted directly, and the micro-humans' world is only revealed through a special computer program that produces a virtual reality.

An absence of visibility is also found in *The Three-Body Trilogy*, in which, first of all, bodies remain unseen. A central character of the third volume, Yun Tianming, who later becomes a nearly messiah-like figure to help humans survive, is rendered literally bodiless, in the sense that only his brain is sent into deep space for the purpose of establishing contact with the alien civilization. Whether the alien species that captures his brain will be able to reproduce his body remains a mystery throughout most of the narrative. Even when he finally reappears, supposedly with a body, the other central character, his lover, does not get to see him after an accident separates them forever.

The human race's clash with the first known alien species, called "Trisolarans," drives the trilogy's main plot. But the physical appearance of the Trisolarans is never described.[16] Instead, the unseen bodies are replaced by humanoid self-images in a virtual-reality game called "Three Body," in which human players, through incarnations in real historical figures like King Wen of Zhou; Mozi; the First Emperor; Copernicus; Newton; and von Neumann gradually come to grasp the reality confronting the Trisolarans, the truth of the lawlessness and formlessness of the Trisolaran world. At the end of the first volume, two small intelligent particles known as sophons are sent by Trisolarans to Earth to spy on human civilization. Sophons are invisible to humans, but when their creators increase their dimensionality, they may grow into giant three-dimensional geometric solids, or unfold both inside and outside of any space in six dimensions, or even become completely unobservable in eleven dimensions.

Through the contact with alien species and human diasporas across the galaxies, some characters in the novel approach the truth of the universe, which has multiple hidden dimensions beyond human perception. In the final volume of the trilogy, when the first human spaceship leaves the solar system, it encounters a mysterious four-dimensional "bubble" within which space appears timeless and beyond measure:

> This depth was not a matter of distance: it was bound up in every point in space. Guan Yifan's exclamation later became a classic quote:
> "A bottomless abyss exists in every inch."
> The experience of high-dimensional spatial sense was a spiritual baptism. In one moment, concepts like freedom, openness, profundity, and infinity all gained brand-new meanings.[17]

This passage recalls Liu Cixin's description of his response to Arthur C. Clarke's *2001: A Space Odyssey*: "I went out to look at the sky after closing the book. Everything around me suddenly disappeared. The ground under my feet turned into a smooth flat geometric plane that extended limitlessly to the beyond. I stood alone under the splendid starry sky, confronting the enormous mystery that the human mind could not understand. From then on, the starry sky has completely changed in my eyes, a sensation like when one leaves a pond to see the ocean."[18] What Liu is describing here is, in effect, the Kantian sublime: infinite, formless, boundless, overwhelming, with a magnitude beyond the human ability to measure and grasp. By the end of *The Three-Body Trilogy*, human survivors have just begun to piece together the story of our universe, which is said to have had originally eleven dimensions—a paradise, or a world that was timeless and endless. However, it was soon lowered to ten dimensions, and then to nine and to eight, all the way down to three dimensions. Reducing the dimensions or changing the physical rules of the universe are the most powerful ways to wipe out entire worlds, and the novel reveals our three-dimensional universe to be the ruins of wars dating to the beginning of time.

On the astronomical scale, the unfathomable magnitude of the universe transcends good and evil. For *The Three-Body Trilogy*—which asks whether the morally self-aware humans could survive in a fiercely hostile and amoral world—the unknown, invisible dimensions of the universe present a gateway to transcendence. Whether the morally self-aware humans could survive in an amoral universe also becomes a moot question toward the end of the narrative, because the entire universe comes to an end when dimensions are finally reduced to zero, absolute nothingness.

The climax of the novel is the collapse of our solar system. A mysterious higher intelligence that patrols the universe, whose body again remains unseen or undescribed, passes by the solar system and our neighboring Trisolaran system and accidentally discovers the civilizations that had developed in this remote area of the galaxy. The alien projects an extraordinarily thin sheet into the solar system. Called "dual vector foil," this sheet changes the structure of the space-time continuum, reducing the three-dimensional solar system to two dimensions. The entire solar system begins to fall into an infinitely large flat picture: planet by planet, object by object, molecule by molecule, the Sun, Jupiter, Saturn, Venus, Mars, the Earth, and all humanity turn two-dimensional.

At this moment, the surviving humans are cast into a diasporic state wherein they may observe the hostility and rivalry among intelligent existences populating the universe. For the surviving characters in the novel, this marks the beginning of humanity's apprenticeship with an intelligent maturity that matches the sophistication of the universe itself. The universe is sublime, fearsome, and hostile, and humanity seeks survival and tries to sustain itself in a war that it has virtually no chance of winning.

From the perspective of narrative poetics, this moment also illustrates Liu Cixin's attempts to render the sublime visible. The entire process of the solar system's two-dimensionalization is displayed with dazzlingly concrete details—each drop of water is depicted as though it were as large and complex as an enormous two-dimensional ocean. Liu depicts this imagined and miraculous catastrophe as directly and precisely as if it were real. Three survivors stationed on Pluto observe this reality, awed by the moon-size snowflakes that are the two-dimensional water molecules. The two-dimensional imagery of the solar system provides a thrilling moment that concretizes sublime invisibility.

This is a telling moment in Liu Cixin's writing, which may be compared to the "dual vector foil." The two-dimensional picture epitomizes Liu's artistic approach to sf: a sublime world image is created out of precise details. His work speaks directly to the infinity of the universe, but he also seeks to transform the invisible and infinite into a plausible physical reality. By the end of the trilogy, he enlivens his work with a wondrous sensation that lifts science fiction from determinism or national allegory (or whatever is rooted in certainty) into a transcendental imaginary realm that opens up to possibilities and perceptions beyond ordinary reality. Yet he also renders the sublime visible, as the very magnetic force of science fiction.

The Amoral Universe in *The Three-Body Trilogy*

The most important work that Liu Cixin has written so far, *The Three-Body Trilogy*, portrays the universe as the darkest forest, in which the only moral imperative is the recognition of zero morality, and all intelligent species compete to destroy other species. The most advanced intelligence in the universe dares to change the laws of physics to eliminate its rivals. The question that Liu Cixin asks is whether the human beings who are morally conscious can survive in a universe that has no place for morality. In other words, can humanity be preserved in a world that only obeys the inhuman principles of "hard science"?

This vision is no doubt a historicized image deeply rooted in the memory of China's recent past. Mao's conviction that men find endless pleasure in the eternal battle against heaven and earth as well as against other human beings is the very root of a utopian vision of social revolution, human progress, and cosmic change that are forever energized by struggles that transcend "morality" as defined by humanness. What stays central to the utopian discourse of the

People's Republic—Mao's ideal for a permanent revolution—is the foundational belief in the possibility of revolutionizing humanity through dehumanizing the revolutionaries.[19]

The Three-Body Problem opens with a cruel moment in the Cultural Revolution: Red Guards humiliating and torturing a distinguished scientist, whose daughter, Ye Wenjie, after witnessing her father's death, becomes completely disillusioned with human goodness. She later joins a secret science project that is tasked by the supreme leader to search for extraterrestrial intelligence, which aims to compete with the Americans and Russians who are doing the same. But the Chinese SETI team is miserable, for they lack both the proper technology and equipment. Ye Wenjie finds a way to bypass the political prohibitions to shoot the signal directly to the sun, which serves as an amplifier to broadcast the message from the Chinese communist leaders to the entire galaxy. Eight years later, Ye receives a reply that reads: "Do not answer! Do not answer! Do not answer!"[20]

What Ye receives is a message coming from the closest planet, located in Alpha Centauri only four light years away. The message is sent by a self-identified pacifist living in a dying civilization that faces the harshest conditions for survival. In their star system, a lone planet orbits three suns. This situation testifies to the three-body problem, which is a real astronomical problem: how three bodies move under the influence of their mutual gravitational attractions is uncertain. In the novel, the Trisolaran world has an unpredictable fate, alternating between Stable Eras when the planet orbits one sun and Chaotic Eras when the planet loses its normal orbit. The Trisolaran civilization has been destroyed many times by either being scorched by three suns rising together or being frozen by the lack of any sunlight. The Trisolarans are eager to emigrate to other planets, readying themselves for interstellar invasion. The pacifist, a listener by profession stationed in a post to search for habitable planets, happens to have received Ye's message, and out of a moral compassion it warns the Earthling that as soon as an answer is sent back to space, the source of the transmission will be located, which means that an invasion will be imminent. Ye Wenjie ignores the warning and replies immediately, inviting the Trisolarans to come to Earth, because "our civilization is no longer capable of solving its own problems."[21]

The epic story of the space war begins at this moment. Trisolarans target Earth for their invasion. The first volume depicts how humans gradually learn about the truth of the Trisolaran world: that it is chaotic, unpredictable, and cruel. The contact with Trisolaris is fatal, for the rivalry between the two civilizations can only end with one wiping out the other. The question that serves as a leading thread in the trilogy emerges: is the universe a place for morality, for a humanity with a moral consciousness? The second volume, *The Dark Forest*, sheds light on the darkest rules of the universe. Before Ye Wenjie dies, she passes her reflections on Earth's encounter with Trisolaris to a student of sociology, Luo Ji, who later invents cosmic sociology. The axioms of cosmic sociology are: "First: Survival is the primary need of civilization. Second: Civilization continuously grows and expands, but the total matter in the universe remains constant."[22] These axioms present a negative answer to the above question: the universe does not have room for morality; it is a dark forest ruled mercilessly by the laws of the jungle.

Luo Ji figures out why the universe is silent and why, though it is filled with civilizations, humans had never discovered extraterrestrial intelligence before. It is because nothing is more dangerous than exposing yourself in the dark forest. The chain of suspicion decides that anyone seeing you cannot determine whether you are benevolent or malicious:

> The universe is a dark forest. Every civilization is an armed hunter stalking through the trees like a ghost. . . . The hunter has to be careful, because everywhere in the forest are stealthy hunters like him. If he finds other life— another hunter, an angel or a demon, a delicate infant or a tottering old man, a fairy or a demigod—there's only one thing he can do: open fire and eliminate them. In this forest, hell is other people. An eternal threat that any life that exposes its own existence will be swiftly wiped out.[23]

In postwar (and post-Stalin) Western science fiction, it is an overwhelmingly popular motif that the utopian has irreversibly become Orwellian, in which the institutional oppression of individuals, on the one hand, represents the arch-evil of the twentieth century, and, on the other hand, the individual heroes' battles with totalitarianism in one way or another represent a belief in the integrity of individuality in spite of the institutional corruption. This sort of plot line testifies to the strength of humanism versus institutional corruption. However, in *The Three-Body Trilogy*, there is even no space for an Orwellian institution, because the dark forest is the battlefield where there is no winner.

Actually in the trilogy, the Orwellian society is not considered to be evil, and heroes are those who are resistant to individualism. The specters of collectivism, communism, and Maoism particularly linger in what Liu Cixin describes as the "Starship Earths," which may look like the true equivalent of Utopia on surface: isolated "islands" in the ocean of stars, extremely well-organized societies that can operate automatically without the intervention of individuals. But a further twist of the utopian/dystopian dialectics shows that none of these

Starship Earths is a paradise for humans. An extremely hostile universe forces the Starship Earths to prioritize survival to such an extent that collectivism legalizes cannibalism, which Liu's characters nevertheless defend as necessary to sustaining the "civilization" that has, however, already become inhuman.

In the second volume of the trilogy, *The Dark Forest*, Liu Cixin creates the character Zhang Beihai, the founder of one of the first Starship Earths. After a simple Trisolaran probe, nicknamed "droplet," destroys nearly all the human starships as well as the last hope for humanity to survive confronting the unfathomably advanced alien invasion, Zhang's starship flees the battlefield near Jupiter and leaves the solar system forever. He is the first architect for a new type of civilization that must confront the posthuman uncertainty in a totally hostile environment with rather limited resources. In the beginning, the officers of the starship have a debate about how to constitute the new civilization. While the majority opinion is to keep the military dictatorship, Zhang Beihai says absolutely not; and when others suggest democracy as an alternative, Zhang Beihai hesitates, saying: "Earth's history during the Trisolar Crisis has demonstrated that, in the face of such disasters, particularly when our world needs to make sacrifices in order to preserve the whole, the humanitarian society you have in mind is especially fragile."[24]

Zhang hides his defeatism deeply in his heart. He does not believe that humanity could survive this treacherous space war. He rather believes that only the sacrifice of the part, perhaps even the majority of humanity, is the condition for the eventual survival of the species, even when it is no longer a civilization. Zhang Beihai does not lament his own death or the destruction of the starship he leads when another starship attacks it for the purpose of obtaining supplies from it, including the nutrition extracted from the human bodies.

Both Liu Cixin and another major new-wave writer, Han Song, write about cannibalism. Han Song takes it as a cultural metaphor for social evil, like Lu Xun, the founding father of modern Chinese literature, did, though with an even more grotesque obsession with anatomical details.[25] But Liu Cixin openly talks about cannibalism as a necessary step for the survival of the species,[26] a step certainly necessary for the development of the Starship Earth. The members of one Starship Earth, captured by Earth humans in the third volume of the trilogy, are charged with committing cannibalism, but the defender questions what the bottom line of morality is when stuck in the lack of all the essential resources for life. The cannibals are executed, but the true punishment is not a moral one in Liu Cixin's narrative. The position Liu lets his characters take when facing the moral indictment is based upon a posthuman imperative for the sacrifice of self. In another story by Liu Cixin, "Ren yu tunshizhe" (Man and devourers), the entire human race is wiped out when an alien species exploits all the resources of the Earth. The last standing soldiers lie down on the ground, dying peacefully with a faint hope that the nutrition from their bodies will at least enable small insects to survive so that the Earth may not be a completely dead world. Liu is obviously not a humanist, and his concerns with the fate of humanity are stuck in a deadlocked conflict between development and morality, or the universe (as the moral vacuum for infinite development of intelligence) and humanity.

To prepare for the release of the English translation of the trilogy's first volume, *The Three-Body Problem*, Liu Cixin shared some of his own thoughts on the novel with English readers. He says: "Science fiction is a literature of possibilities. The universe we live in is also one of countless possibilities. For humanity, some universes are better than others, and *Three Body* shows the worst of all possible universes, a universe in which existence is as dark and harsh as one can imagine."[27] The worst of all possible universes is a place where every civilization is a hunting tribe set out to eliminate rivals. The only way to survive is to avoid exposing oneself. Liu's statement without a doubt presents *The Three-Body Trilogy* as the darkest possible dystopian novel in terms of humanism.

Ye Wenjie's disciple, Luo Ji, the main character of the trilogy's second volume, invents the principles of so-called cosmic sociology, which combines Social Darwinism with the Maoist mandate for self-defense and preemptive attack. Thus Luo Ji finds the key to human survival in the moral vacuum of the universe. A well-coordinated defense system is established, which will expose the locations of the Earth and the home planet of the Trisolarans so that some even more highly intelligent creatures will certainly destroy both. The Trisolarans' military invasion is stopped by Luo Ji's threat of mutual assured destruction. Civilizations on Earth flourish, and a postapocalyptic age of decadence begins to emerge in a world that lives on a thin thread of hope. However, it is completely unprepared for the end that comes through the reduction of the number of dimensions of the solar system. Any living creatures in the system adapted to the three-dimensional universe die like fish thrown to dry land. It proves that the nature of the universe is fundamentally amoral: changing physical rules bring not only the demise of the rivals but also inevitably their mutual assured destruction. So even the superior godlike creatures are also victims of lowering the number of dimensions in the universe; they also have to decrease the number of dimensions of their own physical world.

Foregrounding the destiny of an incredibly dystopian future, Liu's narrative sometimes remains ambiguous with regard to the conflicts between morality and survival, humanity and technology, hope and despair. Liu makes it clear through the overall plot development that the universe is a cold place with little room for morality. However, the most magical power of the trilogy may still come from the sustaining of humaneness that can be found even in the coldest moments and places. One of the only two persons who survive until the end of the universe is Cheng Xin, a kindhearted woman who is sarcastically nicknamed the "saint mother" by Liu Cixin's fans to show their dislike of this character who succeeds Luo Ji to become the chief defender of the Earth but submits to the tender feelings that swell in her heart when facing the alien invasion. She does not have the heart to push the buttons that will set off the mutual assured destruction of the invading Trisolarans and all species on Earth. Her failure to act nevertheless makes her morally self-conscious. Against the backdrop of life-and-death struggles, Cheng Xin constantly reminds us of the moral principles of compassion and mutual aid. She makes a moral choice in an amoral universe.

Cheng Xin also plays an even more important role in the making of Liu Cixin's saga. By the end of the trilogy, billions of years in the future, the last surviving species begin to broadcast throughout the universe, asking all the intelligent creatures to leave their self-made small universes, like Cheng Xin's, so those materials could return to the flux of time and space. In this way, the universe will be collapsing to nonexistence, or "returning to zero," from where a new universe will begin. Cheng Xin and her companions (another human being and a Trisolaran robot) decide to join this movement of "returning to zero," so they eliminate the small universe where they have been hiding themselves. However, here the narrative leaves some questions unanswered as it comes to its end.

Cheng Xin resorts to writing to pass on some messages about humanity to the next universe. Thus, Liu ends the novel from Cheng Xin's perspective and renames the trilogy "Remembrance of Earth's Past." The ending paragraph of the novel, merely about two hundred characters long, is an enchanting description of a small "ecological system" left by Cheng Xin in "our universe" that has come to an end, in which a small fish swims swiftly, and the morning dew on grass reflects the fresh sunshine. The small ball that contains the lively ecological system may well be the last trace of a utopian space in the moral vacuum of the universe in Liu Cixin's space saga.

However, with Cheng Xin secretly leaving behind an ecological glass ball, in which a fish is swimming and her entire memory of the human civilization is encoded, the novel ends on a cliffhanger. Does this mean that the new universe will not happen? Because, obviously, if something is still left there, even within five pounds of glass ball, the universe will not complete the process of collapsing itself into "zero." Or, despite this apparent logical conflict, the ending paragraph may only suggest the goodwill of showing that there is a slight hope that the memory of humans will survive even the end of the universe. If the latter is the case, this moment can be recognized as a manifestation of poetic justice. It shows a human being's determination to balance the entire universe's power to leave behind something personal, a memory that keeps alive the civilization created by humans.

Seen from outside the narrative frame of "Remembrance of Earth's Past," all the words, all the literary descriptions, and all the storylines in the three novels can also be viewed as the testimony to a human morality that cannot survive in an amoral universe. Like "The Poetry Cloud," which depicts how a godlike alien creature that ruthlessly destroys the entire solar system becomes obsessed with classical Chinese poetry and spares the life of a Chinese poet, the ending of *The Three-Body Trilogy* also resorts to the literary imagination as the most powerful manifestation of humanity. An advocate for technology and "hard sf," Liu Cixin nevertheless reserves a soft space in literary imagination where hope survives.

Compared with other Chinese science-fiction writers, Liu Cixin is the most cold-minded about the limitations of humanity, a critic of humanism and a disbeliever in optimism. Yet, his world is also the most marvelous, with a stirring power to attract readers to question and explore the unknown, and his narrative displays a profound curiosity about the infinity beyond what we thought we knew. Above the enormous darkness of an amoral universe, there is indeed a light of utopian vision that transcends the interests of nations and peoples and expands on the scope of light years. It is a posthuman universe that, contrary to optimistic expectations for realization of certain ideals, thrives on unpredictably infinite possibilities. Liu Cixin says that he writes about the worst possible universe, but he also leaves us the space for imagination of the best.

A Posthuman Future

In Liu Cixin's 1999 novella *Micro Era*, the posthuman Micro Era is twenty-five thousand years in the future. A world without worries and sorrows, it is populated by youths—only youths, and they will never grow up to adulthood. Actually, they are tiny, cute, beautiful people, the so-called micro-humans, who have been genetically regenerated, with their size reduced to roughly one trillionth of an ordinary human being. These micro-humans are the only surviving species after the Earth has been torched by the sun. Their microscopic size enables them to escape the apocalyptic explosion of the sun and emerge as the new rulers of the planet, building cities as small as water drops and creating a monument to extinct humanity that is as light as a strand of hair. Their era is characterized by "lightness" and "weightlessness," and their sense of anxiety is proportionate to their extremely small size. Their life is completely carefree and joyous. Correspondingly, they have no burden of responsibilities, no memory of the past, no sense of history, and no necessity for self-development. Living in a sort of eternal carnival, the micro-humans are indulged in a dreamy ecstasy of enjoying a childish, innocent, and forever youthful life.

The story is told from the perspective of the last man, or the last "macro-human," who returns to the Earth after a seventeen-thousand-year space odyssey searching in vain for another Earth. Called "the pioneer" in the story, he is saddened by the total extinction of the human race, but also surprised by what he sees with the aid of a special amplifying technique: a microcosm, a utopia of youth, with paradise-like settlements wrapped in water drops, floating freely on the surface of the Earth. He is warmly greeted by the micro-humans and treated as a patriarch, mentor, and leader. The "chief executive officer" of the future utopian world, a pretty and cheerful young girl elected to the office exactly because of these qualities—who actually is not unlike the female leader in *China 2185*, also called the "chief executive officer" in that novel—engages in a dialogue with the pioneer. She informs him that in her world, melancholia and grief are only found in museums. But after seeing the true sadness in the pioneer's eyes, she is moved to tears, and at the same time thrilled by the electrifying imagination of an older world full of tragic, grandiose, and sublime historical events, which she considers to be beautiful, almost like an idyllic romance. However, she and her people will never truly appreciate that sadness, for their feeling of sadness is groundless and so elusive, and during their lifetime, they will only be "growing more and more childish, becoming happier and happier."[28]

This story reminds me of modern China's foremost writer Lu Xun's allegory about the ancient hero who "burden[s] himself with the weight of tradition and shoulder[s] up the gate of darkness," giving "unimpeded passage to the children so that they may rush to the bright, wide-open spaces and lead happy lives henceforward as rational human beings."[29] But in Liu Cixin's story, the pioneer does a simpler job than is required for the ancient hero. He is confronted with two choices: should he revive the human genes stored in his interstellar ark so that the ancient "human" civilization could be restored? Or should he just quietly accept the demise of his species and let the childlike micro-humans continue to prosper, without ever burdening them with the knowledge of the eventful, tragic history of the macro-humans? After only a second of hesitation, he chooses to vaporize all the human genes he carries from the older world and keep the Micro Era untouched. Thus the pioneer ends the history of the human race, and he celebrates the arrival of a posthuman utopia.

Contextualized in China's cultural changes since 1989, this story of a Micro Era predicts the popular novelist/filmmaker Guo Jingming's cinematic representation of a less scientific "tiny time" that speaks volumes to the lack of sorrow and memory in China's "new age." "Micro Era," a technologically positive image of a posthuman future for Liu Cixin, and the "tiny time," a hedonist version of a post-socialist present-time for Guo Jingming and his fans, may both serve to terminate the enlightenment ideas concerning development, progress, self-cultivation, and psychological growth, the very core values of humanism. Such a cultural phenomenon may correspond to a paradigm shift of political engagement since 1989. The loss of political innocence, the faded idealism, and a common cynicism are all contextualized as a part of social conspiracy (in the unsaid post-1989 political environment) that constructs subjectivity without giving it much free space.

The oblivion of history in Liu Cixin's story and the self-indulgence in Guo Jingming's "tiny times" have both pointed to cultural symptoms of the post-1989 era, in which the forgetting of history is sanctioned by economic development and political indifference. Liu Cixin wrote *Micro Era* in 1999, and his vision of the posthuman utopia of youth became "reality" in Guo Jingming's *Tiny Time* tetralogy (released in 2013–15). Liu's story brilliantly comments on the emerging trend of a hedonistic celebration of the new age. Through his literary imagination, Liu depicts the future offspring of humanity as a generation of "new human beings"—the same word being used to name the generation depicted in Guo Jingming's films, who enjoy a life full of pleasures and happiness but have completely lost historical consciousness. An apocalyptic story, it nevertheless points to a future that evokes a seemingly sweeping optimism. The pioneer sheds happy tears as he looks at the cheerful faces of humanity's micro-children—do we not all hope that our descendents will live happily ever after?

Liu Cixin's story does not hide the hideous side of human extinction: the paradise is built upon the complete oblivion of the abysmal darkness of all the past traumas and tragedies. The Micro Era comes after the end of humanity's history. Is this posthuman future a blessing or a betrayal? Or, in a more general sense, does Micro Era prove Liu's fundamental posthumanist position? No matter what the answer is, Liu has truly captured as well as transcended China's recent changes in political and cultural spheres. He speaks to infinity as well as to China's immediate reality, which he aims to transcend through a

science-fictional imagination that challenges conventional moral and episte-
mological ideas about the self and society. Between the sublime cosmos and
the Micro Era, Liu Cixin creates a diverse, splendid, and multilayered vision
of the universe and humanity, as well as of posthuman potentials.

Notes

Acknowledgement: This chapter contains paragraphs that have previously appeared in my
other published writings on Liu Cixin, particularly Mingwei Song, "Variations on Utopia
in Contemporary Chinese Science Fiction," *Science Fiction Studies* 40.1 (2013): 86–102;
Mingwei Song, "After 1989: The New Wave of Chinese Science Fiction," *China Perspectives*
1 (2015): 7–13; and Mingwei Song, "*The Three Body Trilogy: The Three-Body Problem, The
Dark Forest, Death's End*," a book review published online by MCLC Resource Center in
December 2015 (http://u.osu.edu/mclc/book-reviews/mingweisong/). The author is
grateful to the editors of *Science Fiction Studies, China Perspectives*, and MCLC Resource
Center for granting the permission to reprint or rewrite paragraphs in the articles and
book review previously published.

1. Yan, "Glory and Dreams," 3.

2. For research on late Qing science fiction, see Wang, *Fin-de-siècle Splendor*, 252–312;
and Isaacson, *Celestial Empire*. For research on Chinese sf during the early Reform era,
see Wagner, "Lobby Literature." The works of several writers from this generation were
translated into English and anthologized in Wu Dingbo and Patrick Murphy's collection
Science Fiction from China.

3. Hsia, *Gate of Darkness*, 533.

4. I have coined the term "new wave" [xin langchao] for this recent revival of the genre.
For my discussion on the new wave of Chinese science fiction, see Song, "After 1989."
For a more general survey of the revival of the genre in China, see Song, "Variations on
Utopia."

5. Geng, "Chinese Sci-Fi Novel."

6. The first volume was serialized in *Science Fiction World* from May to December 2006
and later published by Chongqing Press in book form in 2008. The second volume was
published by Chongqing Press in 2008. The third volume was published by Chongqing
Press in 2010.

7. I guest edited this special issue, *Chinese Science Fiction: Late Qing and the Contemporary*.

8. Liu, *Liu Cixin on Science Fiction*, 88.

9. The nightmarish mutation of the government-promoted "Chinese dream" can be
found in Han Song's writings, particularly his 2011 novel *Ditie* [Subway] and short story
"Zaisheng zhuan" [Regenerated bricks] from 2010, as well as his unpublished short story
"Wo de zuguo bu zuomeng" [My fatherland does not dream]. For analysis of the motif and
mutation of Chinese dream in Chinese sf, see Song, "After 1989" and "Between Genres."

10. Between April 15 and June 4, 1989, Beijing saw the largest pro-democracy protest in

the history of the PRC. The protest began as a student demonstration and later involved millions of citizens. The movement ended when the Liberation Army entered the city and cleared Tiananmen Square, the center of the protest, with violence on the morning of June 4, 1989.

11. The text is available at kehuan.net.cn. A Taiwanese publisher, Owl Press, proposed to publish the novel in Taiwan, but Liu refused.

12. Liu, *Liu Cixin on Science Fiction*, 46.

13. Wu, *On Science Fiction*, 107–12.

14. Liu, "End of Morality," B20.

15. Liu, *Three Body Problem*, 46. All citations from this novel are from Ken Liu's translation.

16. "The Trisolaran data contained no descriptions of the biological appearance of Trisolarans," observes the narrator in the first volume of the trilogy. Liu, *Three Body*, 347.

17. The translation is Ken Liu's, quoted from the unpublished manuscript of his translation of *Death's End*.

18. Liu, *Three-Body*, 88.

19. For a comprehensive discussion of Mao's philosophy, see Wakeman, *History and Will*.

20. Liu, *Three-Body*, 272.

21. Ibid., 276.

22. Liu, *Dark Forest*, 13.

23. Ibid., 484.

24. Ibid., 442.

25. Such grotesque cannibalism can be found in Han Song's novella *Meiniu shoulie zhinan* (The guide to hunting beautiful women), which was published for the first time, after having been only available on the internet for many years, in his recent short-story collection *Yuzhou mubei* (The tombs of the universe), 275–373.

26. In a conversation with the historian of science Jiang Xiaoyuan, Liu directly challenges Jiang to answer the question whether they should eat the moderator of the conversation if they have to do it for survival. Jiang argues for the humanism, but Liu presents his absolute preference for survival to civilization. See Liu, *Liu Cixin on Science Fiction*, 42.

27. Liu, "Worst of All Possible Universes."

28. Liu, *China 2185*, 100 (translation mine).

29. Hsia, *Gate of Darkness*, 146–47.

Bibliography

Clarke, Arthur C. *2001: A Space Odyssey*. London: Hutchison, 1968.

Geng, Olivia. "Chinese Sci-Fi Novel, 'The Three-Body Problem,' Touches Down in U.S." *Wall Street Journal*, November 4, 2014. Accessed September 28, 2017. https://www.wsj.com/articles/chinese-sci-fi-novel-the-three-body-problem-touches-down-in-u-s-1415122369.

Han Song. *Ditie* [Subway]. Shanghai: Shanghai renmin chubanshe, 2011.

———. "Meiniu shoulie zhinan" [The guide to hunting beautiful women]. *Yuzhou mubei* [The tombs of the universe]. Shanghai: Shanghai renmin chubanshe, 2014. 275–373.

———. "Zaisheng zhuan" [Regenerated bricks]. *Wenyi fengshang* 1 (December 2010): 59–71.

Hsia, C. T. *A History of Modern Chinese Fiction*. Bloomington: Indiana University Press, 1999.

Hsia, T. A. *The Gate of Darkness*. Seattle: University of Washington Press, 1968.

Isaacson, Nathaniel. *Celestial Empire: The Emergence of Chinese Science Fiction*. Middletown, Conn.: Wesleyan University Press, 2017.

Liu Cixin. "Cong dahai jian yidishui" [Seeing a drop of water in the ocean]. In *Liu Cixin tan kehuan* [Liu Cixin on science fiction]. Wuhan: Hubei kexue jishu chubanshe, 2014. 45–54.

———. *The Dark Forest*. Trans. Joel Martinsen. New York: Tor, 2015.

———. *Death's End*. Trans. Ken Liu. New York: Tor, 2016.

———. "Daode de jintou jiushi kehuan de kaishi" [The end of morality is where science fiction begins]. *Nanfang dushi bao* [Southern Metropolitan Daily], August 31, 2008, B20.

———. *Liu Cixin tan kehuan* [Liu Cixin on science fiction]. Wuhan: Hubei kexue jishu chubanshe, 2014.

———. *Liulang diqiu* [The wandering earth]. Wuhan: Changjiang wenyi chubanshe, 2008.

———. "The Poetry Cloud." Trans. Chi-yin Ip and Cheuk Wong. In *Chinese Science Fiction: Late Qing and the Contemporary*. Ed. Mingwei Song. *Renditions* 77/78 (2012): 87–113.

———. *Santi* [The three-body trilogy]. 3 Vols. Chongqing: Chongqing Press, 2006–10.

———. "Shan" [Mountain]. In *Weijieyuan* [Micro-era]. Shenyang: Shenyang chubanshe, 2010. 225–58.

———. "SF jiao—lun kehuan xiaoshuo dui yuzhou de miaoxie" [The cult of SF: On depictions of the universe in science fiction]. In *Liu Cixin tan kehuan* [Liu Cixin on science fiction]. Wuhan: Hubei kexue jishu chubanshe, 2014. 86–89.

———. *The Three-Body Problem*. Trans. Ken Liu. New York: Tor, 2014.

———. "The Village Schoolteacher." Trans. Christopher Elford and Jiang Chenxin. In *Chinese Science Fiction: Late Qing and the Contemporary*. Ed. Mingwei Song. *Renditions* 77/78 (2012): 114–43.

———. *Weijieyuan* [Micro-era]. Shenyang: Shenyang chubanshe, 2010.

———. "Weijiyuan" [Micro-era]. In *Weijieyuan* [Micro-era]. Shenyang: Shenyang chubanshe, 2010. 85–108.

———. "The Worst of All Possible Universes and the Best of All Possible Earths: *Three Body* and Chinese Science Fiction." Trans. Ken Liu. October 30, 2014. Accessed August 1, 2017. http://www.tor.com/2014/10/30/repost-the-worst-of-all-possible-universes-and-the-best-of-all-possible-earths-three-body-and-chinese-science-fiction/.

———. *Zhongguo 2185* [China 2185]. 1989. Unpublished ms. kehuan.net.cn.

Orwell, George. *1984*. New York: Harcourt Brace and Co., 1949.

Song, Mingwei. "After 1989: The New Wave of Chinese Science Fiction." *China Perspectives* 1 (2015): 7–13.

———. "Zai leixing yu weizhi zhijian: kehuan ji qita xingshi" [Between genres and the unknown: Science fiction and other forms]. *Shanghai wenxue* [Shanghai literature] 12 (2015): 72–75.

———. "*The Three Body Trilogy: The Three-Body Problem, The Dark Forest, Death's End.*" MCLC Resource Center (December 2015). Accessed August 1, 2017. http://u.osu.edu/mclc/book-reviews/mingweisong/.

———. "Variations on Utopia in Contemporary Chinese Science Fiction." *Science Fiction Studies* 40.1 (2013): 86–102.

Song, Mingwei, ed. "Chinese Science Fiction: Late Qing and the Contemporary." *Renditions* 77/78 (November 2012).

Wagner, Rudolf. "Lobby Literature: The Archaeology and Present Functions of Science Fiction in the People's Republic of China." In *After Mao: Chinese Literature and Society, 1978–1981.* Ed. Jeffrey Kinkley. Cambridge, Mass.: Harvard University Press, 1985. 17–62.

Wakeman, Frederic, Jr. *History and Will: Philosophical Perspectives of Mao Tse-Tung's Thought.* Berkeley: University of California Press, 1973.

Wang, David Der-wei. *Fin-de-siècle Splendor: Repressed Modernities of Late Qing Fiction, 1849–1911.* Stanford, Calif.: Stanford University Press, 1997.

Wu Dingbo and Patrick D. Murphy, eds. *Science Fiction from China.* New York: Praeger, 1989.

Wu Yan. *Kehuan wenxue lungang* [On science fiction]. Chongqing: Chongqing Press, 2011.

Yan Feng. "Guangrong yu mengxiang" [Glory and dreams]. In *Liulang diqiu* [The wandering earth], by Liu Cixin. Wuhan: Changjiang wenyi chubanshe, 2008. 1–6.

Laurent McAllister

Rhizomatic Space and the Posthuman

AMY J. RANSOM

It seems only fitting that a volume on contemporary masters of science fiction should include an author who is himself something of a science fiction. The son of two fathers, born in 1987 but mature enough to be published two years later, Laurent McAllister is the "symbionym" of the French-Canadian writers Yves Meynard (b. 1964) and Jean-Louis Trudel (b. 1967). The back-cover blurb of their epic space opera *Suprématie* (2009)—for which their collaborative alter ego won both a Canadian Aurora and a Boréal Award in Québec—describes McAllister as resulting from "the encounter between two very different but complementary authors . . . : Jean-Louis Trudel, a specialist in astrophysics, who places his rigorous and precise narration in the service of an overflowing scientific imagination, and Yves Meynard, with his sumptuous writing style, his sense of character psychology and his humor."[1] This essay first surveys McAllister's career, situating it within the contexts of science fiction in Québec (SFQ)[2] and the larger context of science-fiction and fantasy writing. It then analyzes how the *Suprématie* cycle (comprised of the novel by McAllister and several solo short stories by Trudel) presents a fictional universe best understood through the lens of Gilles Deleuze and Félix Guattari's "rhizome." Finally, it examines the cycle's engagement with contemporary science fiction's most compelling topics, transhumanism and the posthuman.

Jean-Louis Trudel, Yves Meynard, and Science Fiction in Québec (SFQ)

The commonly accepted narrative for the development of science fiction in Québec as a self-conscious "literary movement" and "cultural milieu" situates the genre's origin in 1974 with the foundation of the fanzine *Requiem* at the Cégep Édouard-Montpetit by professor Norbert Spehner (b. 1943) and some of his students.[3] Professionalized in 1979, it became *Solaris* and hired Élisabeth Vonarburg (b. 1947) as its literary director. That same year, Jean-Marc Gouanvic (b. 1944), Jean-Pierre April (b. 1948), Esther Rochon (b. 1948), and others began publishing a competing magazine, *imagine*. . . . Although their birthdates place Trudel and Meynard in the "second generation" of SFQ writers, Jean-Louis Trudel published his first stories and a serialized novel in *imagine* . . . as early as the mid-1980s, while still in high school. He had become a regular contributor to *Solaris* by the early 1990s, publishing twenty-three short stories in its pages to date, more than any other writer. Trudel cemented his position as a founding figure by organizing the annual Congrès Boréal in 1989, a task he has repeated twelve times over the years since. Similarly, Meynard published several stories in the fanzine *Samizdat* in the mid-1980s, breaking into the pages of *Solaris* in 1988, and later serving as its literary director from 1994 to 2002. Although not quite as prolific as Trudel, Meynard still shares the rank of third-most number of stories published in *Solaris* with Élisabeth Vonarburg (seventeen each, including a collaboration between the two of them).

Among the vanguard of Quebec's sf milieu, Meynard and Trudel thus helped found the genre and its institutions in Canada's majority francophone province, collaborating with and building on the work of mentor figures like Vonarburg, Rochon, and Daniel Sernine (b. 1951). Trudel's solo short fiction reveals a significant political engagement; a bilingual Franco-Ontarian living and working in Quebec for much of his career, Trudel interrogates the commonplaces of Québécois franco-nationalism and contests the Anglocentric nature of life on the North American continent.[4] Although less consciously interested in using his sf for political allegory, the native Montrealer Meynard's fiction is also marked by the context in which it developed: the rise of the Parti Québécois and two failed referenda for sovereignty in his home province. Collectively, they have authored over 150 short stories, six adult novels, thirty-three young-adult novels, and several story collections, winning thirteen of Canada's Aurora Awards and Quebec's Prix Boréal eight times, and

Meynard and Trudel have each won the province's Grand Prix de la Science-Fiction et du Fantastique Québécois, in 1994 and 2001, respectively.

Trudel's and Meynard's efforts to bridge the solitudes in Canadian sf remain significant as well.[5] Writing in both of Canada's two official languages, they are uniquely positioned to ensure at least some level of communication between the northern nation's two sf communities. Above and beyond their active and central roles in SFQ, they have attended cons in Anglophone North America and regularly contributed to the *Tesseracts* series of Canadian anthologies of speculative fiction founded by Judith Merril in 1985. Together, they have published twelve stories in various *Tesseracts* volumes, and each coedited a volume; McAllister even has a translation credit in the series for Michel Martin's "La tortue sur le trottoir" ("Tortoise on a Sidewalk"; 1989, trans. 1996).

Publishing not only in Quebec and Canada but also in francophone Europe and the United States, Trudel, Meynard, and their alter ego McAllister reach out to an international audience. In addition to their bilingual Canadian careers, they have maintained ties with francophone Europe's sf community. Trudel's first two novels, *Pour des soleils froids* (For cold suns; 1994) and *Ressuscité de l'Atlantide* (Risen from Atlantis; 1994), were published in France under Fleuve Noir's prestigious Anticipation imprint. Having sold two fantasy novels to New York's Tor, *The Book of Knights* (1998) and *Chrysanthe* (2012), Meynard is arguably more of an international success than any other Québécois sf writer, with the exception of Élisabeth Vonarburg. Indeed, Gene Wolfe dedicates his own recent fantasy diptych, *The Wizard Knight* (2005), to Meynard.

From their very first stories through significant cycles of young-adult novels, Meynard and Trudel, separately and writing together as McAllister, reveal great generic flexibility, constantly pushing the envelope of genre constraints. The desire for novelty and experimentation appears in the introduction to McAllister's story collection, *Les Leçons de la cruauté* (Lessons of cruelty; 2009): "Already one of the functioning rules for Laurent McAllister became clear to us: to never repeat ourselves. If the first story had respected the rules of classic science fiction, the second should choose something more slipstream [*éclaté*]."[6] The mastery of generic conventions necessary for their successful disruption appears in the novels of Trudel's five-volume youth cycle, *Les Saisons de Nigelle* (The seasons of Nigelle; 1997–2000), each of which explores a different genre—sf, fantastic, mystery, and heroic fantasy—and which remains to date the only work of science fiction or fantasy published in Quebec that has been the object of a monograph-length study, Sophie Beaulé's *Jean-Louis Trudel* (2009).

The Birth of a Modern Master

Unlike most pseudonymous writers, thanks to advanced imaging software, Laurent McAllister has a portrait—a composite image morphed from photographs of Meynard and Trudel—which appears on the Éditions Alire website (alire .com). He first saw the light of day as a fictional character in Meynard's story "Sans Titre" (No title), published in 1988. In his literary début, McAllister is a plagiarist, scouring the ruins of a postapocalyptic landscape for texts for which he then takes credit.[7] He reappears a few years later in the fanzine *Samizdat,* somewhat overshadowed, however, by his parallel world avatar named Romain in Trudel's "L'Homme qui n'avait plus de remords" (The man without remorse; 1992).[8] Trudel's literary hoax, "Le Deuxième Carnet de Villard" (Villard's second notebook; 1998), also implicates "Romain McAllister," who—a "note" informs us—adapted the text of a thirteenth-century notebook found in the home of a fictional con-man featured in Trudel's *Nigelle* cycle.[9] This ludic penchant for inside jokes and intertextual references marks the entire McAllister corpus, comprised to date of nine short stories and yet another literary hoax (three of which have been published in English), an unfinished young-adult cycle, *Les Îles du Zodiaque* (The islands of the zodiac; 2001), and the masterful novel *Suprématie.*

In the introduction to *Lessons of Cruelty,* Trudel and Meynard outline their collaborative philosophy as follows: to completely blur the lines between reality and fiction, to disrupt generic codes, and never to repeat themselves.[10] Whereas this last goal results in a rather heteroclite oeuvre, the desire to play with, and even blow up, genre conventions lends a certain homogeneity to their project, which is characterized by the appropriation of a genre type, resulting in a ludic play of intertextual and self-referential allusions, with the recurrence of significant themes found in the respective imaginary universes of Trudel and Meynard. As can be imagined from this description, McAllister's aesthetic is soundly postmodern while at the same time largely refusing to abandon the art of good storytelling.

Reflective of the irony, self-referentiality, and intertextuality that typify the McAllister style, his first publication, "Les Protocoles du désir" (The protocols of desire; 1989), whose title was inspired by a line in Meynard's "No Title,"[11] did not appear under his name, because of an editorial miscommunication.[12] Instead, the story's byline reads, "Yves Meynard et Jean-Louis Trudel."[13] This brilliant tale about cross-cultural misunderstandings and the difficulties of interspecies encounters in the space-colonization setting occurs within the imaginary universe of Trudel's *History of the Future* cycle, featuring an early human attempt to negotiate a relationship with the Glogs, the latter's take on the "little green men" trope.[14] Later, Trudel quotes with irony McAllister's title in his "Contamination" (1994, trans. 1996), another brilliant exploration of this classic sf trope.

The contents of *Lessons of Cruelty* further illuminate the nature of the McAllister corpus. The collection begins with the French version of "Kapuzine and the Wolf: A Hortatory Tale," originally published in English in Claude Lalumière and Marty Halpern's anthology *Witpunk* (2003).[15] Reworking Charles Perrault's classic fairy tale "Little Red Riding Hood" (1697), it transposes the plot and narrative trajectory onto a far-future dystopian landscape. In "Le Pierrot diffracté" (The diffracted Pierrot; 1992), the three adolescent daughters of Richard Philips (named after P. K. Dick)[16] complete their education with guerrilla training at the hands of a sadistic robot that resembles Pierrot, a stock character of the *commedia dell'arte*. Its generic inspiration, completely subverted by its dark and violent narrative, derives from 1920s French didactic fiction by Berthe Bernage.[17] "En sol brûlant" (In burning soil; 1999) pays homage to the iconic French sf writer Serge Brussolo, whereas "Le Cas du feuilleton *De Québec à la Lune, par Veritatus*" ("The Case of the Serial *From Quebec to the Moon*, by Véritatus"; 1994, trans. 1998) is a full-blown hoax. McAllister poses as a literary historian who has discovered a lost work of proto-SFQ—a tongue-in-cheek representation of Trudel himself, who has published several articles on early French-Canadian sf.[18] Preceded by a pseudo-scholarly introduction with footnotes and all, he "excerpts" a comically ultranationalist, ultra-Catholic steampunk narrative in which Quebec has gained its independence thanks to the work of a mad scientist and then launches a rocket to the moon in order to claim colonial territory, like any other "civilized" nation of the time. The story riffs on actual works of proto-SFQ like Napoléon Aubin's "Mon Voyage à la Lune" (1839) and Jules-Paul Tardivel's *For My Country* (1895), referencing at the same time Trudel's fictional planet colonized by French Canadians, alternately called Nu-Québec or Nou-Québec. *Lessons of Cruelty* closes with *Sur la plage des épaves* (2007), which won both Boréal and Aurora Awards, and whose English title, *Driftplast* (2001), nods to Samuel R. Delany's "Driftglass" (1971).

This brief survey reveals the ludic versatility of McAllister's creators, and this shared alter ego represents in some ways a liberating device, allowing them free rein to let their imaginations go and to explore to the fullest their desire to appropriate, rework, and pay homage to an array of genres through the lens of sf. Arguably, however, McAllister's (and even Trudel's and Meynard's) most significant opus to date has been the massive hard-sf space opera *Suprématie* (2009), published by France's Éditions Bragelonne.[19] The novel develops a universe first outlined in several solo works by Jean-Louis Trudel, a corpus that I will refer to collectively here as the *Suprématie* cycle: "La douzième vie des copies" (The twelfth life of copies; 1992), "Les ponts du temps" (Bridges of time; 1993), "Stella Nova" (1994), "Le Choix du lion, le festin des chacals" (Lion's choice, jackal's feast; 1997), "Scorpion dans le cercle du temps" (A scorpion in the circle of time; 1998), and "L'Arche de tous les temps" (Ark of ages; 2000).[20] In the remainder of this essay, I will build on previous scholarship in Québec that identifies the rhizomatic nature of the *Suprématie* cycle (Beaulé, "La Plaie et le couteau") and which has begun to explore the treatment of the posthuman in McAllister's work (Gaudreault).

"The Rhizome as a Form of Creative Resistance"

The Supremats first appeared on the literary horizon in the early 1990s via somewhat fleeting mentions in two Trudel short stories, the time-travel narrative "The Bridges of Time" and "The Twelfth Life of Copies." "Stella Nova," however, offers a full-fledged image of the Supremats and their agenda, and Trudel introduces readers to the ship and some of the crew featured in *Suprématie*. In the fictional chronology of this universe, however, humanity first learns of the Supremats' existence in "A Scorpion in the Circle of Time," one of Trudel's most masterful tales.

"Scorpion" illustrates Trudel's control of the conventions of sf and related genres, as it blends the virtual reality of cyberpunk with time travel and alternate history, as well as a brilliantly engineered first-encounter scene capable of generating the "sense of wonder" in even the most jaded sf reader. Opening with a sequence in which a crew member of a massive space vessel is immersed in a virtual-reality simulation of post–World War I Berlin and meets Werner Heisenberg, this complex narrative lays out precisely how Terran humanity has its first encounter with an extraterrestrial race. These advanced beings, which they name the Sagashi, bring word of the Supremat threat and seek an alliance against a régime that the translating devices can only vaguely describe: "We are explorers, are researchers. We seek refuge, look [for] you. Others seek you, seek your integration. You flee with us, will flee your integration."[21] The crew of this ship, the *Finisterrae*, a vessel of the First Volkswanderung (the peoples' wandering)—humanity's first wave of space colonization—learn that "the Supremats' desire was to assemble all the civilizations in this region of the Galaxy under their aegis, by will or by force,"[22] and they do so by "manipulating minds and cultures to rule over the stars."[23]

Trudel had thus already worked out the hegemonic nature of the Supremat agenda in the mid-1990s: "where the Supremats found an opening, they *infected*. ... They manipulated virtual reality inputs and electronic interfaces to mould minds in their image."[24] McAllister develops this concept further, describing how the régime injects "reality filters" into the computer systems of vessels and entire worlds targeted for conquest.[25] These filters impose a Supremat vision of reality that elides all conflict, opposition, dissonance, and difference in favor of a falsely rosy vision of full employment, zero homelessness and hunger, but also bereft of freedom and individuality. For the as-yet-unvanquished planets of the "Amas," the star cluster in which the novel's action largely occurs, "fighting the Supremats had become a desperate struggle to defend diversity and liberty in the cluster. The Supremats were not an empire, they were an ideology."[26] The *Suprématie* cycle, above all else, thus represents a narrative of resistance to a form of totalitarian power that would reduce all of its citizens to a state of passive homogeneity. It offers an oppositional discourse to the economic and cultural power structures prevalent in contemporary Western civilization's mechanisms of consumer society and tacit state support of a capitalist global economy. This critique echoes those of the French thinkers Michel Foucault,[27] and of Gilles Deleuze and Félix Guattari.

Following somewhat in the wake of Sylvie Bérard, who applied this notion to the work of Élisabeth Vonarburg as early as 1998, Sophie Beaulé applies Deleuze and Guattari's rhizome model to this fictional universe.[28] She describes the *Suprématie* cycle as follows: "at the heart of a rhizomatic space marked by hostility and death, characters act like so many bodies without organs riven by desires, who participate in war machines linked to late capitalism or rejecting it."[29] As we shall see, the metaphor of the rhizome functions on several levels throughout the Supremat universe. First of all, the literary cycle can itself be viewed as structured like a rhizome, although in this case it developed conversely from how we envision a rhizome in botany. Rather than the short fiction shooting off from the novel in random ways, the various shorter texts converge upon the larger body of the novel, feeding into and developing different elements of the history and characters that make it up. Similarly, the fictional space configured in the universe, "l'Amas," a cluster of star systems inhabited by an array of intelligent life forms, is itself a rhizomatic space. Indeed, human migration from "Erd" (Earth) into space, referred to as the "Volkswanderung," develops rhizomatically, according to Beaulé.[30] Finally, in the last section of this essay, we will see how the rhizome metaphor contributes to a theory of the posthuman. The *Suprématie* cycle envisions the future of humanity, contact with other sentient races, and the development of artificial intelligences, all of which are referred to without discrimination by the term "sophonts."[31] This inclusiveness suggests that the authors consider all of these various branchings, of terrestrial, biological, or mechanical origin, as fully "human" if they are endowed with self-consciousness.

The French philosopher Gilles Deleuze, working collaboratively with the psychoanalyst Félix Guattari, builds upon Michel Foucault's work to elaborate a theory of power structures in Western civilization that has been repeatedly applied to the study of literature since the 1980s. One of the key concepts from their two-volume *Capitalism and Schizophrenia* (1972–80), the rhizome, has taken off to enter the jargon of literary and cultural criticism. Drawn from botany and best known to gardeners fond of irises, a rhizome is a fertile root stub that can grow roots, branches, and stems on its own; for the French thinkers the rhizome functions differently than the tree, a frequent metaphor in Western thought that, for them, describes a hierarchical, vertical relationship between its various branches. In contrast, the rhizome spreads horizontally and can provide, they argue, a new metaphor and structure for a human society and relationships beyond the current hierarchical system. Their introduction to *A Thousand Plateaus* (1982) concludes:

> Let us summarize the principal characteristics of a rhizome: unlike trees or their roots, the rhizome connects any point to any other point, and its traits are not necessarily linked to traits of the same nature; it brings into play very different regimes of signs, and even nonsign states. The rhizome is reducible neither to the One nor the multiple. . . . It is composed not of units but of dimensions, or rather directions in motion. It has neither beginning nor end, but always a middle (*milieu*) from which it grows and which it overspills.[32]

In an enlightening essay on Deleuze and technology, Verena Andermatt Conley asks if "we [can] take the rhizome as a form of creative resistance to the more controlling aspects of electronic media."[33] This question appears particularly pertinent to a discussion of a body of science-fiction literature that uses the figure of an extrapolated form of today's wireless digital technologies and the development of increasingly compelling virtual realities as a tool for intergalactic domination, the Supremat's "reality filters." Conley also asks if "the rhizome and the war machine help us resist—if resistance is either warranted or possible— new mechanisms of control that are put in place."[34] Although a discussion of the war machine is beyond the scope of this essay, I argue that the *Suprématie* cycle constructs a rhizomatic form of resistance to totalitarian power in a number of ways. Its use of the rhizome as a form of creative resistance appears in its depiction of the starship, the *Doukh/Harfang* and its crew; it also appears in the Ville d'Art's use of art itself to resist the Supremats; finally, it recurs in the alliance formed by the remaining free planets and orbitats of the Amas.

The trope of the space vessel resonates in a number of ways with the rhizome as it is linked to the concepts of territorialization and deterritorialization central to Deleuze and Guattari's project. Staffed by a heterogeneous crew that includes an array of human types and "exos," like the warrior race of Rapunzels and the aviform Dikkiks, the *Doukh/Harfang* resists territorialization as it travels nomadically across the star cluster. The French philosopher and the psychoanalyst privilege not only the nomadic existence as deterritorialized and therefore less likely to be totalitarian, they above all reject and critique those institutions and powers connected to the "State."[35] As a mercenary vessel, Captain Alcaino's ship refuses any permanent, essentialized state or national identity, selling its services to various bidders in turn.

Significantly, the narrative also denies the ship a fixed or unitary identity through its back story. As the authors conceptualize it, the physical vessel is inseparable from Mnémosyne, the AI who controls it, forging a sort of hybrid existence. Furthermore, even the ship's function and name are not static; in "Stella Nova" Mallia captains the *Doukh*, which means "ghost" in Russian, but we learn that it "had been a first class warship of the Second Volkswanderung" but was then junked, becoming in sequence "a low-rent orbital housing complex," a "heavy-hauler," then a "luxury liner," before becoming again a battleship.[36] *Suprématie* further forces a shift in this signifier. The novel's opening sequence depicts the *end* of the story, at which point the ship is called the *Harfang*, after Quebec's national bird, the snowy owl, a name restored to it by Alcaino as an act of resistance, its original name when built during the Second Volkswanderung. After the prologue, however, the narrative flashes back in time, restoring the ship's Russian name for a good bit of the novel.

Finally, significant military strategies of resistance for starships in the *Suprématie* cycle invoke Deleuze and Guattari's privileging of "lines of flight."[37] Although the *Doukh/Harfang* is a supergiant battleship capable of taking on numerous smaller ships, it nonetheless frequently finds itself at a numerical disadvantage because of the vast resources available to the rapidly growing Supremat forces. In Trudel's solo stories of the cycle, various vessels paradoxically flee for victory, employing strategies that involve jumps in hyperspace to escape a Supremat chokehold, often also using local astrophysical phenomena. For example, "Stella Nova" depicts the *Doukh* engineering a double star system to "go nova" in order to destroy an enemy force, jumping away to avoid its own destruction.[38] Similar strategies recur in "A Scorpion in the Circle of Time,"

"Lion's Choice, Jackal's Feast," and "Ark of Ages." *Suprématie*'s tour de force plot pivots upon Alcaino's strategic implementation of a looped series of faster-than-light jumps to a moment in time before the ship's repeated destruction, until finally they have acquired enough information from each jump to penetrate the Supremat defenses and destroy one of its key home worlds, Canterna.

Central to the narrative's development in *Suprématie* is a unique colony planet, la Ville d'Art (the City of Art), which hires the *Doukh* to break a Supremat blockade. The Ville d'Art—a society reminiscent of Les Organiques in *Étoiles mourantes* (Dying stars; 1999) by Ayerdhal and Jean-Claude Dunyach—resists the conformity required by the Supremats (or any other totalitarian society) by valuing the unique and rejecting art as a commodity.[39] When the planet is ultimately destroyed by the Supremats, a handful of survivors who had witnessed their home world's destruction from space record the event and disseminate it around the Amas. Reminiscent of the media's oversaturation of the tragically destructive images of the terrorist attacks on the World Trade Center towers on September 11, 2001, this intentionally exploitative work of art functions in some ways like memorials to the Holocaust or the exhibits at the Hiroshima museum, as it seeks to energize surviving populations to resist. The genocide perpetrated on the Ville d'Art illustrates the destructive nature of totalitarian power, but this final act of resistance—the recording of the planet's destruction—spreads virally, or rhizomatically, if you will, around the cluster and makes Alcaino more determined than ever to resist the Supremats.

Finally, the remaining alliance of free planets in the Amas represents a rhizomatic structure of resistance. The extradimensionality of space lends itself to conceptualization as a rhizome in that, unlike the vertical directionality of the tree, it can spread across any direction through any plane. Given the heterogeneous nature of the community of the "Twenty Races,"[40] no starting point can be designated, as each of these races has its own homeworld (some of which have now been assimilated into the Supremat régime), as well as various colonies on planet surfaces, in orbital structures around them and even in nomadic vessels. The formation of the alliance constantly changes throughout the struggle with the Supremats; it thus forms "a multiplicity that is never a one," as Conley describes the rhizome.[41]

One of the central projects of SFQ from its inception has been to assert *le fait français*, the French fact, and its continued existence in Canada and North America as a whole. Whether or not SFQ narratives imagine dystopian futures for the French-speaking minority or extrapolate its survival and even hegemony—as does Trudel in his *History of the Future*, particularly with the colony planet of Nu-/Nou-Québec—they consistently propose the value of respecting difference, a sensibility deriving, of course, from French-Canadians' minority position on the continent. *Suprématie* repeatedly and explicitly espouses an ideology of difference through the narrator's or crewmembers' assertions of resistance against the oppressive, totalitarian force of conquest whose power appears to be growing exponentially. Indeed, the narrative suggests that Supremat hegemony may be reaching a critical point at which all of the worlds of the Amas and beyond may be converted, thus effacing all opposition and forcing full compliance and conformity to its agenda. Indeed, the Cycle itself might be viewed as an act of creative resistance on the part of its authors. Writing science fiction in French in North America becomes their contribution to promoting the value of difference in the face of dominant and seemingly monolithic cultural and economic structures.

In the end, through its complete erasure of difference and individuality, the Supremat order proves antithetical to humanity itself. As Vera Conley asserts, "When people are homogenised and their desires controlled, possibilities of resistance are, [Deleuze and Guattari] claim, if not rendered impossible, at least strongly diminished."[42] In *Suprématie* and other works by Trudel, resistance as a human right is a recurring theme: Vivaine, the freedom fighter/terrorist of Trudel's "Tirés d'une même chair" (Pulled from the same flesh; 1999), argues that "revolt is an inalienable right for true humans."[43] Indeed, the definition of humanity is itself tied to the ability to resist.[44] The notion of the nature of humanity and explorations of post- and trans-humanity are not only central to contemporary science-fiction studies, they are central to the work of Trudel, Meynard, and the two writing as Laurent McAllister, as we shall see in the final section of this essay.

The Critical Posthumanism of Laurent McAllister

In *Suprématie*, the alliance of the "Vingt Races" is comprised of humans (various populations descended from "Erd" after the First and Second Volkswanderungs) and other extraterrestrial species, referred to as "exos."[45] McAllister precedes each chapter of *Suprématie* with an epigraphical "citation" from a fictional reference work, providing wiki-like descriptions of various neologisms and cultural aspects of its fictional universe, including ones on the human diaspora.[46] The great ships like the *Finisterrae* in "A Scorpion in the Circle of Time," *Sibylle* in "The Twelfth Life of Copies," and the *Doukh/Harfang* in *Suprématie* and "Stella Nova" were instrumental in this process: "The ships in the Tree of a Thousand Stars had had more than one vocation and their military vocation had not always been the most important at first. Among other things, they had served as sites of memory after the First Volkswanderung. For the farthest branches of the Tree, Erd had become a more and more distant world. In order to preserve part of the human heritage, the ships had housed the vestiges of Erd's ancient civilizations."[47] Not only does this passage employ botanical imagery invoking the arborescent or rhizome-like, as Beaulé points out,[48] it appears to limit the term "humanity" to the diaspora from Earth. However, by the time of *Suprématie*'s action, millennia into the future, humanity itself has both "naturally" evolved or genetically engineered itself into a number of diverse forms, including implanted technological enhancements.

Pramod K. Nayar offers an invaluable outline of the various ways sf media engage with the question of the human and the notion of our potential to transcend the current limits of our species. Today more than ever, rapid advances in computer technologies, artificial intelligence, virtual realities, genetics, biochemistry, and so on have made this potential appear much more near and real. Nayar explains the difference between two terms that have become increasingly present not only in science fiction and its criticism but in mainstream literature and popular culture: transhumanism and posthumanism. Nayar—as does Christina Bieber Lake[49]—cautions against the pseudo-utopian transhumanism propounded by Ray Kurzweil and others, who see *homo sapiens* as already at the top of the evolutionary scale, but gifted with the potential for further perfection via controlled evolution and the use of bio- and computer-aided technologies.[50] Transhumanism, rooted in Western, capitalist, evolutionary notions of the individual as a discrete and independent unit, represents, for its critics like Nayar, the simple continuation of current conceptions of the human within a hierarchical system of power relations, which allows a process of othering to exclude not only animals or nonbiological life from the category of the human, but also groups and individuals (slaves, women, Jews, and so on) to be deemed as less human than others (white males). Instead, he adopts Stefan Herbrechter's term "critical posthumanism," adding the modifier for further clarity, as both a practice and a worldview, which explicitly rejects the transhumanist desire for simply a new and improved status quo.

Derived from poststructuralist feminist theory, critical race theory, disability studies, and monster studies, critical posthumanism draws upon cutting-edge scientific research as well, but does so in order to interrogate the binaries upon which Western civilization has developed its notion of the human, binaries that are then used to exclude and define various groups as less-than-human.[51] Posthumanism focuses on humanity's emplacement in its natural and technological environment and propounds an ethics of relationality rather than one of perfection and individual freedom. Whereas transhumanism reinforces and reinscribes human as Self and then identifies its imperfect, lesser Others, critical posthumanism embraces difference and multiplicity; and—as one might expect—it also draws from Foucault[52] and Deleuze and Guattari, describing the posthuman in terms of the rhizome and an assemblage.[53]

Nayar uses examples from science-fiction literature, and both Nayar[54] and Lake[55] argue for the significance of literature and reading as critical practices that help us define what is the human and now, of course, the posthuman. Nayar invokes such figures as clones, cyborgs, artificial intelligences, *homo sapiens* that have been genetically engineered or "enhanced," symbionts, and even animals that portray emotions and advanced mental capacities as potentially posthuman. Trudel, Meynard, and the two writing as McAllister exploit all of these types of characters in their work, generally for the same reasons that writers examined by Nayar, like Margaret Atwood, Octavia Butler, Ursula K. Le Guin, Kazuo Ishiguro, and so many others, do: to question and stretch the current definition of the human.

An array of posthuman beings populates McAllister's work, from the werewolf Volkodave and the batracian Visques in *Les îles du zodiaque* (The isles of the zodiac; 2003) novels, to the android title character and cloned daughters of "Le Pierrot diffracté" (Pierrot diffracted; 1992). Marc Ross Gaudreault devotes an article to the transhuman in McAllister's novella *Driftplast*, which concludes that "McAllister associates transhumanism rather as a loss, that of humanity in its natural form; the transhumanist project is totally rejected."[56] As we shall see in the following analysis of the *Suprématie* cycle, McAllister rejects the transhumanist project as critiqued by Nayar (a nuance that Gaudreault fails fully to tease out), but he also embraces a number of forms of critical posthumanism. Thus, through the variety of sentient beings—organic and nonorganic—portrayed and the variety of iterations into which various branches of the human rhizome have developed, the novel clearly embraces difference, multiplicity, the not-One.

Trudel's early novellas in the cycle set the stage for the critical posthumanism of the novel that culminates it. "Ark of Ages" is a technically difficult story, opening on two main characters, Scaramella and Maang, engaging in a philosophico-religious debate about the nature of reality and relativity. They are traveling on a vessel that mirrors the biblical Noah's Ark, in that representatives of seventeen surviving groups of sophonts have been gathered there, having apparently fled the Supremats. Trudel's narrator notes that humans were the sixteenth group to arrive, thus decentering them in a critically posthumanist manner.[57] The rhizomatic nature of the human diaspora and the development of an array of posthuman types appears in the description of Scaramella, the "descendent of an archaic branch of humanity."[58] Although he has accepted computer-interfaced implants—and thus is, in some ways, a cyborg—these are hidden under his browned skin, and his face "did not betray any sign of genetic intervention. The velvety skin of an ephebe, a thick and black moustache, straight nose, eyes with very dark irises. . . . Such traits could be found all over the solar system from the terrestrial arcologies to the transmartian orbitats."[59] In some ways, then, Scaramella represents a certain human "norm" found across the Amas; indeed, his form is "closer to the original model debuted by the first hominids in the African savannahs."[60] His appearance is contrasted with that of Maang, who has accepted surgical enhancements (or genetic modifications) that have transformed the joints of his elbows and knees so that they bend in both directions.[61] Paradoxically, it is Maang who is temporally closer to those first hominids originating in Africa; he has been rescued by the Ark, having been catapulted into a future "in which all of his own kind were already dead" via a space-time wrinkle while he was carrying critical parts for a gluon projector meant to protect Earth from the Supremat invasions.[62]

The apparent paradox is explained, however, as it is revealed that this ship, the *Vatican*, is actually from the First Volkswanderung and has itself been caught in the wrinkle called the "Ring" for millennia.[63] Maang is told that they, too, are fighting the Supremats, and he is introduced to the captains of the groups of sophonts represented on the *Vatican*, including ones that are implicitly "exos"— nonhuman lifeforms that have evolved on planets other than Erd. He thus meets "the humans' Captain, the androgyne Avishai Dekel with a smooth, flawless face and long black hair";[64] the Captain of the "Aboriginals," "the mysterious intelligent species that presided over the colonization of the Ring during an epoch so long ago that the Ring was still outside the local Cluster of galaxies";[65] "the Captain of the Esnanardies [who] resembled a hybrid between a mole and a millipede,"[66] and "the Captain of the Rationalists [who] was a quadruman whose body evoked less a gorilla than a leopard."[67] After a number of peripeteia involving whether or not the *Vatican* is after all in league with the Supremats, Maang escapes with the help of his ship's AI, Jichaak. Once again, resistance at all costs against the threat to difference posed by the Suprématie is stressed, and the story closes with an interesting comment on the posthuman: "the humans of the Arc were outdated models. . . . From the time of the First Volkswanderung, the majority of humans had opted for symbiosis with integrated nano- and bio-systems and could remodel themselves on demand."[68] This image of a posthuman race living in symbiosis with other organisms of mechanical and biological origin aligns precisely with the models of cooperation and mutual responsibility for the posthuman proposed by Nayar.

The *Doukh/Harfang* resembles just such a posthuman symbiotic organism, an assemblage of differences rather than a monadic individual. Nomadic rather than territorial in nature, the physical vessel of concrete, metal, and electronics represents a body that can externally interface with other ships and docking units, but which is internally interfaced with a number of different sentient species of organic beings and rendered itself sentient by its AI, Mnémosyne. Significantly, Trudel's terminology across his *History of the Future* indicates the increasing sophistication of computer-aided technologies, so that works set earlier in the fictional chronology refer to an "artificial semi-intelligence" running a ship,[69] whereas Mnémosyne is herself referred to as a "sophont"—a thinking being, the equivalent perhaps of the notion of the "person" in philosophy/ethics (although this term is a bone of contention for posthumanists)— capable of interacting with and feeling emotion for not only her own kind but others as well. Tragically, the Supremats eventually destroy all other ships in her class, so she has only "others" to communicate with. Indeed, in reference to Mnémosyne, the term "transhuman" acquires a more inclusive application. On the one hand, to distinguish biologicals from herself, Mnémosyne makes reference to "organic sophonts."[70] However, she herself is included in the set of "transhuman" by the narrator: "When the *Harfang*'s soul expressed herself in these terms, it was in order to distinguish clearly between transhuman entities like herself and simple biological beings."[71] Organics can interface in turn with Mnémosyne at various levels, from the full immersion of Première Communion in which Lynga loses all notion of her embodied self, mentally joining Mnémosyne for tasks and problem solving, to simple consultations for data via implants. Within the ship, then, reside a variety of species of beings who interact with her and with each other in various ways. Furthermore, if she is damaged and life-support systems fail, they are all at risk, forming an immense, complex, symbiotic organism.

As their treatment of the posthuman in the *Suprématie* cycle demonstrates, Trudel, Meynard, and the two writing as McAllister engage in their science fiction the most compelling of sf's contemporary tropes in a highly sophisticated but most definitely critical manner. Their work combines the best of hard sf—space has forced me to limit discussion of McAllister's incorporation of astrophysics and cybernetics—with the best of soft sf in its interrogations of the notions of the human itself. Published in Canada, the United States, and France, translated into a number of languages, their truly "speculative fiction," as defined by Judith Merril, explores all of the dimensions and genres proper to the modern master of international sf.

Notes

1. This and subsequent translations are my own; whenever possible, however, I cite the published translations listed in the bibliography to this chapter.

2. For further information on the careers of Trudel, Meynard, and McAllister, see Ransom, "Bridging the Solitudes," "Parabolas of SFQ," and "History Making and Canon Fodder"; and Paroski, "Jean-Louis Trudel." For a more thorough history of the development of science fiction in Québec, see Lord, "Architectures"; Ransom, "History Making and Cannon Fodder," "Parabolas of SFQ," and *Science Fiction*, 33–59.

3. Sernine, "Historique," 42.

4. In part for this reason, Trudel's work is among the most frequently treated in academic studies of SFQ; for more extended discussions of his sf as national allegory, see Baker, "Politics of Language"; Beaulé, *Jean-Louis Trudel*, "La Plaie," "Regards"; Ransom, "(Un)Common Ground" and "Oppositional Postcolonialism"; Serruys, "Xénototalité."

5. The "two solitudes" is a frequently used, because so apt, metaphor for the (lack) of communication between English- and French-speaking Canada, coined after a 1945 Hugh McLennan novel that explores the theme in relation to Montréal.

6. McAllister, *Lessons*, 32.

7. Morin, "Sans Titre," 105.

8. Laurent McAllister, of course, shares his name with the great river running through the province, so named because Jacques Cartier reached the gulf on St. Lawrence's feast day. Trudel uses a brilliant "what if" renaming for this fictional writer of science fiction in the parallel world "Romain," speculating that Cartier reached the gulf a day earlier (e-mail to the author, January 25, 2015).

9. Trudel, "Villard's Second Notebook," 67.

10. McAllister, *Lessons*, 32.

11. Ibid., 31.

12. Ibid., 32.

13. McAllister, "Protocols," 207.

14. Trudel published an essay on the topic, "Looking for Little Green Men," in the *New York Review of Science Fiction* in 2005.

15. Lalumière is another interesting case: born in the working-class, francophone Montréal neighborhood of Hochelaga, he writes and publishes almost uniquely in English and has referred to himself as a "lapsed Francophone."

16. McAllister, *Lessons*, 33

17. Ibid., 33.

18. Trudel, "Science Fiction in Francophone Canada," "French-Canadian Science Fiction and *Fantastique*," and "Une littérature de passage."

19. Apart from Daniel Sernine's *Les Méandres du temps* [Time's wanderings] (1983, 2004–8) trilogy and Alain Bergeron's *Phaos* (2003), I know of no other hefty sf novel published in Québec to rival the scope and quality of McAllister's *Suprématie* in terms of its hard science, action, and speculative power. Whereas Élisabeth Vonarburg and Esther Rochon have both constructed massive and compelling science-fictional and fantasy worlds, their work,

which privileges sociology, individual psychology, and moral development, would largely be considered "soft" sf. Its flawed hero, Constantin Alcaino, also something of a trickster figure, recalls Lois McMaster Bujold's Miles Naismith Vorkosigan or Commander William Adama of the *Battlestar Galactica* (2004–9) reboot. Its plot focuses on a turning-point moment in a larger epic saga that Jean-Louis Trudel began to develop in the early 1990s in a cycle of stories that include his best work, certain aspects of which compare favorably to M. John Harrison's *Light* (2002) and the French *Étoiles mortes* trilogy (Dead stars; 1991–92) by Ayerdhal and Jean-Claude Dunyach (a writer whose work Trudel has translated).

20. Unfortunately, of this corpus, only "Stella Nova" is available in English.

21. Trudel, "Scorpion," 398.

22. Ibid., 404.

23. Ibid., 406.

24. Trudel, "Stella Nova," 34.

25. McAllister, *Suprématie*, "filtres de réalité," 62, 158, 165.

26. Trudel, "Stella Nova," 34.

27. Sophie Beaulé's survey of the presence of violence in Trudel's work ("Violence et tourments") begins to suggest this connection.

28. Beaulé, "La Plaie," 299.

29. Ibid., 299.

30. Ibid., 300.

31. Trudel attributes the coinage to Karen Anderson, whose husband Poul used it in a number of stories beginning in the 1960s (e-mail to the author, January 25, 2015).

32. Deleuze and Guattari, "Introduction," 21.

33. Conley, "Rhizomes," 35.

34. Ibid., 32

35. See Massumi, "Foreword," xiii.

36. Trudel, "Stella Nova," 34.

37. Deleuze and Guattari, "Introduction," 3–4.

38. Trudel, "Stella Nova," 35.

39. McAllister, *Suprématie*, 70.

40. Ibid., "Vingt Races," 29.

41. Let us recall Verena Andermatt Conley's useful definition of the rhizome here: "Rhizomes are made of lines, not points. Without beginning or end, they connect from a *milieu*, not a given place, but a middle, a median space and a complex environment. While the tree always grows into the same form, rhizomes are constantly changing. They are part of a multiplicity that is never a one (n-1). They thrive on alliances and heterogeneous connections that replace the ubiquitous either/or with *and*" (Conley, "Rhizomes," 33; original emphasis).

42. Ibid., 36.

43. Trudel, "Pulled from the Same Flesh," 121.

44. Both Trudel's "Tirés de la même chaire" ["Pulled from the Same Flesh"] and "L'Éclat brûlant de la lune" ["The Burning Glare of the Moon"] feature characters whose humanity

is somehow compromised by the societies in which they live (clones, genetically engineered beings, slaves), but who demonstrate their full humanity by performing acts of resistance to the power structures that would seek to bind them.

45. McAllister, *Suprématie*, 149.

46. Ibid., 269, 639.

47. Ibid., 83.

48. Beaulé, "La plaie," 300–301.

49. Lake, *Prophets*, ix–xiv, 2–4.

50. Nayar, *Posthumanism*, 6–8.

51. Ibid., 2–13.

52. Ibid., 13.

53. Ibid., 69–71.

54. Ibid., 32–33.

55. Lake, *Prophets*, xvi.

56. Gaudreault, "Humain?" 36.

57. Trudel, "Ark of Ages," 267.

58. Ibid., 255.

59. Ibid.

60. Ibid., 256

61. Ibid.

62. Ibid.

63. Ibid., 259.

64. Ibid., 264.

65. Ibid., 265.

66. Ibid.

67. Ibid.

68. Ibid., 288.

69. Trudel, *Un trésor*, 79.

70. McAllister, *Suprématie*, 201.

71. Ibid.

Bibliography

Aubin, Napoléon. "Mon Voyage à la lune" [My trip to the moon]. In *Napoléon Aubin*. Ed. Jean-Paul Tremblay. Montréal: FIDES, 1972. 31–40.

Ayerdhal and Jean-Claude Dunyach. *Les Étoiles mourantes* [Dying stars]. Paris: J'ai lu, 1999.

Baker, Neal. "The Politics of Language in Science Fiction from Québec." *Contemporary French Civilization* 28.1 (2004): 33–53.

Beaulé, Sophie. *Jean-Louis Trudel*. Ottawa: David, 2009.

———. "La Plaie et le couteau: Formes du pouvoir et de la violence dans l'univers de *Suprématie* de Laurent McAllister" [The wound and the knife: Forms of power and violence in the universe of Laurent McAllister's *Suprématie*]. *@nalyses: revue de critique et de théorie littéraire* 8.2 (Spring 2013): 298–319.

———. "Regards sur le Québec dans un numéro spécial de la revue *Solaris*" [Gazes on Quebec in a special issue of *Solaris*]. In *La Francophonie panaméricaine: état des lieux et enjeux* [Francophone Pan-America: Present state and challenges]. Ed. André Fauchon. Winnipeg: Presses Universitaires de Saint-Boniface, 2000. 103–21.

———. "Violence et tourments dans la science-fiction de Jean-Louis Trudel." In *La Littérature franco-ontarienne: voies nouvelles, nouvelles voix* [Franco-Ontarian literature: New paths, new voices]. Ed. Lucie Hotte. Ottawa: Le Nordir, 2002. 253–74.

Bérard, Sylvie. "Fictional Arborescence and Allusive Coherence in Élisabeth Vonarburg's Universe." In *Perspectives on the Canadian Fantastic: Proceedings of the 1997 Academic Conference on Canadian Science Fiction and Fantasy*. Ed. Allan Weiss. Toronto: ACCSFF, 1998. 35–45.

Conley, Verena Andermatt. "Rhizomes, Smooth Space, War Machines, and New Media." In *Deleuze and Technology*. Ed. Mark Poster and David Savat. Edinburgh: Edinburgh University Press, 2009. 32–44.

Delany, Samuel R. "Driftglass." In *Driftglass*. New York: Nelson R. Doubleday, 1971. 112–29.

Deleuze, Gilles, and Félix Guattari. *Anti-Oedipus: Capitalism and Schizophrenia*. Trans. Robert Hurley, Mark Seem, and Helen K. Lane. 1972; reprint, Minneapolis: University of Minnesota Press, 2000.

———. "Introduction: Rhizome." In *A Thousand Plateaus: Capitalism and Schizophrenia*. Trans. Brian Massumi. Minneapolis: University of Minnesota Press, 1987. 3–25.

Gaudreault, Marc Ross. "Humain? Transhumanisme chez Isaac Asimov et Laurent McAllister" [Human? Transhumanism in Isaac Asimov and Laurent McAlister]. *Québec français* 167 (2012): 33–37.

Herbrechter, Stefan. *Posthumanism*. London: Bloomsbury Academic, 2013.

Lake, Christina Bieber. *Prophets of the Posthuman: American Fiction, Biotechnology, and the Ethics of Personhood*. Notre Dame, Ind.: University of Notre Dame Press, 2013.

Lord, Michel. "Architectures de l'imaginaire: Le Récit fantastique et de science-fiction au Québec depuis la Révolution tranquille." In *Panorama de la littérature québécoise contemporaine* [Architectures of the imaginary: The fantastic tale and science fiction in Quebec since the Quiet Revolution]. Ed. Réginald Hamel. Montréal: Guérin, 1997. 241–81.

Marchildon, Daniel. "De la science-fiction qui chauffe" [Science fiction that heats up]. Rev. of *Pour des soleils froids* [For cold suns], by Jean-Louis Trudel. *Liaison* 79 (November 1994): 39.

Martin, Michel. "Tortoise on a Sidewalk." Trans. Laurent McAllister [Yves Meynard and Jean-Louis Trudel]. In *Tesseracts 5*. Ed. Robert Runté and Yves Meynard. Edmonton: The Books Collective, 1996. 135–51.

Massumi, Brian. "Foreword: The Pleasures of Philosophy." In *A Thousand Plateaus: Capitalism and Schizophrenia*, by Gilles Deleuze and Félix Guattari. Trans. Brian Massumi. Minneapolis: University of Minnesota Press, 1987. ix–xix.

McAllister, Laurent. "Le Cas du feuilleton *De Québec à la Lune*, par Veritatus." *Les Leçons de la cruauté* [Lessons of cruelty]. Lévis, QC: Alire, 2009. 131–60. Translated as "The Case of the Serial *De Québec à la lune*, by Veritatus." In *Arrowdreams*. Ed. Neil Shainblum. Winnipeg: Nuage, 1998. 173–91.

———. *Le Chemin des tornades* [The path of tornadoes]. Montréal: Médiaspaul, 2003.

———. *Driftplast* and "Sur la plage des épaves." In *Les Leçons de la cruauté* [Lessons of cruelty]. Lévis, QC: Alire, 2009. 161–243.

———. "En sol brûlant" [In burning soil]. In *Les Leçons de la cruauté* [Lessons of cruelty]. Lévis, QC: Alire, 2009. 87–130.

———. "Kapuzine and the Wolf: A Hortatory Tale." In *Witpunk*. Ed. Claude Lalumière and Marty Halpern. New York: Four Walls Eight Windows, 2003. 317–35. French version: "Kapuzine et les Loups: une légende dorée." In *Les Leçons de la cruauté* [Lessons of cruelty]. Lévis, QC: Alire, 2009. 1–30.

———. *Les Leçons de la cruauté* [Lessons of cruelty]. Lévis, QC: Alire, 2009.

———. *Le Maître des bourrasques* [Wind master]. Montréal: Médiaspaul, 2006.

———. *Le Messager des orages* [Storm messenger]. Montréal: Médiaspaul, 2001.

———. "Le Pierrot diffracté." In *Les Leçons de la cruauté* [Lessons of cruelty]. Lévis, QC: Alire, 2009. 31–86.

———. *Suprématie*. Paris: Bragelonne, 2009.

Meynard, Yves. *The Book of Knights*. New York: Tor, 1998. Trans. by the author as *Le Livre des Chevaliers*. Beauport: Alire, 1999.

———. *Chrysanthe*. New York: Tor, 2012.

———. "Sans Titre" [No title]. *Solaris* 80 (1988): 34–38.

Meynard, Yves, and Jean-Louis Trudel. "Les Protocoles du désir." In *L'Année de la Science-Fiction et du Fantastique Québécois 1988* [The Year in Québécois science fiction and fantasy, 1988]. Ed. Denis Côté, Claude Janelle, and Jean Pettigrew. Québec: Le Passeur, 1989. 207–20.

Morin, Lise. "Sans Titre" [No title]. In *L'Année de la Science-Fiction et du Fantastique Québécois 1988* [The Year in Québécois science fiction and fantasy, 1988]. Ed. Denis Côté, Claude Janelle, and Jean Pettigrew. Québec: Le Passeur, 1989. 105.

Nayar, Pramod K. *Posthumanism*. London: Polity, 2014.

Paroski, Dan S. "Jean-Louis Trudel." In *The Dictionary of Literary Biography: Canadian Science-Fiction and Fantasy Writers*. Vol. 251. Ed. Douglas Ivison. Westport, Conn.: Gale Research, 2002. 273–81.

Perrault, Charles. "Le Petit Chaperon rouge." In *Contes*. 1697; reprint, Paris: Librairie Générale Française, 2006. 207–12.

Ransom, Amy J. "Bridging the Solitudes: The Bilingual Canadian SF & F of Yves Meynard, Jean-Louis Trudel, and Laurent McAllister." *New York Review of Science Fiction* 285 (May 2012): 13–18.

———. "History Making and Canon Fodder: The Battle of SFQ." *Foundation* 112 (2011): 7–26.

———. "Oppositional Postcolonialism and the Science Fiction of Québec." *Science Fiction Studies* 99 (July 2006): 291–312.

———. "Parabolas of SFQ: Canadian SF in French and the Making of a 'National' Sub-

Genre." In *Parabolas of Science Fiction*. Ed. Brian Attebery and Veronica Hollinger. Middletown, Conn.: Wesleyan University Press, 2013. 89–105; 265–67.

———. *Science Fiction from Québec: A Postcolonial Study*. Jefferson, N.C.: McFarland, 2009.

———. "(Un)common Ground: National Sovereignty and Individual Identity in Contemporary SF from Québec." *Science Fiction Studies* 82 (November 2000): 439–60.

Sernine, Daniel. "Historique de la SFQ" [A little history of SFQ]. *Solaris* 79 (1988): 41–47.

Serruys, Nicholas. "Xénototalité: l'utopie, l'uchronie et l'anticipation canadiennes-françaises et québécoises dans l'optique de l'allégorie nationale" [Xenototality: French-Canadian and Québécois utopia, uchronia, and anticipation as national allegory]. *Voix plurielles* 5.2 (2008): 28–44.

Tardivel, Jules-Paul (1895). *For My Country*. Trans. Sheila Fischman. Toronto: University of Toronto Press, 1975.

Trudel, Jean-Louis. "L'Arche de tous les temps" [Ark of ages]. In *Escales 2000* [Layovers 2000]. Ed. Serge Lehman. Paris: Fleuve Noir, 1999. 253–92.

———. "Le Choix du lion, le festin des chacals" [Lion's choice, jackals' feast]. In *Etoiles vives I*. Ed. Gilles Le May. Le Plessis Brion: Orion, 1997: 123–55.

———. "Contamination" (1990). Trans. Donald McGrath. In *Tesseracts Q*. Ed. Jane Brierley and Élisabeth Vonarburg. Edmonton: The Books Collective: 1996. 26–46.

———. "Demain l'espoir" [Hope tomorrow]. In *Demain, les étoiles* [Tomorrow, the stars]. 1987; reprint, Saint-Laurent: Pierre Tisseyre, 2000. 211–35.

———. "Le Deuxième Carnet de Villard" [Villard's second notebook]. In *SF 98: Les Meilleurs Récits de l'année* [SF 98: Best stories of the year]. Ed. Olivier Girard and Philippe Curval. Luisant: Bélial/Orion, 1998. 65–78.

———. "La Douzième Vie des copies" [The twelfth life of copies]. In *Au Nord de Nulle-Part* [North of nowhere]. Liège: Groupe Phi, 1992. 11–22.

———. "L'éclat brûlant de la lune" [The burning glare of the moon]. *Solaris* 151 (2004): 77–118.

———. "French-Canadian Science Fiction and *Fantastique*." In *French Science Fiction, Fantasy, Horror and Pulp Fiction*. Ed. Jean-Marc Lofficier and Randy Lofficier. Jefferson, N.C.: McFarland, 2000. 460–70.

———. "L'Homme qui n'avait plus de remords." *Samizdat* 22 (1992): 4–9.

———. "Les Instincteurs de cruauté." *Solaris* 102 (1992): 7–14.

———. "Looking for Little Green Men." *New York Review of Science Fiction* 18.3 (2005): 1, 6–11.

———. "Lukas 19." *Demain, les étoiles*. 1987; reprint, Saint-Laurent: Pierre Tisseyre, 2000. 237–63. English translation: "Lukas 19." In *What IF…? Amazing Stories Selected by Monica Hughes*. Toronto: Tundra, 1998. 162–80.

———. *Nigelle par tous les temps* [Nigelle in all seasons]. Montréal: Médiaspaul, 2000.

———. "Les Ponts du temps" [Bridges of time]. *Solaris* 107 (1993): 36–46.

———. *Pour des soleils froids* [For cold suns]. 1991–92; reprint, Paris: Fleuve noir, 1994.

———. "Proscripts of Gehenna." In *Tesseracts³*. Trans. John Greene. Ed. Candas Jane

Dorsey and Gerry Truscott. Victoria, B.C.: Porcépic, 1990. 372–91. Trans. of "Proscrits de Géhenna." *Solaris* 71 (1991): 12–17.

———. *Le Ressuscité de l'Atlantide* [The resuscitated Atlantan]. 1985–87; reprint, Paris: Fleuve noir, 1994.

———. "Science Fiction in Francophone Canada (1839–1989)." In *Out of This World: Canadian Science Fiction and Fantasy Literature*. Ed. Allan Weiss and Hugh Spencer. Kingston, Ont.: Quarry Press and the National Library of Canada, 1995. 51–65.

———. "Scorpion dans le cercle du temps" [A scorpion in the circle of time]. In *Escales sur l'horizon* [Layovers on the horizon]. Paris: Fleuve Noir, 1998. 387–469.

———. "Stella Nova." *On Spec* 16 (1994): 31–43. French translation: "Nova Stella." *Galaxies* 13 (1999): 15–30.

———. "Tirés d'une même chair" [Pulled from the same flesh]. In *Transes Lucides* [Lucid trances]. Ed. René Beaulieu and Guy Sirois Roberval. Québec: Ashem Fictions, 1999, 97–126.

———. *Un automne à Nigelle* [Fall in Nigelle]. Montréal: Médiaspaul, 1998.

———. *Un été à Nigelle* [Summer in Nigelle]. Montréal: Médiaspaul, 1997.

———. *Un hiver à Nigelle* [Winter in Nigelle]. Montréal: Médiaspaul, 1997.

———. "Un papillon à Mashak" [A butterfly in Mashak]. *Solaris* 105 (1993): 5–15.

———. *Un printemps à Nigelle* [Spring in Nigelle]. Montréal: Médiaspaul, 1997.

———. *Un trésor sur Serendib* [A treasure on Serendib]. Montréal: Médiaspaul 1994.

———. "Une littérature de passage: la science-fiction et fantastique franco-ontariens de 1885 à nos jours" [A Literature in passing: Franco-Ontarian science fiction from 1885 to today]. *@nalyses: revue de critique et de théorie littéraire* 8.2 (2013): 40–80. Accessed August 2, 2017. https://uottawa.scholarsportal.info/ojs/index.php/revue-analyses/article/view/880/759.

Wolfe, Gene. *The Wizard Knight*. London: Gollancz, 2004.

Olatunde Osunsanmi and Living the Transatlantic Apocalypse:

The Fourth Kind

ALEXIS BROOKS DE VITA

American-born, Nigerian-identified Olatunde Osunsanmi has written and directed films that might be classified as traditional European/American sf. On the Internet Movie Database, a Nigerian member, IDEASmi, places Osunsanmi sixth on a list of nine "Nigerian Directors to Watch Out For": "Olatunde Osunsanmi was born on October 23, 1977 in the UNITED STATES. He is known for his work on *The Fourth Kind* (2009), *Smokin' Aces 2: Assassins' Ball* (2010) and *The Cavern* (2005)."[1] An up-and-coming name, Osunsanmi is also the screenwriter/director of the apparently overly innovative *Dark Moon*, shelved by Warner Brothers in October 2010 within weeks of being picked up by it, and Akiva Goldsman's *Weed Road*, as well as the director of "Saturday Night Massacre" and "Space Oddity" for the fourth and final season of the sf television series *Falling Skies*. Goodreads carries the very promising October 2014 announcement that Robert Buettner's bestselling debut novel *Orphanage*—the 2004 Quill Award nominee for Best SF/Fantasy/Horror novel, called the post-9/11 generation's *Starship Troopers* and "one of the great works of modern military science fiction"[2]—has been adapted for film by Osunsanmi for Davis Entertainment. Osunsanmi's sf reputation is steadily growing, and with such credits accumulating, his vision and controversial delivery merit analysis.

Attempting to summarize why seemingly few Africans write science fiction may be analogous to explaining why no women dress as drag queens and parade down the catwalk in *Paris Is Burning,* or why so few African Americans paint themselves in blackface outside of the film *Bamboozled.* An academician approaching an adequate analysis of this or similar prompts regarding Africans and sf, if s/he is somewhat knowledgeable about both African literary and cultural studies and the porous genres of speculative fiction, may find her/himself facing a disruptive opportunity: the existence of the prompt signifies the need for a broader, vastly more defamiliarizing and reconstructive conversation than the subject matter may at first appear to invite. An anticonfrontational alternative of silently sifting through a few meager names for one that fits the requisites of youth, non-European/American nationality, and sf genre may be more tempting than pausing to suggest, "Let us highlight an African/Diaspora writer while concurrently pointing out relevant issues implicit in the question."

In "Africa Has Always Been Sci-Fi," Zambian Namwali Serpell reintroduces Mark Dery's 1994 analysis of apparent African American and implicit African absence from sf in her analysis of twenty-first-century Nigerian-American author Nnedi Okorafor's work. Serpell points out that Dery introduces his concept of Afrofuturism as an answer to seeming African/American absence from sf. Serpell expands upon Dery's premise that African Americans are, historically and in reality, descendants of people who were abducted by aliens, inhabiting a nightmarish sf realm that threatens intolerance, dismemberment, experiments, and the use of weaponry; this latter circumstance is expanded to include continental Africans. With a passing reference to Mark Bould's implication in his introduction to *Paradoxa*'s African sf issue that African sf is "nascent," Serpell speculates that perhaps African literature is focused instead on the real-world exigencies of survival and rebuilding. However, if Dery and Serpell's assertions that African and African American history may represent actual alien abduction and colonization are to be seriously considered, then it follows that African and African American literature might also be postulated as having progressed from describing centuries-old alien encounters to represent the ongoing postapocalyptic reconstruction that must follow hostile alien takeover. Why would Africans and African Americans feel inspired to write themselves into a genre of literary speculation about what alien encounters might possibly be like if their literature already imagines sustainable self-reconstruction in the aftermath of attempted annihilation?

Dery has pointed out a possible African/American sf future, as Serpell recounts and expands: that African/American communities whose pasts have been deliberately occluded and who have been forced to expend their energies in efforts to reconstruct and redefine their lost and distorted civilizations might profitably turn their creativity to the imagining of futures. Serpell proposes

African sf as a futuristic investment in deconstructing and reconstructing an intercontinental postapocalyptic wasteland, creative work she sees in what Nnedi Okorafor has coined as her own distinctly "Naijamerican" (Nigerian and American) sf voice.[3] Inspired to respond to Neill Blomkamp's widely popular film *District 9*, which Okorafor perceived as racist, and moved by real-world headlines about a swordfish destroying an oil pipeline, Okorafor penned *Lagoon*, which Serpell characterizes as a song that sings "Africa has always been sci-fi." Hope Wabuke's Okorafor interview confirms the author's reactive inception of *Lagoon* and her concerns about a lack of African/American presence in sf: Okorafor states to Wabuke that Africans tend to only appear as they have been conceptualized in sf by those of European descent, compromised or minimized until their presence is not perceived as problematic to that audience. Wabuke expands upon the theme of hostility to vibrant or central characters of African descent in sf by listing hostile audience responses to the recent *Star Wars* stormtrooper of visibly African descent, hostility toward a *Harry Potter and the Cursed Child* Hermione Granger of African descent, and audience hostility to the depiction of *Hunger Games'* Rue as being of African descent.

Wabuke contends that such hostility to characters of African descent in sf makes no sense if, as she asserts, sf-fantasy is based upon experiences of the global African Diaspora: enslavement, colonization, genocide, and rape. Okorafor's post for *Science Fiction and Fantasy Writers of America*, "Can you define African Science Fiction?" encapsulates the racially layered dilemmas of exclusion faced by those of visibly African descent who attempt to participate in sf by pointing out that the first major African sf film was directed by and starred South Africans of European descent. "The first major African science fiction film" to which Okorafor is referring is, of course, *District 9*, which Serpell, Wabuke, and Okorafor's writings have all agreed is problematically racist. What is of particular note, however, for this essay is that, within months of the appearance of *District 9*, what might be considered the second major African science-fiction film—Olatunde Osunsanmi's *The Fourth Kind*—also hit theaters worldwide. Critical and, to some extent, audience response mirrors the racial divide these women writers of African descent describe, with critics of European descent almost unilaterally praising *District 9* while disparaging *The Fourth Kind*. This essay will propose an explanation of this perceptual disparity by closely analyzing the Nigerian influences potentially informing and impacting Osunsanmi's creative lens and influencing the film's cross-cultural immersive impact on viewers.

Okorafor cautions in "African Science Fiction" that addressing Africanness is a sensitive topic to be treated with respect. Okorafor raises questions of who speaks for whom, cultural appropriation, authenticity, history, and spirituality. All these questions can be confronted in comparing critical reception of *District 9*, written and directed by and starring descendants of South Africa's European colonizers, to *The Fourth Kind*, written and directed by a descendant of one of Africa's invaded and colonized regions: Nigeria. For example, 90 percent of 296 critics' responses to *District 9*, as summarized by the website *Rotten Tomatoes*, is that the film is "Technically brilliant and emotionally wrenching," featuring "action, imagination, and all the elements of a thoroughly entertaining science-fiction classic." *The Fourth Kind*, later that same year, according to *Rotten Tomatoes*, struck only 19 percent of its 112 critics positively, earning it a critical summary of "hokey and clumsy and makes its close encounters seem eerily mundane."[4] Mindful of the racialism pointed out by Serpell, Wabuke, and Okorafor, who are all women of African descent, a scan of the photos of the Top Critics and Super Reviewers acknowledged by *Rotten Tomatoes* shows that most if not all of them weighing in with the greatest reputational influence on these two films are of European descent and male, apparently potential members of the group Wabuke quotes Okorafor as calling "gatekeepers" of the sf genre.

As potential examples of criticism-as-gatekeeping, rating *The Fourth Kind* 2/5 in comparison to *District 9*'s 4/5, Joshua Rothkopf, a Top Critic whose work appears in *Time Out*, offers the bizarre reassurance that *District 9* features "too many gory vaporizations to qualify as a serious statement on race relations," so the viewer is free to sit back and "thrill to the cleanly cut action sequences" (November 17, 2011). Tom Charity, a Top Critic of CNN .com, praises *District 9*'s "sharp, inventive detail" (August 25, 2014). Anthony Lane, a Top Critic writing for *New Yorker*, assures the viewer that "you don't feel bamboozled, fooled, or patronized" by *District 9* but, instead, "winded, shaken, and shamed" (September 7, 2009). *District 9* undeniably offers the viewer sympathetic immersion in the sense of loss, vulnerability, disorientation, and helplessness of a lethal Other alien invader. *District 9* makes it easy for the audience to transpose its massive shiploads of huddled, starving, stranded, frightened aliens needing succor and shelter in and reorientation to their targeted new homelands as metaphors for Europe's ousted religious practitioners, prisoners, and government-sponsored pirates who landed along American, African, Pacific, and Caribbean coastlines, carrying infectious epidemics and armed with Chinese explosives. *District 9* focuses an empathetic lens on the disempowered and embarrassed invader, mistrusted and unwanted, though nonetheless being assisted to survive by populations that may soon find themselves colonized or wiped out of existence altogether, as a consequence. Those taught from elementary school to see European colonists who founded such segregated nations as the United States, South Africa, and Australia as having done a unilaterally good thing—genocide and segregation notwithstanding—may be predisposed to root for an underdog alien invader cowering in a floundering giant ship. Just as *District 9*'s protagonist comes to sympathize with, see himself as, and become the uninvited and unwelcome but powerful, regenerating alien invader, capable of annihilating the invaded civilization that struggles to isolate and contain him even as he seeks love and belonging, so may that movie's predominant audiences.

Conversely, true to the historical roots of its writer and director, and in diametric opposition to the creative impetus of *District 9*, *The Fourth Kind* immerses its viewers in an empathetic experience of being violently colonized, which this essay will further explore. The preponderance of Top Critics and Super Reviewers featured at *Rotten Tomatoes*, whose photos show them not likely to be of indigenous African descent, are apparently predisposed to sympathize with a historical view that ratchets up the terror of invasion. These critics' comments regarding *The Fourth Kind* include such patronizing dismissals as "dull, clumsy little movie" and "No, no, no, no," by *At the Movies* Top Critics A. O. Scott and Michael Phillips (November 9, 2009), "badly acted" and "insipid" from the *New York Daily News* Top Critic Joe Neumaier (November 6, 2009), and "laughable" by Ian Buckwalter, a Top Critic from *NPR* (July 4, 2010). Amy Biancolli, a *San Francisco Chronicle* Top Critic, hyperbolically accuses *The Fourth Kind*'s narrative segments of being "too glossy and over-stylized," suffering from "obvious melodrama" (November 6, 2009). In an unblushing celebration of wholly missing the point, even the usually intelligible Roger Ebert indulges in a level of snarky joking about the film's Afrocentric symbolisms that communicates little capacity for analysis on the critic's part but nevertheless generates enthusiastic putdowns as recently as 2016: "This film was more found-footage style garbage. Good review by Roger," weighs in TheLulzyHunter. And yet, Jenna Busch of the *Huffington Post* cared enough about the film not only to rate it in March 2010 but to return and update her rating in May 2011: "*The Fourth Kind* was one of the scariest things I've seen in years," Busch states; "*The Fourth Kind* made horror fun again." Busch pointedly goes after apparent Top Critics and Super Reviewers who claim that the audience is "too sophisticated" to believe that *Fourth Kind* features real found footage with a resounding, "Yeah, so what?" Busch thus implies that such heavy-handed, pointless complaints about the existence of the film seem to communicate nothing except that the critics who wrote them have missed—for whatever motive—what the movie is about and what it accomplishes. *The Fourth Kind* unself-consciously manages a genuine cross-cultural historical experiential immersion, destroying perceptual boundaries. Anyone who cares to know what alien invasion probably feels like to the invaded and colonized now has a filmic vehicle for that gut-wrenching, confusing, overwhelmingly horrifying, and decidedly nonheroic experience, thanks to Osunsanmi's rootedness in the historicity, authenticity, and spirituality that Okorafor pinpointed as necessary to African sf.

Like a planet in orbit, controversy loops infinitely around Osunsanmi's *The Fourth Kind*. For example, in answer to the seemingly innocuous message board question on the Internet Movie Database, "Is he nigerian [*sic*]?" One IMDb member, Nikfyst, quotes and responds to commentary deleted by adminstrators:

> I guess Nigerians make deceptive filmmakers (RACIST BULL) who are looking to rip off the public with hoaxes (WHEN IT COMES TO HIS FILM THE FOURTH FIND [*sic*] I DEFINITELY AGREE THAT HE RIPPED OFF AND TRIED TO DECEIVE HIS AUDIENCE WITH RIDICULOUS HOAX LIES).[5]

Negative reflection upon Osunsanmi's work tends to toy with the allegation that it is unethical to persuade an audience to believe that historically documented tragedies prove a fictional tale to be a factual documentary. This double-standard against Osunsanmi's work raises the question of why such vilification has not continually attended and increasingly modified the legacies of not only Orson Welles's infamous Halloween radio broadcast of *The War of the Worlds*, remembered as "original, and so convincing" by *History Today* contributor Dean Nicholas,[6] but also such filmic standouts as *The Blair Witch Project*, purportedly found footage of a team's exploration of the legend of a murderous witch, and—even more fittingly—*The Mothman Prophecies*, whose book and film claim that at least one historically explicable tragedy resulting in forty-six actual deaths may have been the result of unexplained paranormal activity. If American movie critics and filmgoers are concerned about breaching the irreconcilable division of fact and fiction in Osunsanmi's *The Fourth Kind*, why is their condemnation of filmic line-crossing apparently inconsistent?

Reversing the lens of condemnatory mixing of fact and fiction in film, one might go so far as to question the lack of popular and critical American media coverage about the racially selective serial killer whose atrocities were not widely known—even in Los Angeles, his hunting ground—until the release of *Tales of the Grim Sleeper*. Not only were necessary alerts about this serial killer of African American women silenced for two decades in a predominantly African American neighborhood, effectively creating a false sense of security for women who might be out at night for any number of reasons; but once the killer was stumbled upon by police and arrested, and his murders documented by a British film crew, American audiences continue to respond laconically to the exposed coverup. These widely varying responses to the convergent topics of truth and silence in filmmaking lead this cultural analyst to propose that, perhaps, what an individual film consumer and his or her ethnic community may consider material fit to cross sensitive lines between the factual, fictional, sacrosanct, or silenced may prove to be a matter of cultural perspective. More summarily put, if Osunsanmi's use of factual tragedies to create interest in his fictional film is reprehensible, then all such filmmakers should be in for an equal share of censure, and negligent silence about such tragedies should be equally problematic. Otherwise, selective condemnation appears to indicate that some other issue may be the actual cause of critical attack in Osunsanmi's case.

It was not until recently beginning to study African American literature that, one of my Nigerian students has written, she finally understood why her grandfather disappeared and his family never learned what happened to him during World War II—a war in which Nigeria did not declare itself a participant— and why her own back remains crisscrossed with scars from public whippings at her Nigerian school.[7] While her family was irrevocably traumatized by the international quicksand effect of World War II, they had little or no objective information about the patterns of conscripting colonized or ethnic-minority laborers (or prisoners) against their will to supply a wartime workforce. Regarding her scarred back, like many descendants of the victims of colonialist or racist brutalities, parents and school administrators who were flogged or whipped for infractions against a colonizing or enslaving power may have relied upon these same methods when disciplining their own children and charges, even if they loved them. Survivors of persecution may have little or no discriminatory ability to identify which of the treatments to which they have been subjugated are reasonable and which are excessive or even brutal. Therefore, lack of access to widespread information about international atrocities may place a double imposition upon those who suffered and, decades later, continue not to understand, when filmmakers could candidly explain to them the historical maelstroms in which they and their families found themselves entrapped. The valid issue of truth-disseminating in film production, distribution, and availability should have a much wider breadth of discussion and weightier international content than what appears to be ongoing finger-pointing at Osunsanmi's *The Fourth Kind*.

Choosing Osunsanmi rather than a novelist or short-story writer for the *Lingua Cosmica* collection also raises a question about cross-cultural concepts of authorship. Osunsanmi writes screenplays and creates worlds as a director, necessitating a culturally sensitive choice. Ought the scholar proposing an African author ignore authorship in the broader African perspective as described by Nigerian Nobel Literature Laureate Wole Soyinka, who explains that "contraction of the cosmic envelope"[8] re-creates and interfaces with the universe, collapsing theater, spirit, and words into "man's fearful awareness of the cosmic context of his existence"?[9] Or might an analyst bring a host of (mostly Nigerian) African authors into comparative consideration of Osunsanmi's (perhaps unconscious) portrayal of inherited, culturally specific legacies of storytelling to explain a crucial interpretive point: that Osunsanmi's sf appears to retell the experience of the Transatlantic Human Trade? Osunsanmi's immersion of the viewer in the deeply unsettling experiences of horror and incredulity that foreshadow the revelation of a genocide that has already taken place—his culturally specific take on alien invasion and the futility of resistance to it—may be cathartic for some viewers, while it is profoundly disturbing to others.

And yet, disturbing or not, this is our living world history of alien invasion: creeping incursions into the minds, laws, and habits of the abducted and colonized and the internal erosion of their values and practices, resulting in what Ayi Kwei Armah refers to as zombies: "What a scene of carnage we have come to live here! Here we have had quarrels, bitterness, strife, so that the life of our people is become a tattered thing and we are everywhere in shreds."[10] Osunsanmi softens intercultural calluses enough to make each of his viewers feel the terror and know the helplessness of those living through the realization that they, their loved ones, and their communities are already victims of an alien invasion, a feat in keeping with the legacy of the Father of African Literature, Chinua Achebe.

In "African SF 101," Mark Bould cautions about the need for sensitivity to perceptual recolonization: the critical viewer may assume that evaluative superiority belongs to European and American perception of sf and thus label or ghettoize African sf as insufficiently developed or otherwise lacking because it is not recognizably European/American in perspective. But even as he acknowledges the dangers of evaluating the science-fictional quality of African art through an American or European lens, Bould goes on to state that the only African sf written before World War II of which he is aware is by South Africans of European descent. However, a study of sf authors from outside the United States and Europe might well start with the first published African novel, wherein Thomas Mofolo's spirit/man Isanusi appears before Chaka at will, across space, time, and worlds, infusing the exiled boy emperor with the power to crush together kingdoms into a new creation—not quite what is assumed to be sf, though this synopsis is certainly the predecessor of *Star Wars*. Mofolo's

Chaka could well be subtitled *An Original African Alien-Invasion Epic*. Or one might highlight Olaudah Equiano's *Interesting Narrative*, an alien-invasion epic about being carried off from his home through what alien colonizers would soon rename Nigeria, to an ocean he had never seen, there to be corralled in the pitch-black belly of a monstrous vessel that would take him to unknown lands, where strangers mate with women and girls of his nation by force as he finds himself also exploited for purposes of alien-species survival: the African progenitor of Octavia Butler's "Bloodchild" and her *Xenogenesis* (*Lilith's Brood*) series. One might include in the subgenre of African and Diaspora sf an analysis of Achebe's *Arrow of God* and the maddened spiritual entity who has rescued six Nigerian villages from slavery but whose villagers still prefer to worship the millennia-old snake god. The vengeful younger god has brought alien Christian invaders to Nigeria to wipe out the worship of the snake from the African continent, once and for all: an African inversion of *Stargate*. Or, to comply with *Lingua Cosmica*'s requisite parameters of youth, one might simply analyze Ben Okri's *The Famished Road*, a spirit-child's navigation of postcolonial postapocalypse, as the definitive Nigerian *Roadside Picnic*: survivors in the aliens' dumping ground must eke out a living in their denatured homeland, at their own physical and spiritual peril. While African and Diaspora authors and analysts have read, thought, and written on both sides of what social analyst W. E. B. DuBois describes as a veil between the human of African descent and the object others may think him or her to be,[11] they have also learned to sunder it advisedly before speaking plainly to cross-cultural audiences. The *Lingua Cosmica* collection presents an exciting opportunity for plain speaking, excavating a cross-cultural African/sf perceptual chasm while attempting to bridge it.

Respecting anthology guidelines of age and purity of genre, it becomes clear that as a screenplay writer, director, and producer, Osunsanmi creates in that space of potentiality that Soyinka calls a "cosmic entirety."[12] Osunsanmi was frequently the vindicating sf voice chosen by Nigerians offended by their portrayal in *District 9*. Osunsanmi gives a predominantly European/American sf audience an opportunity to consider what was already made evident in H. G. Wells's alien-invasion sf prototype, *The War of the Worlds*, which Félix J. Palma imagines was invented to get European and American readers to experience how their countries' no-holds-barred quests for wealth were felt by the targeted, pillaged, predominantly agricultural, hunting/gathering, nomadic, and highly philosophical ancient civilizations of Africa. In a section called "The New Overseas Empires of Steamship and Railway" in his *Outline of the History of the World* (1921), and again in his *Short History of the World* (1922), Wells excoriates Europe for carving up and exploiting Africa. Introducing "European Aggression in Asia," Wells continues to express incredulity at the European/American assumption that the systematic exploitation of Africa represents the new normal arrangement of global financial affairs. Wells goes on to blame such Eurocentric complacency on what he describes as the nineteenth-century European mind's "shallow historical background," compounded by "no habit of penetrating criticism"[13]—in short, greed-fueled bigotry founded upon historical ignorance. It is reasonable to conclude that Wells may be reflecting upon such studies as Sir Harry H. Johnston's *A History of the Colonization of Africa by Alien Races* (1899). While vividly relating horrific atrocities against Africans captured and enslaved by Europeans that lead him to conclude that races should only enslave within themselves, not enslave others, and listing traditional African nations that proved to be impervious to mass enslavement by Europeans, Johnston nevertheless accuses Africans of being apelike and blames fictitious African "heedlessness" for the continent's being overrun by aliens.[14] Johnston's study demonstrates so poor a grasp of historical facts antecedent to and broader than his period of observation and Eurocentric viewpoint, and such incapacity to weigh his biases against what he has seen with his own eyes, that his Cambridge University Press publication fully vindicates Wells's denunciations of European colonial enthusiasm in his *Histories* and Palma's fictionalized theory about Wells's intent for *War of the Worlds*.

Osunsanmi portrays an African/Diaspora reality in a genre and via a medium created by and of interest to Europeans and Americans, exposing a reality the latter may not have explored from the candid perspectives of the peoples traumatically affected. Following a heightened Nigerian/sf rupture in response to the international popularity of *District 9*, I propose to take this challenging opportunity at its face, as a wonderfully cross-cultural scholarly point of intersection, and at its implication, as an ethically responsible teachable moment, to visit Osunsanmi's most well-known work.

It is perhaps Osunsanmi's writing and directing of 2013's *Eden* that best argues for reading his sf against his Nigerian inheritance of literary voices describing and decrying the Transatlantic Human Trade and the colonization of the African continent that the nearly genocidal stripping of its populations made possible. Dave McNary of *Variety* heralds a second collaboration between Gold Circle Films motion-picture and video production company and Osunsanmi on *Eden*, the story of an escaping family trying to get to a free city, following their earlier work together on *The Fourth Kind*. It is perhaps worth pausing to note that the seeming disappearances of Osunsanmi's *Dark Moon* and *Eden* into the cutting rooms or storage closets of Hollywood may strike a curious observer as eerily similar to a series of alien abductions "in the reel world."

Cultural Cyborgs: Reading Science Fiction
in African/Diaspora Literature and Art

In Hannah Hall, the central administrative building of Texas Southern University—a university founded for the advanced education of African Americans in the *de jure* segregated United States—many walls are covered with historical murals painted by some of the university's twentieth-century graduating Art majors. Like much of classic African literature, many of these African American students' murals are dramatically sf in theme. One such mural, the work of David Smith in 1978,[15] depicts the Middle Passage and includes stylized male and female African figurines apparently carved of wood, similar to those referenced as carrying spiritual power in Achebe's *Arrow of God*. However, where the figures' genitalia should be, Smith has painted stripped-away rectangles, as though those parts of his mural were sliced off or torn out and dropped just above the floor of the Hannah hallway, evoking actual historical aggression against traditional sexual identities and gendered community roles of chattel slavery's victims. The male statue appears to have been completely castrated, including full penectomy, and the female aggressively excised. Squares of frayed-edged genitalia rest on their sides by the painted statues' feet, as if the male has suffered traditional American castration/lynching as recounted in Trudier Harris's *Exorcising Blackness*, and the female the kind of sexual self-mutilation believed to have been practiced by some chattel enslaved women attempting to avoid rape and forced breeding, as artistically depicted in Gayl Jones's *Corregidora*. In the exposed rectangle between the man's thighs sits a typewriter in place of a penis and testicles. Between the woman's thighs appears to have been inserted what may have been a 1970s version of the computer, its printer churning out dot-matrix paper, in place of a vagina issuing forth menstrual blood or a newborn baby. An analyst might read this mural as implying that traditionally held roles of men and women and, indeed, the very definitions of manhood and womanhood have been so irrevocably excised and permanently altered by African subjugation to European technology as to have been replaced by it. This interpretation would argue that the man of African descent post–chattel slavery functions as a man only if he can reproduce European learning without obtruding his Africanness into the product, and that the woman of African descent post–chattel slavery is a woman only if she can produce future reproducers of European learning. To be functional, Smith's mural implies, the person of African descent who has been stripped not only of culture and the legal claim to humanity but of gendered functionality in his or her society must serve as a sterilized reproducer of the alien technology and alien culture that have effectively dehumanized and denatured him or her. This argument mirrors those regarding colonized identity, belonging, and the capacity for functionality in Frantz Fanon's *Peau noire, masques blancs* (*Black Skin, White Masks*) and *Les damnés de la terre* (*The Wretched of the Earth*). The traditional African male, in Smith's depiction, has become analogous to a eunuch guarding the technological harem of his castrators and the traditional African woman a sterilized breeder of technological products, rather than being allowed to remain sexually functional acculturated people, capable of regenerating their own cultures and communities, post-invasion.

When I teach African and African American literature courses, I bring students to see the Hannah Hall murals, particularly this one. At some point in the semester, the class may observe Nigerian novelist Buchi Emecheta's karma-plagued Igbo heroine, Nnu Ego, trying to maintain the traditional roles of senior wife and mother in the face of intersecting, mutually undermining, colonized African gender-role shifts. This pan-African problem of self and social role unrecognizably redefined by European colonization is consummately described by Ugandan author Okot p'Bitek's fictional Acoli narrator, Lawino, who makes this observation to her Europeanized husband, Ocol:

> There is not one single true son left, [...]
> For all our young men
> Were finished in the forest,
> Their manhood was finished
> In the class-rooms,
> Their testicles
> Were smashed
> With large books![16]

Lawino has observed the process of her husband's deculturation as an Acoli and acculturation as a member of the British Commonwealth through the perspectives of her traditional education. Lawino interprets Ocol's European education as sorcery leading to a demonic possession that has turned him into a zombie-like enemy of his own people. P'Bitek's epic poem of Lawino's lament serves as a cautionary tale for young Africans in the European colonies, warning them—despite their European education—to continue to respect their African traditions, their African ancestors and parents, or suffer earthly consequences:

> All misfortunes have a root, [...]
> They do not fall anyhow,
> They do not fall at random,

They do not come our way by accident,
We do not just run into them.[17]

Lawino warns that self-destructive insanity is caused by hostile European ghosts that displace African voices and traditions:

The deadly vengeance ghosts
Of the writers
Will capture your head,
And like my husband
You will become
A walking corpse.[18]

In p'Bitek's poem, Europeanization is similar to the infections in the films *28 Days Later*, *28 Weeks Later*, and *World War Z*: a fatal, seemingly demonic possession that appears to be untreatable. Contact with those infected triggers a raging, mindless hatred of all that is reflective of the former—now altered and self-despising—original self: for the zombies, this hated, obsessively sought former self is found in uninfected humans; for the Europeanized African, this now-despised, obsessively denigrated former self is the traditionally educated, tradition-practicing African. To her husband, who has become "a dog of the white man,"[19] Lawino defamiliarizes the objects and practices of European enchantment that obsess him while they estrange and terrify her: not only books of magic and brainwashing but also clocks, electric stoves, coal stoves, tables, plates, chairs, rosaries, ballroom dancing, and the chanting of Christian prayers, all accoutrements of functionality within the parameters of European colonization. "Ignorance and shame provoke you / To turn to foreign things,"[20] Lawino warns. Ghanaian novelist Ayi Kwei Armah has one of his anticolonial characters decry "those needing the white destroyers' shiny things to bring a feeling of worth into their lives," those who "uttered their deep-rooted inferiority of soul, and called them lacking in the essence of humanity; womanhood in women, manhood in men. For which deficiency they must crave things to eke out their beings, things to fill holes in their spirits."[21]

Osunsanmi's 2005 *The Cavern*, originally titled *WIthIN*, is a filmic meditation on the apprehension of selfhood through love and loss, a reflection on betrayal's impact on catastrophic survival. Reflecting on whether wholeness is possible for a man who has chosen life over self-sacrifice for his beloved, the haunting and self-definitive choice of the expedition's leader, a shaman enters a cave and senses its spirit's personification. The cave's spirit has personified in its foster son and acolyte, Petr, the Beast. In *Hopes and Impediments*, Achebe explains the Igbo creative viewpoint that "the practical purpose of art is to channel a spiritual force into an aesthetically satisfying physical form that captures the presumed attributes of that force."[22] Osunsanmi's fire-scarred, plane-crash-surviving orphan, Petr, who has grown into the spiritually possessed Beast, vicariously experiences two cavers' covert sexual act the night before their expedition begins. This experience sets in motion his cannibalistic devastation of the entire team, except for the woman he chooses to fill the developmental sexual hole in his own possessing spirit: a ravenous craving that he may not have previously known he had. As the penultimate surviving woman and the woman the Beast will rape to complete the last stage of his adult development stumble upon the relics of Petr, the audience is given a chance to see that the film has been an excursion into the dichotomy of ultimate betrayal versus survival: Petr, the viewer realizes, must have cannibalized his fire-charred parents' bodies in order to survive the crash, learning to use fire to cook otherwise inedible meat and warm himself from the same disaster that killed his parents and their pilot and left him scarred but alive, even as he learned to shelter in the cavern. Killing and roasting the expedition's members must ritualistically return the Beast to that moment of devolutionary choice at which he left the developmental trajectory established by his parents' intended socialization of him and became the product of its catastrophic interruption: the cannibalistic boy destined to become the adult Beast. Ironically, the Beast's prolonged cannibalistic feast upon the expeditioners also reunites his distorted psyche with what remains of the preadolescent Petr he once was, who must, in his normalcy, have idealized his parents' intimacy and that relationship's creation and protection of him, even as their nurturing of him was horrifically extended by his presumed consumption of their burned corpses. Stalking the expeditioners has not only provided the Beast with another cannibalistic feast and opportunities to reflect upon his emergence as Beast but also a chance to make the only living human contact that he may still feel has potential worth for him: the as-yet-unexplored sexual act. Though Petr's memories may stir the Beast's yearnings, Petr the socialized child no longer guides the Beast's enactment of those desires. Petr as a potentially socialized adult was destroyed in the survival choices the child was forced to make following the plane crash. The Beast who devolved from those choices evidently retains Petr's memories and attendant longings but is not the adult product of that socialized child. The Beast is an antisocialized product of Petr's catastrophic survival.

The Beast's deeply ingrained habit of cannibalism as a rite of survival that resurrects the last traces of his contact with his parents also tragically ensures that he can never be discovered and rescued; no cavers can ever return from his mountain to tell rescuers where to find the man who was once Petr. As the last two women survivors of the expedition realize that the Beast is roasting—and they are eating—the remains of the self-torturing expedition leader whose life was rebuilt on his abandonment of a lover in a flooding cave as he saved himself, the Beast returns to his camp to enact the final stage of his maturation: the rape that is the sole sexual communion of which he, under these aggregate circumstances, is capable. Osunsanmi's linking of the expedition leader's comparatively esoteric survivor's guilt with the Beast's aggressive psycho-physical immersion in his interpretation of a survivor's rites echoes a common African/Diaspora literary theme, as debated by Novella Brooks de Vita regarding Octavia Butler's *Kindred* in "Beloved and Betrayed: Survival and Authority": how much betrayal can a survivor survive? On the other side of one's devolutionary choices to survive, how much of the original socialized being who wanted to survive will actually remain? Has the catastrophically threatened being been destroyed in the process of choosing to embrace psycho-social betrayal in order to survive?

Osunsanmi's Beast may be conceptualized as the spirits of Fire and Earth not titled in any of the chapters of William Golding's *Lord of the Flies*, embodied in a literally Caucasian boy grown in isolation to manhood, now hunting human prey of mixed ethnicities. A sexualized adult Petr (meaning "Rock") cannot emerge through the devolution that has become the Beast, even though it must be Petr's memories that inform the Beast's observation of adult human sexual interaction sufficiently to bestir him to want to experience sexual human contact himself. Unfortunately for his victim, the Beast's sexual communion must follow the patterns established by Petr's trauma, a bravado embracing of acts that must have originally caused the orphaned boy shame, as symbolized by the covering of Petr's fiery disfigurement with his elaborate skull mask commemorating the Beast's exploits. The Beast's sexual act reflects and consummates his embracing and reenacting of the taboos that have defined his emergence into being. How else could Osunsanmi's take on Golding's Beast incorporate sexual coming of age? Of interest for Osunsanmi's career as a writer and director of sf films in a European/American market reluctant to ethnically integrate that genre, how did film critics react to the devolution of a Caucasian male in juxtaposition to his socialized ethnic-minority prey, who cannot fail to have appeared comparatively more civilized than the Beast?

In the same way that the Beast has reached a point at which his socialized boyhood self is unattainable to him, even as it prods and informs his adult desires, the desexed and denatured African/Diaspora cyborgs David Smith has depicted will not be able to resurrect their original selves or reproduce their original communities on the other side of their catastrophic removal from their destroyed homelands. These issues of survival and betrayal confronting the cavers and the Beast, as is the case with much of Osunsanmi's speculative work, throw light on the question of Transatlantic Human Trade survivors' capacity for self-reconstruction upon arrival in their incomprehensible, hostile, and degrading new homelands: the European colonies. Osunsanmi's films may be said to argue that there can be no so-called postcolonial era if postcolonialism implies renaissance; Smith's cyborgs, like Osunsanmi's Beast, have been irrevocably altered by their survival of what has destroyed their capacity to pass on the legacies they once stood to inherit.

A Closer Look at *The Fourth Kind*

In "Academia and the Advance of African Science Fiction," Nick Wood postulates that African sf already exists and is poised to take over the planet, a position statement that acknowledges African sf is not always recognized. After pointing out in "African Science Fiction is Still Alien" that African sf is not analogous to sf that takes place somewhere in Africa, Nnedi Okorafor indicates a desire for more African exploitation of the sf literary tool potentially designed to address if not redress political and social ills. Following her welcome if rare recognition of Amos Tutuola's unforgettable *The Palm Wine Drinkard* as Nigerian sf based on a traditional Yoruba folktale, Chinelo Onwualu adds to this discussion in "African Science Fiction and Literature" the perceptual problem that African sf and African scientific innovation are often neither recognized nor credited. Seen in that light, it seems significant to point out that, apparent ongoing critical and popular denigration of the film and its writer notwithstanding, Osunsanmi's *The Fourth Kind* grossed $47.7 million worldwide and continues to be the first credit listed after its writer/director's name, for purposes of popular identification. Such a potential perceptual dichotomy suggests that cross-cultural analysis of the film may be socio-academically useful. However, even Bould's introduction to *Paradoxa*'s Africa SF edition overlooks *The Fourth Kind* in his recognition of other 2009 sf films by African filmmakers: Kenyan Wanuri Kahiu's visually entrancing and poignant *Pumzi* and Blomkamp's *District 9*. While *Pumzi* and *District 9* are set in potentially recognizably African landscapes, *The Fourth Kind* is not, nor does it purport to be; though the two spokesmen guiding and explaining the viewer's immersion in *The Fourth Kind*'s story are both identifiably of African descent, most of the other actors are visibly European American, as has been most of the film's audience. Bould's neglecting to recognize *The Fourth Kind* as an African sf film, apparently because its story is not located on the African continent or because only its two guiding narrators are of obvious African descent, points out a potential European/American privileging of perception. In "WHO Is the Monster," Novella Brooks de Vita explain that Osunsanmi appropriates the continental African definition of the trickster: he leads the audience into vicariously experiencing a Nigerian story through Nigerian mythical and historical perspectives in an American setting; Osunsanmi as trickster/storyteller has so fitted his Nigerian story to his American audience that storytelling and spirituality seem to belong to the American genre that Osunsanmi has (re)appropriated.

In *The Fourth Kind*, Osunsanmi creates a double film that comes across as a documentary about a psychologist, Dr. Tyler, caught up in a spate of alien abductions, disappearances, mental and emotional breakdowns, and deaths. The film explores how "homicides and missing persons" in Alaska may have been miscategorized alien abductions, presenting jarring supposed found footage of survivors undergoing hypnotic regression. Osunsanmi's *The Fourth Kind* takes the viewer into the moments of unbearable understanding, horrific experience, and irresistible recall of suppressed memories that must have attended the devastation of traditional cultural structures for both Transatlantic Human Trade survivors and the African progenitors of the popular television series *The Leftovers*—ravaged communities left scrambling in chaos to reform and function back on the African continent, indelibly traumatized by apparently random loved ones' disappearances. For Osunsanmi writes alien invasion without peaceful lulls, successful retaliations, or potentially happy endings. *The Fourth Kind* is no *Independence Day*, no *Mist*, and no *Avatar*. In Osunsanmi's universe, the cavalry is not coming. There is no respite from increasing disclosures of devastation and unforeseen new tragedies. Osunsanmi projects intimately and invasively mass devastation heaped upon personal devastation, a process of regional destruction that will landslide into apocalyptic cultural destruction, carrying everything and everyone hopelessly and helplessly before it. Osunsanmi re-creates an uncomfortably familiar *Underworld* not of Lycans and Vampires but of other pseudoscientifically divided beings, supposedly so essentially different as to be theoretically incapable of interbreeding; in a "might-makes-right" historical replay, a self-proclaimed master race of technologically violent parasites exploits those whom they have self-servingly categorized as lesser beings to be enslaved, tortured, maimed, probed, or killed, evoking chattel slavery's theories of "Drapetomania."[23] *The Fourth Kind*'s suicidal father shooting his family reflects African Diaspora men and women who aborted offspring and murdered loved ones rather than allow them to be treated as enslaved cattle (as in Toni Morrison's *Beloved*). Its traumatized psychologist comes across as a reminder of those voice-in-the-wilderness victims who fail to persuade their countrymen that something unseen and repugnant about their society is deeply, irremediably wrong (as in Kazuo Ishiguro's *Never Let Me Go*). Its nebulous denouement returns the audience to the world as they know it but may have preferred not to see it. Watching *The Fourth Kind* is like standing on a beach to view an incoming tsunami, knowing there will be no resistance, no bulwark against annihilation, and no reprieve. *The Fourth Kind* may raise disquieting specters in the minds of anyone familiar with the history of how the United States and Western Europe became superpowers; the film suggests that, whatever God is, It is not a hand that stays the oncoming destruction. All that will remain to be explored, following *Deep Impact* and return to consciousness, will be an unrecognizable landscape of desolation: *Cloverfield*.

The Fourth Kind's European/American audience immersion in antiformulaic absolute helplessness and antiheroic terror may be compared to the apocalyptic sf-esque stories told by Nigerian authors Olaudah Equiano in his memoirs of the atrocities of chattel slavery, Buchi Emecheta in recounting the rapid deculturation of African kingdoms and cultures in the *The Rape of Shavi* and *The Joys of Motherhood*, Chinua Achebe's description of the incremental breaking down of apocalypse survivors in *Arrow of God*, and Ben Okri's spirit-child's view of Nigeria's continual postapocalyptic cultural and economic disintegration in *The Famished Road*. In his portrayal of terrorist-style sneak attacks, bedroom abductions at 3:33 A.M. (half of the reputedly diabolic 666, in diametric opposition to the time of the Christ's death on the cross at 3:00 P.M.), captives abducted, imprisoned, scarred, branded, and tortured by their abductors, the use of damaging and sexually assaulting probes,[24] and even in the abductors' claim to speak for or stand in for God, Osunsanmi's *The Fourth Kind* is a cultural crossover bridging African and European perceptions of alien abduction as the twenty-first-century reenactment of the actual eighteenth- and nineteenth-century Transatlantic Human Trade that annihilated traditional cultural structures and communities on the African continent. Traditionally Nigerian metaphysical or supernatural metaphors, such as those attached to the filmic tropes of the owl, its coloring, an abducted victim's blindness, and the protagonist's imprisonment, may benefit from cross-cultural translation.

Before their abductions, the hypnotized victims recall the appearance of a strange owl. Tellingly, in the ancient Yoruba (predominantly based in Nigeria) religion of Ifá, the owl carries double significance as one of the bird avatars of the shape-shifting goddess of chaos and transformative change, Oya, as well as, according to Deanne Quarrie, a symbol of the androgynous god/dess of elevated consciousness, Obatala. Obatala's color is white; so is the owl, upon its first mention in a *Fourth Kind* therapy session. Awo Fá'lokun Fatunmbi describes

Oya's function within Obatala's realms of existence as providing "those changing conditions that force consciousness to grow, expand and transcend its limitations," creating "empathy and deep spiritual bonding with many different
dimensions of reality" as she "shifts between manifestation as human and animal," teaching "the lesson of tolerance, acceptance and compassion."[25] Fatunmbi
credits Oya with "disrupting complacency" as she "brings the unexpected, the
chaotic, the transformative and the overwhelming" to "shatter the illusion" and
"give human consciousness a sense of mortality and humility."[26] As spirit of the
wind and a dweller in cemeteries, Oya brings insights from the ancestors in the
realms of the dead to the polarity of Obatala as "expansion and contraction";
Fatunmbi thus describes Obatala embracing "both forms of primal force in
the universe" as, simultaneously, the "light which is moving in on its source"
or "Consciousness," and the "light which is moving away from its source" or a
"Womb that generates Character."[27] Quarrie explains that Obatala represents
and teaches the "highest ethical standards" and is both "forgiving and vengeful, brilliant and retarded, perfect and deformed"; it is Obatala who "whips
the arrogant and blesses them with humility."[28] The mythatype,[29] meaning the
concurrently mythical, historical, and personal African/Diaspora symbol of the
white owl darkening to beige as it gazes out of *The Fourth Kind* at the viewer
before increasingly alarming scenes of abduction, signals that the beneficiaries
of global economic colonization—both in the cast of abducted actors and in the
transfixed audience—are being offered a lesson from the ancestors. Obatala's
white cloth darkens with a deliberate spill of palm oil from Esu, the messenger
god, as Obatala journeys toward humility; s/he must detour to ancestral waters
to be cleansed. Oya's dark link to ancestral wisdom thus complicates Obatala's
whiteness and makes elevated consciousness possible. Blinded, falsely accused,
imprisoned, and humiliated—as will be Dr. Tyler and her daughter in *The
Fourth Kind*—Obatala achieves humility and, with it, profound insight. Like
Obatala, *The Fourth Kind*'s cast is drawn into unjust suffering and humiliation
and its concomitant opportunities to learn, stumbling away from the chaos to
desolation's wisdom.

In the course of the film, the psychologist is discovered to have already been
abducted by Sumerian-speaking aliens. Dr. Tyler bravely pieces together the
evidences and memories of her experience, including flashbacks of invasive
probes. One of her distraught patients describes the dehumanizing experiences of abduction as, "You'd have to have seen it, felt it. . . . The worst you
could ever imagine." This concurrent fear and drive to articulate the horror left
in the minds of survivors of abduction echoes the historical memoir of kidnap
and enslavement written by a Nigerian ancestor: *The Interesting Narrative of*

Olaudah Equiano or Gustavus Vassa, the African, Written by Himself. Eleven-year-old Equiano is stolen from his farming community by Africans who sell him to a steadily changing stream of Africans, who treat him as a servant or a family member, depending upon their household needs. Eventually, Equiano is carried to the West African coast, where he discovers Europeans who buy cargo-loads of humans as cattle. At the sight of the strange cargo ship, the miserable human beings chained and terrified all around him, and the violent creatures he takes to be "bad spirits" who have just paid for him, Equiano is "quite overpowered with horror and anguish" and convinced that he and his fellow human beings have been bought to "be eaten by those white men with horrible looks, red faces, and loose hair":

> I had never experienced any thing of this kind before. . . . I asked them if these people had no country, but lived in this hollow place (the ship): they told me they did not, but came from a distant one. 'Then,' said I, 'how comes it in all our country we never heard of them?' They told me because they lived so very far off. . . . I asked how the vessel could go? they told me they could not tell.[30]

Osunsanmi translates Equiano's shock and fear by defamiliarizing historical tropes of European invasion, using aliens from outer space telepathically speaking Earth's first recorded language.

Recall of interactions with the aliens forces Dr. Tyler to confront suppressed memories of her own abduction. During her series of reenactments and cringe-worthy flashbacks in hypnotic regression, the psychologist vents the aliens' claim to be "god," a not infrequent claim of enslavers and colonizers. However, the seemingly real, institutionalized Dr. Tyler confides to the film's real director Osunsanmi that she does not believe this to be true, considering that the aliens' possession of her filled her with "hopelessness." Dr. Tyler resists the aliens' control but, by the film's end, she is nevertheless defeated, wasted away and disbelieved by everyone but Osunsanmi posing as a documentarian. Dr. Tyler insightfully confides to Osunsanmi her theory that the alien can only "pretend to be" the god that it is not. This theorizing by the psycho-emotionally broken and socially isolated Dr. Tyler might place this statement of relative power in perspective as analogous to the life-and-death control Europeans legislated for themselves over enslaved Africans and colonized freemen in many of Europe's colonies. But Dr. Tyler, like the viewer, is only beginning to learn that, as Achebe teaches, "'No condition is permanent'": "In Igbo cosmology even gods could fall out of use; and new forces are liable to appear without warning in the temporal and metaphysical firmament . . . It stands to reason, therefore, that new forms must stand ready to be called into being as often as new (threatening) forces appear on the scene. It is like 'earthing' an electrical charge to ensure communal safety."[31] After the psychologist's trauma-blinded daughter is abducted "in a beam of light," Dr. Tyler decides to pursue her stolen child "directly to the source." Taking children, with the goal of more effectively colonizing the community by indoctrinating its most susceptible members to love and admire or at least fear their colonizers, is repeatedly addressed by writers of invaded cultures: not only Achebe in *Arrow of God* and p'Bitek in *Song of Lawino*, but Ngugi wa Thiong'o in *The River Between*, Ferdinand Oyono in *Une vie de boy* (*Houseboy*), Tsitsi Dangarembga in *Nervous Conditions*, Linda Hogan in *Mean Spirit*, Frantz Fanon in *Black Skin, White Masks*, Ken Bugul in *Le baobab fou* (1984, translated as *The Abandoned Baobab: The Autobiography of a Senegalese Woman* in 1991), and Carter G. Woodson in *The Mis-education of the Negro* (1933), to name a few classics. The abduction of Dr. Tyler's daughter proves to be a convincing act of verisimilitude, if Osunsanmi is to depict a realistic takeover. The loyal child's bond with her remaining parent must be broken and her faith in her mother and community systematically dismantled by persuading her, in her naïveté, to perceive the invading culture as both nurturing and superior to the culture in which she was being raised, a concept both pro- and anticolonially explored in M. R. Carey's sf/horror masterpiece, *The Girl with All the Gifts* (2014).

Whatever ultimate authority the child believes her mother and cultural leaders answer to (such as God), the aliens must persuade her that they are or speak for that authority; cultural indoctrination inculcates in children the idea that the alien or its religion is the mouthpiece of the only God, an assertion the adult Dr. Tyler has immediately rejected. In contrast, Dr. Tyler's son is not abducted during the course of the film; the viewer may surmise that Dr. Tyler's son was previously abducted and indoctrinated against his mother, or that his hostility toward her serves him as a kind of inoculation, making it unnecessary for the aliens to intervene and splinter him from his remaining family. He is already becoming sufficiently hostile, condemnatory, and abandoning to serve the invading aliens' apparent purpose of divide-and-conquer, a fictionally depicted behavior that colonial education seems historically and realistically to inspire, as in p'Bitek's *Lawino*, Achebe's *Arrow of God,* and wa Thiong'o's *The River Between*. Thus, Osunsanmi's jarring perspective about the atrocities of alien takeover presents a brutal realism.

Surviving cultures may have much to teach a twenty-first century global community about facing encroaching devastation. As Octavia Butler has one of her heroines state: "God / Is Change,"[32] as if foretelling the tragedies of Emecheta's *The Rape of Shavi*, in which a planeload of Europeans fleeing their own self-annihilating civilization crash into a seemingly timeless, previously isolated fictional African kingdom. In this microcosmic reenactment of European settlers accidentally marooning themselves within an older community whose ways they neither understand nor intend to respect, intercultural interaction is consistently disastrous. The dissatisfied, conflicted Europeans are incapable of learning from or coexisting peacefully with the complexities of Shavi civilization: "they must have sounded barbaric to these gentle people,"[33] the Europeans' disillusioned pilot sadly reflects as he realizes the Shavians have treated the refugees to hospitality at the hands of their highest-ranking women:

> "Sometimes I think we should blow ourselves up, and give Mother Africa an opportunity to produce a new set of humans, better equipped to cope with the world. All we've so far produced are instruments of physical and moral destruction," ruminated Flip.... "When we came here, they made the best of their women, the would-be Queen Mother, look after us before they could even be sure we were humans like them. They had no way of knowing, because we don't speak the same language, but they trusted us with their best."[34]

The outnumbering Shavians do not manage to calm the Europeans who have come among them, uninvited but nurtured. Instead, seemingly trivial objects and arguments representative of the alien culture foreshadow destruction of the centuries-old Shavi civilization. Because the Europeans come from a culture of diametrically opposed values and habits, one of their members thinks the queen-to-be must be a servant girl of no account because she has been assigned care of the aliens, so he rapes her, thus infecting the newlywed king with syphilis insanity, symbolizing self-destructive Europeanization. Too late, the reader, the Europeans, and the Shavians realize that the aliens have brought infectious self-annihilation with them; the Shavians' succor of refugees fleeing their countries' threat of nuclear war has been an act of community suicide. Like Osunsanmi's *The Fourth Kind*, Emecheta's *The Rape of Shavi* was criticized in Europe and the United States.

Be European/American rejection of the validity of critical Nigerian sf voices as it may, it is worth noting that the Nigerian storytellers discussed in this essay—including Osunsanmi—have given their colonized victims agency. According to Equiano, Achebe, Nwapa, Emecheta, and Osunsanmi, the actions of the protagonists' ancestors may have drawn alien invasion and takeover; having inherited spiritual responsibility for wars of aggression and other acts of destruction, the colonized can now make decisions about how to navigate their devastated landscape, focusing on the limited empowerment of actionable options, however bleak. Both of the would-be princesses who are the protagonists of Nwapa's *Efuru* and Emecheta's *Joys of Motherhood* find that, caught in the upheaval of British takeover, their inherited royal status means little or nothing to their choice of husbands, vocations, and eventual community status. Only after finding themselves abandoned and scrambling for survival at the lowest levels of their own social hierarchies do these heroines begin the slow recasting of themselves, preparing a way back to tradition. These writers' depictions of Igbo theologies may resist the stasis of racial and gendered hegemonies and feel threatening to some readers. However, as with the story of the vengeance of a young god on an older, more venerated one in Achebe's *Arrow of God*, in Emecheta's *Joys of Motherhood*, it is not European greed but African karma, the spiritual debt of a kingdom bringing down another kingdom, a king enslaving neighboring royalty, that has brought aliens overrunning, colonizing, and debasing the ruling classes of Nigeria. Whatever the cause, the result is the consistent mass self-destruction of the colonized, a neurotic drive to self-erasure resulting in cultural implosion, such as is described in Fanon's *The Wretched of the Earth*.

Finally, not only are unwilling immersion in an unflattering mirror and audience helplessness possible motives for critical resistance to *The Fourth Kind*, but that film, like its predecessor *The Cavern*, notably lacks European/American male leadership. Whatever the double-standard accusations and unsubstantiated criticisms leveled at Osunsanmi, his choosing not to place men of European descent in heroic juxtaposition against ethnic-minority men and against women of any race in his films may be the actual trigger for most critical and popular attack. European-descent male leadership has been a highly visible trope of sf film since its inception. Not only do the European-American men in *The Fourth Kind* lack any discernible capacity for leadership in times of crisis, but they are also exemplary instigators of self-destructive community implosion: one of the psychologist's traumatized patients shoots his family and himself in his distress and confusion; the psychologist learns that her husband has already shot himself, and she has spent the duration of the film in traumatic amnesia about the event; her son blames and abandons her for the disappearance of her daughter; the police chief spends the film in denial about alien invasion and in pursuit of the psychologist for all the above unexplained or suspicious deaths and disappearances. As with Equiano's captured boy self who comes to love and willingly serve some of his captors and only cooperatively pursues what freedom is possible in an international chattel enslavement community, as with Achebe's god-maddened and interrelationally blind chief priest, and as with Emecheta's syphilitic young king, it is the European-American men of *The Fourth Kind* who further the neurotic cultural erosion first introduced by the invading aliens. These men's apparent unwillingness to grasp what is being done to their community means that the aliens' increasing power grows within it unseen, like a house destroyed by termites but still standing. Osunsanmi's European-American men appear to succumb to the comparatively seductive surrender of embracing their brainwashing, like p'Bitek's Ocol and the lethal patriarchs, wa Thiong'o's Joshua and Dangarembga's Babamukuru.

In a genre that has been slow to distribute heroism among differing ethnicities and genders, Osunsanmi's unapologetic presentation of one confused, frightened, or condemnatory European-American male after another, compared to two objectively fact-finding men of African descent and a psychologically destroyed but courageous woman of their own race, may have made of *The Fourth Kind* a sf racial and gendered site of upheaval. If this idea merits closer investigation, then the critical and popular voices deriding Osunsanmi and his most well-known film will need to demonstrate how his use of historical fact to perpetrate fictional verisimilitude differs from that of other creative writers who have used far-fetched or fantastic fictions to explain observable facts. Actually, the fictional explaining of real-world facts is a traditional trope of trickster tales in Nigeria, as demonstrated in Oyekan Owomoyela's collection of *Yoruba Trickster Tales*. Owomoyela explains that the use of the tortoise trickster's incredible adventures to understand factual realities "enables [the Yoruba] to dramatize remarkable qualities that could stand those who possess them in good stead in coping with a difficult world."[35] Notably, in *The Fourth Kind*, it is two African-descent men—inheritors of cultural communities that have repeatedly attempted to rebuild and make sense of their lives after invasion has shattered and scattered them—who fact-gather in the face of the horror. While the film's men of African descent provide an opportunity for characters and viewers to understand the phenomena witnessed in the film, the European-American men—who may have collectively inherited the benefit of their own ancestors' perpetration of alien invasion but apparently not the cultural perspectives learned by surviving it—fall apart.

Osunsanmi's inversion of the assumptions of racial and ethnic superiority of character and intellect seem to fly in the face of traditional tropes of sf. Notably successful compromises of this pattern may be the cooperative interracial leadership of the two men who bomb the aliens' mothership in *Independence Day*, and the ethnically ambiguous (though portrayed by an African American actor) ex-prisoner whose exploits have developed the *Chronicles of Riddick* franchise from *Pitch Black*. Perhaps Osunsanmi's lack of at least one cooperative European-American man in charge of the story's fact-gathering, combined with his lack of racial ambiguity characterizing his knowledgeable, self-assured

African men, has placed *The Fourth Kind* itself in a leadership role as a racially anticolonial sf film ahead of its time.

In *The Map of the Sky*, Palma has H. G. Wells argue that he wrote *War of the Worlds* "to criticize Europe's colonization of Africa," forcing English readers to experience how it is to be treated as though "humans deserved no more consideration than cockroaches":

> Within a matter of days, our neighbors in space had trampled on the Earth dwellers' values and self-respect with the same disdain the British showed toward the native populations in their empire. They had taken control of the entire planet, enslaving the inhabitants and transforming Earth into something resembling a spa for Martian elites. Nothing whatsoever had been able to stand in their way. Wells had intended this dark fantasy as an excoriating attack on the excessive zeal of British imperialism, which he found loathsome.[36]

If, as Palma appears to theorize, alien-invasion sf might conceivably have been invented to communicate the horrors of alien invasion to its earthly beneficiaries, the European communities that sponsored global colonization, then perhaps *The Fourth Kind* succeeds too well at what *The War of the Worlds* was created to do. As an alien-invasion immersion experience created by a descendant of a colonized culture, perhaps *The Fourth Kind* forces too visceral an experience of hopelessness upon an audience seeking to be reassured, conversely, that it has always been destined to triumph.

Toward Inclusiveness of African sf

Though it is popularly supposed that African writers rarely address sf, this essay demonstrates that traditional sf elements are present in twentieth-century African literature that explores the cultural destruction brought about by the Transatlantic Human Trade and European colonization of the African continent. While a single Nigerian text such as Equiano's *Interesting Narrative*, Achebe's *Arrow of God*, Emecheta's *Rape of Shavi*, or Ben Okri's *Famished Road* could furnish substantial material to support this argument, this essay offers for considered inclusion in the sf genre several texts by Nigerian and other African/Diaspora authors. Finally, this essay offers a comparative reading of Osunsanmi's *The Fourth Kind* as the consummate sf re-creation of the experience of community destabilization and personal devastation undergone by survivors of the Transatlantic Human Trade and African continental colonization. This essay demonstrates that, while immersing viewers in the experience of uncovering alien invasion, indoctrination, and cultural destruction, the audience is simultaneously exposed to an antihegemonic overturning of expected racial and gendered tropes of leadership.

Osunsanmi offers blatantly antihegemonic cues to prompt such decoding: none of the European-American men in *The Fourth Kind* evidence leadership capacity, clear-sightedness, level-headedness, or objective detachment. The heroine of European descent, Dr. Tyler, a seeming feminist stand-in for the absent leading male of her race, relies upon the film's two men of obvious African descent for intellectual guidance and moral support. *The Fourth Kind* thereby forces its audience to acknowledge potential socially taught biases by first querying, then overturning, and finally undermining them. Comparative analysis should be undertaken to determine if *The Fourth Kind*'s antihegemony of disempowered European-American males works more disruptively than in *The Matrix*, in which a racially ambiguous male protagonist is led by a male of clearly African descent to an ultimate Godhead that represents primordial Eve, a caretaking mother-figure of African descent, whose teachings are, however, not only resisted but effectively suppressed by the powers of a satanic corporate Anglo-American male antagonist.

Traditional sf elements in *The Fourth Kind* reenact a systematic process of cultural-destruction mirroring what was brought about by the Transatlantic Human Trade and the English colonization of the region that became known as Nigeria. Osunsanmi thereby reinterprets the human trade and colonization of the continent as classic sf: alien invasion. *The Fourth Kind* may therefore feel more informative or experiential than entertaining. It is arguable that Osunsanmi's false documentary risks not being seen as enjoyable because most viewers' dominant European/American culture does not triumph over this particular adversity. *The Fourth Kind*'s alien invasion is not depicted as one more daunting contest that European/American societies are manifestly destined to win. Instead, the film's message seems suddenly distanced and objective, relentlessly demonstrating that it is not the most nebulously "superior" but the most systematically invasive, lethally armed, technologically equipped, and morally ruthless culture that vanquishes its undeclared target. According to Osunsanmi's *The Fourth Kind*, present-day European-America might not only be beaten before it knows it is in a contest by enslaving and colonizing alien invaders similar to those who swarmed Africa; more importantly, European-America might not have any better collective comprehension than did sixteenth-through-eighteenth-century multinational Africans that an undeclared war is under way. Ironically, *The Fourth Kind*'s alien invasion takes place in one of North America's most frigid outposts, where the devastation of biological and ecological warfare waged against indigenous populations has not been masked by forced or coerced replacement by racially targeted enslaved or otherwise subjugated laborers. In this Alaskan environment, the extraterrestrial aliens' victims must of necessity be descendants of North America's European colonizing aliens, calling to mind historical waves of irresistible conquest followed by such empires' eventual implosion.

As the camera pans the Alaskan wilderness in closing, questions linger about the unseen extent of *The Fourth Kind*'s extraterrestrial alien takeover of the Earth's peoples. Iyunolu Folayan Osagie describes Sengbe Pieh's likely devastated return to a chaotic Sierra Leone following his comrades' successful revolt against enslavement aboard the *Amistad*, and their fight for liberty in what was then one of the human-trading capitals of the world, the United States. If such extraordinary historical confluences of courage and serendipity as Joseph Cinqué/Sengbe Pieh's are insufficient to restore to him what invading aliens have precipitously stolen, meaning his family, community, and lifestyle, then the knowledgeable viewer must ask what hope there is for *The Fourth Kind*'s population. Perhaps an audience cannot finish viewing *The Fourth Kind* without feeling deeply unsettled, having caught sight of self and culture in an unflatteringly candid light, just as Félix J. Palma's H. G. Wells seems to have intended his *War of the Worlds* to provide.

Notes

1. IDEASmi, "Nigerian Directors."
2. "*Orphanage* by Robert Buettner," Goodreads, accessed August 2, 2017, https://www.goodreads.com/book/show/395738.Orphanage?from_search=true.
3. See Clayton, "Author Interview."
4. See the *Rotten Tomatoes* pages for *The Fourth Kind* (https://www.rottentomatoes.com/m/district_9) and *District 9* (https://www.rottentomatoes.com/m/district_9).
5. Nikfyst, Message Board.
6. Dean Nicholas, "The 1938 Broadcast of 'The War of the Worlds,'" October 30, 2011, accessed August 2, 2017, http://www.historytoday.com/blog/2011/10/1938-radio-broadcast-war-worlds.
7. Egbuna, "Lashes on a Nigerian Woman's Back."
8. Soyinka, *Myth, Literature, and the African World*, 41.
9. Ibid., 3.
10. Armah, *Two Thousand Seasons*, 203.
11. DuBois, *The Souls of Black Folk*, part. 3, chap. 1, and *Darkwater*.
12. Soyinka, *Myth, Literature, and the African World*, 2.
13. Wells, *Short History*, 984–85.
14. Johnston, *History*, 102.
15. David Smith, *Untitled* (1978), Hannah Hall, Texas Southern University, Houston.
16. P'Bitek, *Song of Lawino/Song of Ocol*, 117.

17. Ibid., 98.

18. Ibid., 115.

19. Ibid.

20. Ibid., 50.

21. Armah, *Two Thousand Seasons*, 202.

22. Achebe, *Hopes and Impediments*, 64.

23. "Drapetomania" was the pseudoscientific psychiatric theory that African-descent captives' efforts to escape enslavement were the result of a mental illness, probably caused by the ability to speak English or other European languages, to read and to reason, all of which led the enslaved to mistakenly believe that they were human and potentially equal to their European-descent captors. The prescribed preventative and cure for Drapetomania was the constant exercise of barbarous acts of cruelty designed to intimidate, humiliate, dehumanize, and break the spirit, to be perpetrated by conscientious captors. See, among other sources, Beard, *Drapetomania*.

24. See, among other sources, Holloway, *Passed On*.

25. Fatunmbi, *Oya*, 3, 10.

26. Ibid., 12–13.

27. Ibid., 16.

28. Quarrie, "Blue Roebuck."

29. See Brooks de Vita, *Mythatypes*.

30. Equiano, *Interesting Narrative*, chap. 2.

31. Equiano, *Hopes and Impediments*, 64.

32. Butler, *Parable of the Sower*, 1.

33. Emecheta, *Shavi*, 54.

34. Ibid., 102.

35. Owomoyela, *Yoruba Trickster Tales*, xiv.

36. Palma, *Map of the Sky*, chap. 1.

Bibliography

28 Days Later. Dir. Danny Boyle. United States: 20th Century Fox, 2002.

28 Weeks Later. Dir. Juan Carlos Fresnadillo. United States: 20th Century Fox, 2007.

Achebe, Chinua. *Arrow of God*. New York: Anchor Books, 1974.

———. *Hopes and Impediments: Selected Essays*. New York: Anchor Books, 1990.

Armah, Ayi Kwei. *Two Thousand Seasons*. Oxford: Heinemann Educational Publishers, 1979.

Avatar. Dir. James Cameron. United States: 20th Century Fox, 2009.

Bamboozled. Dir. Spike Lee. United States: New Line Cinema, 2000.

Beard, Derrick Joshua. *Drapetomania, a Disease Called Freedom: An Exhibition of Eighteenth-, Nineteenth- and Early Twentieth-Century Material Culture of the African Experience in the Americas from the Collection of Derrick Joshua Beard*. Fort Lauderdale: Bienes Center for the Literary Arts, 2000.

Beloved. Dir. Jonathan Demme. United States: Buena Vista Pictures, 1998.

The Blair Witch Project. Dir. Eduardo Sánchez and Daniel Myrick. United States: Artisan Entertainment, 1999.

Bould, Mark. "African Science Fiction 101." *Science Fiction Research Association Review* 311 (Winter 2015): 11–18.

———. "Introduction." *Paradoxa* 25 (African SF). Accessed January 7, 2017. http://paradoxa .com/volumes/25/introduction.

Brooks de Vita, Alexis. *Mythatypes: Signatures and Signs of African/Diaspora and Black Goddesses*. 2000; reprint, Santa Barbara, Calif.: ABC/CLIO, 2009.

Brooks de Vita, Novella. "Beloved and Betrayed: Survival and Authority in *Kindred*." *The Griot* 22.1 (Spring 2003): 16.

———. "WHO is the Monster: Profiling Dr. Who as Antivillain or Antihero." Paper presented at the International Conference for the Fantastic in the Arts. Orlando, Fla., March, 2012.

Bugul, Ken. *Le baobab fou*. Paris: Les nouvelles éditions africaines, 1984.

Busch, Jenna. Rev. of *The Fourth Kind*. *Huffington Post*, March 18, 2010; updated May 25, 2011. Accessed August 4, 2017. http://www.huffingtonpost.com/jenna-busch/emthe-fourth -kindem-revie_b_342812.html.

Butler, Octavia. *Adulthood Rites*. New York: Warner Books, 1988.

———. "Bloodchild." 2d ed. New York: Open Road Media Sci-Fi and Fantasy, 2012.

———. *Dawn*. New York: Warner Books, 1987.

———. *Imago*. New York: Warner Books, 1989.

———. *Kindred*. New York: Doubleday, 1979.

———. *Parable of the Sower*. New York: Warner Books, 1993.

Carey, M. R. *The Girl with All the Gifts*. London: Orbit, Kindle Edition, 2014.

The Cavern. (originally *WIthIn*). Dir. Olatunde Osunsanmi. United States: Spotlight Pictures, 2005.

Clayton, Dhonielle. "Author Interview: Nnedi Okorafor and *Akata Witch*." *Teen Writers' Bloc*, September 10, 2012. Accessed February 12, 2017. http://www.teenwritersbloc.com/ 2012/09/10/nnedi-okafur/.

Cloverfield. Dir. Matt Reeves. United States: Paramount Pictures, 2008.

Dangarembga, Tsitsi. *Nervous Conditions*. Seattle: Seal Press, 1989.

Deep Impact. Dir. Mimi Leder. United States: Paramount Pictures, 1998.

Dery, Mark. *Flame Wars: The Discourse of Cyberculture*. Durham, N.C.: Duke University Press, 1994.

District 9. Dir. Neill Blomkamp. United States: TriStar Pictures, 2009.

"District 9." *Rotten Tomatoes*. Accessed August 4, 2017. https://www.rottentomatoes.com/ m/district_9.

DuBois, W. E. B. *Darkwater: Voices from within the Veil*, 1920; reprint, New York: Oxford University Press, 2007.

———. *The Souls of Black Folk*. 1903. Project Gutenberg. Accessed August 4, 2017. http:// www.gutenberg.org/files/408/408-h/408-.htm.

Ebert, Roger. Rev. of *The Fourth Kind*. *RogerEbert.com*. November 4, 2009. Accessed August 4, 2017. http://www.rogerebert.com/reviews/the-fourth-kind-2009.

Egbuna, Ekwutosi. "Lashes on a Nigerian Woman's Back: An African Woman's Reading of African American Literature." Paper presented at the Seventh Annual Gender, Sex, and Power Conference. University of Houston-Downtown, April 2014.

Emecheta, Buchi. *The Joys of Motherhood*. Portsmouth, N.H.: Heinemann Educational Publishers, 1979.

———. *The Rape of Shavi*. New York: George Braziller, 1985.

Equiano, Olaudah. *The Interesting Narrative of Olaudah Equiano or Gustavus Vassa, the African, Written by Himself*. London: Middlesex Hospital, 1789. Project Gutenberg. Accessed August 4, 2017. http://www.gutenberg.org/files/15399/15399-h/15399-h.htm.

Eurpublisher02. "Deal for Film 'Eden', Modern Take on Underground Railroad." *Lee Bailey's EurWeb.com: Electronic Urban Report*. Accessed August 4, 2017. http://www.eurweb.com/ 2013/03/deal-for-film-eden-modern-take-on-underground-railroad/ #JBHbaJulCmUAuO7q.99.

Fanon, Frantz. *Peau noire, masques blancs* (*Black Skin, White Masks*). Paris: Seuil, 1952.

———. *The Wretched of the Earth* (*Les damnés de la terre*). Trans. Richard Philcox. New York: Grove Press, 2004.

Fatunmbi, Awo Fá'lokun. *Obatala: Ifá and the Chief of the Spirit of the White Cloth*. Plainview, N.Y.: Original Publications, 1993.

———. *Oya: Ifá and the Spirit of the Wind*. Bronx, N.Y.: Original Publications, 1993.

The Fourth Kind. Dir. Olatunde Osunsanmi. United States: Universal Pictures, 2009.

"The Fourth Kind." *Rotten Tomatoes*. Accessed August 4, 2017. http://www.rottentomatoes.com/m/fourth_kind/.

Goldberg, Matt. "Warner Bros. Shelves 'Found Footage' Sci-Fi *Dark Moon*, but Dark Castle May Pick It Up." *Collider*, November 10, 2010. Accessed August 4, 2017. http://collider.com/tag/olatunde-osunsanmi/.

Golding, William. *Lord of the Flies*.London: Faber and Faber, 1954.

Harris, Trudier. *Exorcising Blackness: Historical and Literary Lynching and Burning Rituals*. Bloomington: Indiana University Press, 1984.

Hogan, Linda. *Mean Spirit*. New York: Ivy Books, 1990.

Holloway, Karla F. C. *Passed On: African American Mourning Stories*. Durham, N.C.: Duke University Press, 2002.

IDEASmi. "Nine Nigerian Directors to Watch Out For." Internet Movie Database. Accessed September 28, 2017. http://www.imdb.com/list/ls075800724/.

Independence Day. Dir. Roland Emmerich. United States: 20th Century Fox, 1996.

Ishiguro, Kazuo. *Never Let Me Go*. London: Faber and Faber, 2005.

Johnston, Sir Harry H., K.C.B. *A History of the Colonization of Africa by Alien Races*. Cambridge: Cambridge University Press, 1899. Accessed August 4, 2017. http://scans.library.utoronto.ca/pdf/5/25/historyofcoloniz00johnuoft/historyofcoloniz00johnuoft.pdf.

Jones, Gayl. *Corregidora*. Boston: Beacon Press. 1987.

The Leftovers. Dir. Damon Lindelof and Tom Perrotta. United States: Warner Bros. Television, 2014–.

The Matrix. Dir. Lana Wachowski and Lilly Wachowski. United States: Warner Bros., 1999.

McNary, Dave. "Gold Circle Heading to 'Eden' with Olatunde Osunsanmi." *Variety*. Accessed August 4, 2017. http://variety.com/2013/film/news/gold-circle-heading-to-eden-with-olatunde-osunsanmi-1200329372/.

The Mist. Dir. Frank Darabont. United States: Metro-Goldwyn-Meyer and Dimension Films, 2007.

Mofolo, Thomas. *Chaka*. Trans. Daniel P. Kunene. Oxford: Heinemann Educational Publishers, 1981.

Morrison, Toni. *Beloved*. New York: Alfred Knopf, 1987.

The Mothman Prophecies. Dir. Mark Pellington. United States: Screen Gems Sony Pictures Entertainment, 2002.

Never Let Me Go. Dir. Mark Romanek. United States: Fox Searchlight Pictures, 2010.

Nicholas, Dean. "The 1938 Radio Broadcast of 'The War of the Worlds.'" *History Today*, October 30, 2011. Accessed August 4, 2017. http://www.historytoday.com/blog/2011/10/1938-radio-broadcast-war-worlds.

Nikfyst. Message Board, April 09, 2012. Accessed March 26, 2013. IMDb.com.

Nwapa, Flora. *Efuru*. 1966; reprint, Long Grove, Ill.: Waveland Press, 2014.

Obenson, Tambay A. "Olatunde Osunsanmi Will Write and Direct Sci-Fi Alien Project 'Eden' for Gold Circle Films." *IndieWire*, March 26, 2013. Accessed August 4, 2017. http://www.indiewire.com/2013/03/olatunde-osunsanmi-will-write-direct-sci-fi-alien-project-eden-for-gold-circle-films-136960/.

Okorafor, Nnedi. "African Science Fiction Is Still Alien." Nnedi's Wahala Zone Blog, January 15, 2014. Accessed August 4, 2017. http://nnedi.blogspot.com/2014/01/african-science-fiction-is-still-alien.html.

———. "Can You Define African Science Fiction?" *Science Fiction and Fantasy Writers of America*, March 16, 2010. Accessed August 4, 2017. http://www.sfwa.org/2010/03/can-you-define-african-science-fiction/.

Okri, Ben. *The Famished Road*. New York: Anchor Books, 1991.

Onwualu, Chinelo. "African Science Fiction and Literature." *Omenana*, August 7, 2016. Accessed August 4, 2017. https://omenana.com/2016/08/07/essay-african-science-fiction-and-literature/.

Osagie, Iyunolu Folayan. *The Amistad Revolt: Memory, Slavery, and the Politics of Identity in the United States and Sierra Leone*. Athens: University of Georgia Press, 2000.

Owomoyela, Oyekan. *Yoruba Trickster Tales*. Lincoln: University of Nebraska Press, 1997.

Oyono, Ferdinand. *Une vie de boy*. Paris: René Julliard, 1956.

Palma, Félix J. *The Map of the Sky*. New York: Atria Books, 2012.

Paris Is Burning. Dir. Jennie Livingston. United States: Miramax Films, 1991.

P'Bitek, Okot. *Song of Lawino* and *Song of Ocol*. Portsmouth: Heinemann Educational Publishers, 1984.

Pitch Black. Dir. David Twohy. United States: USA Films and Gramercy Pictures, 2000.

Pumzi. Dir. Wanuri Kahiu. United States: Focus Features, 2009.

Quarrie, Deanne. "The Orishas." *The Blue Roebuck*. 2008. Accessed August 4, 2017. http://www.blueroebuck.com/orishas.html.

"Robert_Buettner." *Goodreads.com*. February 3, 2015. Accessed August 4, 2017. https://www.goodreads.com/author/show/118294.Robert_Buettner.

"Saturday Night Massacre" and "Space Oddity." Dir. Olatunde Osunsanmi. *Falling Skies*. United States: Warner Bros. Television, 2014.

Serpell, Namwali. "Africa Has Always Been Sci-Fi: On Nnedi Okorafor and a New Generation of Afrofuturists." *Literary Hub*, April 1, 2016. Accessed August 4, 2017. http://lithub.com/africa-has-always-been-sci-fi/#.

Soyinka, Wole. *Myth, Literature, and the African World*. Cambridge: Canto, 1992.

Star Wars. Dir. George Lucas. United States: 20th Century Fox, 1977.

Stargate. Dir. Roland Emmerich. United States: Metro-Goldwyn-Meyer and Carolco Pictures, 1994.

Strugatsky, Arkady, and Boris Strugatsky. *Roadside Picnic*. Trans. Olena Bormashenko. Chicago: Chicago Review Press, 2012.

Tales of the Grim Sleeper. Dir. Nick Broomfield. United States: HBO Documentary Films, 2014.

Tutuola, Amos. *The Palm Wine Drinkard*. New York: Grove Press, 1953.

Underworld. Dir. Len Wiseman. United States: Screen Gems, 2003.

Wa Thiong'o, Ngugi. *The River Between*. London: Heinemann Educational Books, 1980.

Wabuke, Hope. "Nnedi Okorafor Is Putting Africans at the Center of Science Fiction and Fantasy." *The Root*, December 29, 2015. Accessed August 4, 2017. http://www.theroot.com/articles/culture/2015/12/nnedi_okorafor_is_putting_africans_at_the_center_of_science_fiction_and/.

Wells, H. G. *The Outline of History: Being a Plain History of Life and Mankind*. New York: Macmillan, 1921.

———. *A Short History of the World*. New York: MacMillan, 1922.

———. *The War of the Worlds*. London: William Heinemann, 1898.

Wood, Nick. "Academia and the Advance of African Science Fiction." *Omenana*, March 5, 2015. Accessed August 4, 2017. https://omenana.com/2015/03/05/academia-and-the-advance-of-african-science-fiction/.

Woodson, Carter Godwin. *The Mis-education of the Negro* [1933]. Ed. and intro. Charles H. Wesley and Thelma D. Perry. *History Is a Weapon*. Accessed August 4, 2017. http://www.historyisaweapon.com/defcon1/misedne.html.

World War Z. Dir. Marc Forster. United States: Paramount Pictures, 2013.

Johanna Sinisalo
and the New Weird

Genres and Myths

HANNA-RIIKKA ROINE AND HANNA SAMOLA

A Versatile Writer

Johanna Sinisalo (b. 1958) is a figure of long standing in the Finnish science-fiction and fantasy scene, and she is also known as a writer of more mainstream literature. Before her career as a professional writer, she started publishing short stories in various Finnish sf fanzines. In 1986 she received her first Atorox Award for the best Finnish sf short story of the year; she has since won the award six times. In 2000, she became the first (and so far, the only) Finnish sf/fantasy writer awarded the prestigious Finlandia Prize for literature, for her first novel, *Ennen päivänlaskua ei voi* (Not before sundown).[1] The same novel was awarded the James Tiptree Jr. Prize in 2004. In 2009, Sinisalo was also nominated for a Nebula Award for the novelette "Baby Doll" (2002). Her work has been translated into several languages, including English, Swedish, Japanese, French, and German.

Sinisalo is a versatile writer: in addition to literary fiction, she has authored numerous scripts and screenplays for comics, television productions, radio programs, and the internationally released sf comedy film *Iron Sky* (2012). Despite the variety, certain themes are prominent, especially in her written fiction. Sinisalo names Tove Jansson's Moomin stories as the most influential books she read at an early age, and Ursula K. Le Guin, Margaret Atwood, Michael Tournier, and Ray Bradbury as her literary heroes.[2] These acknowledged influences are definitely noticeable in the recurrent themes of Sinisalo's novels, which include, among others, topics related to sex and gender (*Auringon ydin* [*The Core of the Sun*]; 2013, trans. 2016), otherness (*Not before Sundown*), and ecological issues (*Enkelten verta* [*The Blood of Angels*]; 2011, trans. 2014; and *Linnunaivot* [*Birdbrain*]; 2008, trans. 2010). The references to Finno-Ugric mythology and folklore often give a special twist to her work, most notably in the *Kalevala*-influenced *Sankarit* (Heroes; 2003). For instance, a path to the mythical life hereafter might appear in the mind of a human being, or concretely in the attic of a shed, where it may be opened with the help of dead queen bees.

Among the most distinctive features of Sinisalo's work is the introduction of fantastic elements into realistically depicted milieus and the self-reflexive combinations of various genres and text-types. In *Not before Sundown*, for example, the protagonist who lives in the urban milieu of contemporary Tampere discovers a troll cub. The contrast between the modern story and its mythical, dark fairy-tale underpinnings is one of the foundations for the novel, and this is realized both at the level of events and characters and in the structure of the work. Throughout the novel, short first-person snippets are intercut with reference material of online and print vintage, recounting the Finnish history of troll sightings and the symbolic significance of the forest creatures in the nation's myth and folklore. *Birdbrain* evokes Joseph Conrad's *Heart of Darkness* (1899) not only thematically but also because the text is scattered with references to the novel.[3] Such self-reflexive references are often the source of Sinisalo's humor: her novels (along with the film *Iron Sky*) wink at readers acquainted with the sf canon and parody the conventions of various text-types, such as commercials and folk poems.

The Finnish Weird as a Challenge to Realist Writing

In the marketing materials for her latest novel, *The Core of the Sun*, Sinisalo is situated as "part of the rule-breaking 'Finnish Weird' genre."[4] This genre—as well as the literary New Weird movement worldwide—has been quite topical over the last decade or so. In addition to Sinisalo, contemporary Finnish writers such as Pasi Ilmari Jääskeläinen, Leena Krohn, Tiina Raevaara, and Maarit Verronen have been mentioned in connection with the Finnish Weird (*suomikumma*). Concrete connections to the New Weird movement can be drawn: for example, an excerpt of Krohn's novel *Tainaron: Postia toisesta kaupungista* (*Tainaron: Mail from Another City*; 1985, trans. 2004) was included in the collection *The New Weird* (2008), edited by Jeff VanderMeer and Ann VanderMeer.

While the writers of New Weird have been outspoken in their goal to "subvert the romanticized ideas about place found in traditional fantasy,"[5] in the context of the Finnish Weird, the subversive features are designed to challenge the tradition of realist writing that has dominated the Finnish literary canon for a long time.[6] In a recent essay, Sinisalo argues that during the twentieth century the genre of realism became the correct way to write in Finland, while the other genres were seen as deviations from this norm: "One could generalize that until recent decades these deviations did not represent 'respectable' literature in Finland—we have had a tradition of reading fiction as if it were always somehow documentary, not as a piece of someone's wild imagination or allegory or satire."[7]

Sinisalo uses the umbrella term "Finnish Weird" to a similar rhetorical end as Jeff VanderMeer, for example, has done with the term "New Weird"—to challenge the old and the canonical, which are only defined in opposition to the new and the original. However, as a former professional in the advertising business, Sinisalo is consciously using the term as a brand, aiming for the same effect that the term "Nordic Noir" evokes as a label for a certain quality of detective and crime fiction originating in the Nordic countries. This is certainly one of the ways Sinisalo acts out her role as a prominent member of the science-fiction and fantasy scene of her home country: she actively promotes Finnish literature by means of a brand that is designed to cover Finnish stories experimenting with the elements of myth, magic, and the fantastic.

It is nevertheless interesting to compare Sinisalo's rhetoric with one of her major literary influences, Le Guin, who recently called upon her fellow fantasy and science-fiction writers, saying: "I think we need writers who know the difference between production of a market commodity and the practice of an art. The profit motive is often in conflict with the aims of art."[8] Le Guin's standpoint is rather polemical, but it can be asked whether Finnish Weird really works out apart from being a marketing category—and perhaps as the means of making writing that deviates from realism more visible.

The larger question of genre is obviously relevant not only from the viewpoint of marketing. Farah Mendlesohn has argued for the view of science fiction as a discussion.[9] In our view, genre can be understood as an ongoing discussion, but of a different kind. The theory of Alastair Fowler stresses the instability of genres and their ability to combine with other genres.[10] He states that a single work modulates the genre in which it takes part.[11] This makes genre less a means of classification than of communication between the author and the reader; the attempt to define the genre(s) of a single work is to try to find different meanings to the work.[12] The understanding of the nature of genre as communication is rather similar to Mendlesohn's view of science fiction as discussion. As with any genre, science fiction invites the reader to take part in a communication process with the work of art, the author, and the other works belonging to the tradition(s) to which a single work refers.

However, Mendlesohn continues: "The reader's expectations of sf are governed less by what happens than how that happening is described, and by the critical tools with which the reader is expected to approach the text."[13] Here, she aspires to describe a feature peculiar to sf: the fact that texts are often written by those active in criticism and can be generated from the same fan base that supports the market—a feature that is quite apparent in the attempts of the weird fiction writers to define or label their writing. Indeed, the field of science-fictional or speculative writing can be "a battleground" also from the viewpoint of readerly interpretation.

Among the defining features of contemporary weird fiction are the crossings of generic boundaries and the casual combinations of various types of texts as well as the radical mix of real and fictional. Various text passages making up Sinisalo's latest novel, *The Core of the Sun*, for example, include genuine historical documents, such as an article on eugenics that was published in a Finnish magazine in 1935. Meanwhile, the back-cover text presents the novel as a "chillingly fiery dystopia." In what follows, we explore the nature or building blocks of such fiction. What kind of elements does Sinisalo's technique make use of, and what do they bring to the readerly interpretation? Is there something unique to the way Sinisalo uses these elements?

Sinisalo in the Context
of Speculative and Weird Fiction

The genre of Finnish Weird, as well as the New Weird movement, has often been dubbed simply "speculative fiction," which has also been offered as an alternate name for the genre of science fiction. Not all science fiction is strictly speculative in this sense, though. The defining feature of speculative science fiction is the thought experiment, the "what if" that Darko Suvin has famously called the *novum*.[14] Mendlesohn notes that it is here that science fiction departs most fully from mainstream literature, because "in science fiction 'the idea' is the hero."[15] These starting points are crucial for most of Sinisalo's writing, but not the Finnish Weird in general, which includes more magical and fantastic stories, too.

Sinisalo's novels are usually built around thought experiment—at the core, she is a science-fiction writer who nevertheless is very flexible in making use of various other elements in her writing. This makes Sinisalo distinctive compared with most writers whose work has been brought up in relation to the New Weird movement. China Miéville, whose novel *Perdido Street Station* (2000) is widely mentioned as the first notable example of New Weird fiction, is an extremely "genre-conscious" writer, but the way he makes use of various genres differs from Sinisalo. In the case of *Perdido Street Station*, the conversation has centered around its defiant unclassifiability, and it was linked to several subgenres such as gothic or dark fantasy, weird fiction, and steampunk.[16] Sinisalo's usage of genres and text types is quite self-reflexive, and it is important to note that more often than not it is aimed at working out the thought experiment, the idea.

One of the main ideas of *The Core of the Sun*, for example, is the possibility of the domestication of human beings in the same way that humans have domesticated other animals. What would happen if only people with certain traits were allowed to reproduce? In this respect, the novel shares features with the traditions of feminist dystopia, feminist speculative fiction, and novels such as *Man's World* (1926) by Charlotte Haldane, *Swastika Night* (1937) by Katherine Burdekin, and *The Handmaid's Tale* (1985) by Margaret Atwood. In a technique similar to the abovementioned narrative structure of *Not before Sundown*, Sinisalo combines the depiction of fictional and fantastic human domestication with documents addressing sterilization and the domestication of silver foxes.

Sinisalo's skill as a writer allows such thought experiments to speak to us despite the fact that they are highly fabulous or fantastical. Robert Scholes has defined "fabulation" as any "fiction that offers us a world clearly and radically discontinuous from the one we know, yet returns to confront that known world in some cognitive way."[17] The point of discontinuity or dissonance with the known world is the Suvinian novum, but Scholes wants to emphasize the fact that despite discontinuity of this kind, science fiction can confront the world of our everyday experience. Similar ideas have been brought up in relation to the view of science fiction as a form of thought experiment where the *consequences* of some or other nova are worked through. This means that it is the scientific method, the logical working through of a particular premise, that is important to science fiction, not scientific accuracy.[18]

Some of the premises and their consequences discussed in Sinisalo's novels are closer to being reality than we would like to think. In *The Blood of the Angels*, the bees disappear suddenly and inexplicably, plunging the world into ecological chaos and the reader into thinking, What if we already have damaged our planet beyond repair? Some thought experiments are subtler or more conceptual: the hiking novel *Birdbrain*, for example, invites the reader to conceptualize the relationship between a man and a woman in terms of the relationship between man and nature—and vice versa. The novel questions the place of human in the ecosystem. Humans have brought the planet to the point where oceans are filled with plastic trash, and only small parts of the globe are still "virgin territory." The main characters are a young couple hiking in Tasmania and New Zealand. The male protagonist has an urge to conquer the land by walking on it. On their journey, he doubts the cleverness and abilities of his girlfriend. The title may refer to the arrogant view of the man, who sees the woman as a birdbrain, but, at the same time, it alludes to the bird Kea who is believed to be the cause of forest fires. In the end, the birdbrain proves to be more clever than the (hu)man brain.

Making the connection between the relationship of the sexes and the relationship of man and nature is probably new to many readers and therefore has the potential to evoke new types of viewpoint in them. One of the most important threads in Sinisalo's fiction is the attempt to confront our "known world" and highlight some of its problems by means of various contrasts and combinations. In this, she certainly follows in the steps of Le Guin, who has written on the subject of why science fiction is not predictive but descriptive: "The purpose of the thought-experiment, as the term was used by Schrödinger and other physicists, is not to predict the future . . . but to describe reality, the present world."[19] As we mentioned earlier, the contrasts are realized both at the level of events and characters and in the structure of the work. On the whole, *The Core of the Sun* aims to connect with the long tradition of discussing themes such as human-led evolution and selective breeding and to update them with contemporary questions linked to sexual discrimination and the idea of women's sexual power.

While the broad genre of speculative writing along with science-fictional thought experiments form a basis for most of Sinisalo's work, the way her novels reach out toward various other traditions and genres—such as satire and fairy tale—creates collisions that are typical of her writing not only stylistically but also rhetorically. Instead of using various genres, traditions, and text-types as sources of inspiration, Sinisalo's works often draw from their collisions and combinations in an original way. As a result, her novels like *Not before Sundown* and *The Core of the Sun* encourage readings from various viewpoints, as they can simultaneously (or alternatively) be read as pure what-if speculations, as satires of contemporary society, or as fairy tales resembling myths.

In addition to confronting the reader, there is also the sense of wonder that Mendlesohn names as a crucial feature of the mode of science fiction.[20]

In Sinisalo's works, the sense of wonder has multiple functions and is connected with different genre traditions, among which are science fiction, fairy tale, mythical story, and dystopia. In the following section, we examine the features of dystopian fiction and fairy tale in *The Core of the Sun*.

A Totalitarian and Dystopian Regime of the Alternative Future

In the context of Johanna Sinisalo's oeuvre, *The Core of the Sun* is her most satirical and most dystopian novel. It is perhaps the culmination of the style peculiar to her writing and a synthesis of the themes discussed in her previous works. It consists of first-person narratives of the protagonist Vanna/Vera and her boyfriend Jare, as well as excerpts from several documents, most of which are pseudo-authentic. On the pages of the novel there are, for example, a lottery advertisement, a folk poem, a retelling of a fairy tale, dictionary articles, and chapters from a guidebook for women. Together, these texts build an alternate history of the twentieth century in Finland under a totalitarian regime. This results not only in a stunning story but also in a satirical picture of contemporary European societies. Dystopia is sometimes understood as a serious genre, as it forewarns its readers of possible disasters, but Sinisalo's novel is linked to the tradition of satirical dystopias, and in this case, satire is perhaps the more dominant element.

The novel takes place in the fictional Eusistocratic Republic of Finland, where the citizens have been categorized into the gendered groups of Eloi and Morlock women and Masko and Minus men.[21] The Eusistocratian regime attempts to maintain the stability of the society by enabling satisfactory and sufficient amounts of sex for all men regardless of their social status or appearance. It is explained that before the sex laws were enacted, unmarried men used to be violent and threatened the stability of the society. This, in turn, is explained by their lack of sexual contact with women. The Eusistocratian state supports heterosexual marriages and high birth rates. To keep the women submissive to men, the state has organized experiments with the selective breeding of women. Those who are motherly, docile, and willing to marry—the Eloi—have a right to have children. Androgynous, independent, and unruly women, or Morlocks, have been forced to undergo sterilization. Some of the unmarried women serve their homeland in state-owned brothels.

The Core of the Sun describes the results of selective breeding several decades after the first domestication experiment. The life of women is depicted through the story of two sisters. The protagonist Vanna/Vera was born as an androgynous Morlock,[22] but her sister Manna/Mira is a stereotypically feminine Eloi. Eloi women embody stereotypically feminine traits with their round heads, curvy bodies, naivete, and tender characters. In short, they are presented as beautifully shaped but empty-headed, and their education encourages these features by limiting their possibilities to gain knowledge about the surrounding world. Meanwhile, Morlock women are depicted as intelligent and independent.

The theme of the manipulation of human beings connects the novel with the tradition of dystopian literature such as Aldous Huxley's *Brave New World* (1932), with its depiction of assembly lines of human embryos. The themes of male control of reproduction and limited sexual autonomy connect Sinisalo's novel to the subgenre of feminist dystopia. Forcing women to the status of breeders and fulfillers of male sexual needs is a means of oppression depicted in several feminist dystopias.[23] The terms "Eloi" and "Morlock" refer to the dystopian/utopian novel *The Time Machine* (1895) by H. G. Wells and its depiction of population divided into two groups: the Morlocks, whose members are ugly, oppressed, and forced to live underground; and the Eloi, who are beautiful, naive, hedonistic, and who exploit the products made by Morlocks.

The reference to Wells's novel connects Sinisalo's novel not only with the particular work but also to its genre and thus widens the interpretations of both works. In Sinisalo's novel, only women are named as Elois and Morlocks, but the idea of the connection between social class and appearance is one of the similarities of the societies depicted in these novels. In Wells's novel, the extremely classist society of the future is to be devastated. In this way, the intertextual reference to *The Time Machine* suggests to the reader of Sinisalo's novel that perhaps the Eusistocratian state is on its way to destruction despite the regime's attempts to convince its citizens that the society is perfectly organized.

Eusistocratian Finland resembles contemporary real-life Finland in multiple ways. The milieu of the novel is the city of Tampere (Sinisalo's hometown), and all the locations in the city are depicted in a realistic way. The welfare state and labyrinthine bureaucracy are common both to the real Finland and its Eusistocratian version, but in Eusistocratia, the health of the population is controlled to an extreme: for example, all alcohol and drugs (including hallucinogenic chili peppers) are prohibited. According to Raffaella Baccolini and Tom Moylan,[24] partial realism and the normality of the nightmare society are crucial elements of dystopian fiction. The way the protagonist begins to feel herself alienated and resists the system is the beginning of the counternarrative to the hegemonic ideology. In Sinisalo's novel, the way Vanna and her grandmother Aulikki differ

from normative femaleness and rebel against hegemonic rule develops a counternarrative for the ideological documents published by the state.

The superiority of Eusistocratia is validated in multiple ways by explaining
its history in a manner that fits the ruling ideology. On the pages of *The Core
of the Sun*, there are chapters from a pseudo-authentic history book called *The
Short History of the Domestication of Women*, published by the State in 1997.
This book presents experiments and research by the Russian geneticist Dimitri
Belyaev in which he bred wild silver foxes by favoring certain features in order
to domesticate them. In this text, the parallel is drawn between the life story
of Belyaev and the history of Finland: "Belyayev was born in 1917, the same
year that Finland gained its independence—an interesting example of how
history is far from random and is in fact filled with beautiful synchronicity! For
Dimitri Belyayev and his life's work are uniquely and inextricably intertwined
with Finland's destiny."[25] The breeding experiments performed by Belyaev are
analogous to the process in which Eusistocratia has forced the female population to obey men. The legislation controlling sex and gender is the cornerstone
of the politics of Eusistocratian bureaucratic society. The diversity of gender
and sexuality and the norms that limit the sexual behavior of humans have been
among the main topics of Sinisalo's works. In *Not before Sundown*, for example,
Sinisalo questions heteronormativity. All of the main characters in the novel are
homosexual men—and one troll. They are all, in their own way, others in the
society. *The Core of the Sun* questions the patriarchal system in which women
and the Minus men who do not fulfill the norms of masculinity are regarded
as inferior and fated to be submissive to the ruling men.

In Eusistocratia, all women have been reduced to their reproductive function. Women are silenced and forced to serve the needs of men. The categoriza-
tion of human beings into gendered groups and the double standard in sexual
politics resemble not only feminist dystopian fiction but also contemporary
Finland, with its ongoing discussions comparing sexual relationships with a
marketplace and conservative versus liberal views on marriage.[26] In the Eusistocratian Republic depicted in *The Core of the Sun*, neoconservatism, xenophobia,
conservative views on gender roles, and sexual selection of human beings are a
crucial part of the politics. By using documents written in the 1930s, the novel
draws a historical analogy between the beginning of the twenty-first century
and the 1930s in Europe, especially in Finland.

Sinisalo's novel is linked to the dystopian tradition by its depiction of the
hierarchical totalitarian regime and the oppression of human beings. What
makes this novel peculiar in the dystopian tradition is the use of mythological

motifs and the crucial role of magic in the survival of the main character. The explanations given for the deviations from our consensus reality are not only scientific or (pseudo)historical but also mythological and magical.

Myths, Magic, and Fairy Tales in Sinisalo's Work

In contemporary Finnish Weird and speculative fiction, mythological themes and fairy-tale elements play a crucial role. Tiina Raevaara, for example, uses fairy-tale motifs in her novels *Eräänä päivänä tyhjä taivas* (One day, an empty sky; 2008) and *Yö ei saa tulla* (Deny the night; 2015), while Pasi Ilmari Jääskeläinen's works also make reference to myths and fairy tales. The worldview of Sinisalo's novels is often mythological, and her novels include references to Finno-Ugric, Scandinavian, Siberian, and even Maori mythologies. In *The Core of the Sun*, those characters who are able to think only rationally may perish, but those having the ability to think outside the rational and normative ideology survive. Two of the characters—Aulikki and her granddaughter, Vanna/ Vera—possess shamanic powers. They have the ability to see and feel things invisible and unreachable to the majority of humans.

The idea of the hereafter or the Otherworld is peculiar to Sinisalo's oeuvre. In *The Blood of Angels*, Sinisalo develops the idea of bees being able to connect the everyday world to the hereafter and to bring knowledge from another world. In Finno-Karelian mythology, bees are considered liminal creatures between different worlds.[27] In *Not before Sundown*, the main character makes a journey into the darkness of the woods accompanied by a troll. They disappear into the forest cover (*metsänpeitto*), unreachable to most humans.[28]

Vanna/Vera is able to contact the Otherworld by using an especially strong variety of chili, prohibited by the Eusistocratian state. During her shamanistic journey, she takes the form of an elk, a wolf, and a bird. The entrance to the shamanistic lower world is in Vanna's mind. The shamanistic rituals of Vanna/ Vera refer to the shaman rites and poems by Chukchi people, who live by the Arctic Sea in northeastern Siberia.[29] The title of the novel may also be explained by the connection to Chukchi shamanism and their belief in the sun as the most powerful celestial character.[30] The extremely strong chili strain, cultivated by Vanna's friends, is named the Core of the Sun, and it opens the door for the protagonist to the freedom outside the totalitarian rule.

In the dystopian tradition, the protagonist's ability to survive in the oppressive society often plays a crucial role in the plot. Moylan and Baccolini discuss the differences between traditional and critical dystopias.[31] In a critical dystopia, the ending may be open, and there is a ray of hope left in the miserable situation. According to Baccolini and Moylan, critical dystopias also tend to cross generic boundaries: "By self-reflexively borrowing specific conventions from other genres, critical dystopias more often blur the received boundaries of the dystopian form and thereby expand its creative potential for critical expression."[32] If hopefulness and crossing genre boundaries are features of critical dystopia, *The Core of the Sun* may be connected with this tradition. Vanna's means of escape is quite unique, though: she escapes by flying away both concretely by plane and spiritually on her shamanic journey with the help of hallucinogenic chili.

In Sinisalo's novels, the elements of Finnish Weird, science fiction, dystopia, and mythologies are often accompanied with fairy-tale features. *Not before Sundown* retells Nordic beliefs in trolls and other mythological forest creatures by combining old tales with new ones. *Sankarit* is a postmodern pastiche of the national epic of Finland, *Kalevala*, with a fairy-tale twist. The characters of *The Core of the Sun* are those typical of many fairy tales: two sisters, a clever one and a stupid one; an old woman who has magical powers; an evil antagonist who is the husband of the stupid girl; and a witty young man as a savior. In the context of fairy tales, chili may be interpreted as a magical tool that helps the protagonist to succeed and survive.

A fairy tale called "Pikku Punanna" (Little Redianna) is one of the texts embedded in Sinisalo's novel. This short tale tells the story of a naive and beautiful girl named Redianna who is told to take medicine to her grandmother. On her way through the forest, Redianna meets a wolf who proposes to marry her. When Redianna turns him down, the wolf runs to the grandmother's house, eats her up, puts her nightgown on, and then lies down on the bed waiting for Redianna. When Redianna arrives, she wonders why grandmother has such weird and big features. The wolf answers and then throws off his wolf skin and reveals that he is a handsome prince who tested the obedience of the girl.

In the Western literary tradition, the fairy tale of a little girl who encounters a wolf in the forest has been retold multiple times and interpreted in many ways. One of the supposedly earliest versions of the story is called "The Story of a Grandmother," where the clever girl escapes the wolf by tricking him into believing that she is just going out for a pee. The versions of the story that have been dominant in Western culture were written by Charles Perrault ("Le Petit Chaperon Rouge"; 1697) and Jacob Grimm and Wilhelm Grimm ("Rotkäppchen"; 1812). Perrault and the Brothers Grimm altered the previous versions of the tale by adding a moral lesson and by depicting the girl as foolish, innocent, and helpless instead of the brave, clever, and active heroine of the folk versions. Perrault and the Grimms adapted the tale to suit the moral norms of their societies, and the latter eliminated erotic playfulness and sexuality from the tale.[33]

"Rotkäppchen" and "Le Petit Chaperon Rouge" have often been interpreted as cautionary tales with gendered warnings.[34] These versions warn girls not to listen to the seductions of strangers who pretend to be friendly. The wolf has usually been understood as representative of men, and the violence of the wolf as sexual violence. Jack Zipes argues that the Grimms and Perrault altered the story about an initiation of a young woman into a tale about sexual violence and the responsibility of a woman to prevent violence.[35] For her part, Christina Bacchilega suggests that in the literary tradition of "Little Red Riding Hood," the girl protagonist is either domesticated or devoured.[36]

The Eusistocratian version of the tale in Sinisalo's novel ostensibly repeats the morals of classical versions, but in the context of the whole novel, the morals of the Redianna tale and classical versions of "Little Red Riding Hood" ("Punahilkka" in Finnish) are ironized. The satirical point of the novel falls upon the absurd ways in which the masculinist society tries to keep women under control by protecting and patronizing them, and "Redianna" is an example of this attitude toward women. "Little Redianna" is published by the Eusistocratian state in the fairy-tale collection for girls titled *The Most Beautiful Fairy Tales for the Eloi Girls*. The name of the book parodies the way fairy tales have been retold to meet the ideals of the time of their publication. The collection of tales is part of the education work of the state that focuses on the behavior of girls and women.

The story of Redianna is a *mise en abyme*, which is analogous with the themes and character positions of the whole work, and as such it provides us pointers for the genre interpretation of the novel. This prospective *mise en abyme* is one of the self-reflexive elements, as it gives instructions for reading and misleads the reader at the same time.[37] Redianna shares common features with the Eloi sister Manna/Mira: the nasal sounds of their names, naivete, beauty, kindness, and willingness to marry a man. The didactic morality of "Little Redianna" is similar to the moral double standard in Eusistocratia: the story warns girls not to be disobedient to any man who may be disguised as a wolf. If a girl turns down a man once, she will never marry, which is the most horrifying punishment for a girl in Eusistocratia. The relation of "Little Redianna" to the classical versions of the tale is parodic in its altered lesson, but all these versions share the message: a girl must be obedient and domesticated, and if she is not, she will be punished.

In Sinisalo's novel, the wolf is also a symbol of the dystopian society that controls and stalks its citizens. At the end of the Redianna tale, the heroine asks the wolf about the size of his eyes and ears.

"Grandmother, what big eyes you have!" Redianna said.
"All the better to see with," the wolf replied.
"Grandmother, what big ears you have!" Redianna said.
"All the better to hear your thoughts with," the wolf replied.[38]

The wolf who hears the thoughts and sees everything around him behaves the same way as the paranoid state with its controlling Health Office. The wolf's answer to the question about the size of his mouth combines control and the greed to own: "The better to gobble you up and make you a part of myself and keep you as my own for the rest of my life."[39] This answer could be read as a representation of a jealous husband, but it also depicts the way in which the Eusistocratian state holds people, especially women, in its grip and tries to forestall the possibilities of escape from the country.

The motif of camouflage is crucial in *The Core of the Sun* and in many versions of "Little Red Riding Hood." In "Little Redianna," the prince uses multiple forms of camouflage: he pretends to be a wolf in the forest and thus tests the obedience of Redianna. In the grandmother's house, he is disguised in the clothes of dead grandmother. Surprisingly, the greatest pretender in Sinisalo's novel is not Manna's evil and murderous husband but the protagonist Vanna/Vera. Compared with the protagonists of the versions of "Little Red Riding Hood," she more closely resembles the resourceful and cunning girl of the old folk tales, but her character can also be associated with the wolf: on her shaman journey, she runs in the forest as a wolf and is able to hear the unstated thoughts of her sister Manna/Mira.[40]

As a wild creature of the forest and as a clever Morlock, Vanna/Vera strays from the path she has been ordered to take. She tries to survive in the Eusistocratian system by behaving womanly, like a true Eloi, with her feminine appearance. She tricks the bureaucrats into believing that she is harmless and innocent, but inside the makeup and dresses she is a clever Morlock who tries to rebel against the gender laws of Eusistocratia. At the end of the novel, she escapes from the state just like the girl escapes the wolf in "The Story of a Grandmother."

In this essay, we have discussed Johanna Sinisalo's fiction and especially *The Core of the Sun* from the viewpoint of generic interpretations that the novel evokes. We have analyzed various elements contributing to this medley and concentrated on the themes that are peculiar to Sinisalo's style. Another goal in our discussion has been to explore the "anatomy" of the genre (or brand) of Finnish Weird, which has been quite topical in the field of Finnish speculative writing.

More often than not, Sinisalo's self-reflexive use of genres and text types is aimed at working out the thought experiment, the idea. Therefore, at the core, she can be considered a science-fiction writer who nevertheless is very flexible in making use of elements drawn from multiple sources in her writing. However, it seems that the way Sinisalo combines various genres and text types and provides the reader with instructions for reading can be regarded as the strengths and the weaknesses of her written fiction. As we have earlier argued,[41] Sinisalo's choice to combine speculative thought experiment with the means of satire in *The Core of the Sun* may sometimes confuse the reader, as the comical side to satire has the potential to eat away the credibility and the terrifying effect of the dystopian society described. *The Core of the Sun* is at its funniest (and hits its satirical target most directly) when it turns to confront the contemporary view of romantic relationships functioning like a market, where certain kinds of men and women can be of "better value" than others.

The strategy of confronting the world of our everyday experience by working through speculative premises also evokes interpretations that are possibly antithetical to the author's message. This occurs, for example, when the traits that are traditionally perceived as feminine (such as maternal urges, helplessness, impressionability, flexibility) are presented in unfavorable light. As a result, the attempt to deconstruct the traditional role of a woman easily turns into a mockery of desire to have a child, for example. Still, the ambiguity is not necessarily a flaw in the novel but rather a characteristic of satire as a genre, the irony of which is often unstable.[42] According to Dustin Griffin,[43] the main function of satire is not to attack a certain target but to provoke, inquire, and play.

What about the Finnish Weird, then? When it comes to Johanna Sinisalo, it is not simply a marketing trick to call her written fiction subversive, imaginative, and something that can evoke new viewpoints in its readers. It is perhaps more natural to connect her with the international traditions such as feminist speculative writing or weird fiction, but in the context of Finnish literary canon, the umbrella term "Finnish Weird" remains one of the most important means of making ways of writing that deviate from realism more visible and more respected.

Notes

1. Translated as *Not Before Sundown* in 2003, it was translated again as *Troll—A Love Story* in 2004 for the American market. When referring to this work, we will use the 2003 title and translation cited in the bibliography.

2. Johanna Sinisalo, email to Hanna Samola, August 31, 2015.

3. Lyytikäinen, "Realismia," 11.

4. This is how *Auringon ydin* is presented in the "Top10+" section, aimed primarily at foreign publishers, on the webpage of the Finnish Literature Exchange. See http://www.finlit.fi/fili/en/books/the-core-of-the-sun (accessed August 4, 2017).

5. See VanderMeer and VanderMeer, *The New Weird*, xvi. By traditional fantasy, the VanderMeers supposedly refer to post-Tolkienian fantasy (or genre fantasy, or epic fantasy, or high fantasy—a dear child has many names, indeed). The writers of New Weird fiction have been proud to announce that they draw their inspiration from a different kind of fantastic narration, such as Mervyn Peake's *Gormenghast* trilogy or M. John Harrison's *Viriconium* series.

6. Kivistö and Riikonen, *Satiiri Suomessa*, 419.

7. Sinisalo, "Rare Exports," 3.

8. Le Guin gave her speech at the National Book Awards when she received the Medal for Distinguished Contribution to American Letters in November 2014. For the text of her speech, see Le Guin, "Ursula K. Le Guin's Speech."

9. Mendlesohn, "Introduction," 1.

10. Fowler, *Kinds of Literature*, 45.

11. Ibid., 20.

12. Ibid. 22, 38, 256.

13. Mendlesohn, "Introduction," 1.

14. Suvin, *Metamorphoses*, 63.

15. Mendlesohn, "Introduction," 4.

16. See Gordon, "Hybridity," 456; and VanderMeer and VanderMeer, *New Weird*.

17. Scholes, *Fabulators*, 2.

18. See also Roberts, *Science Fiction*, 10.

19. Le Guin, "Introduction," n.p.

20. Mendlesohn, "Introduction," 3.

21. Masko men represent normative masculinity in the Eusistocratic Republic, while Minus men deviate from these norms in some way. However, the two groups of men are barely mentioned in the novel.

22. The state of Eusistocratia gives all women Eloi names that have double nasal sounds. The original names of two sisters are Mira and Vera.

23. Mohr, *Worlds Apart?* 36.

24. Baccolini and Moylan, "Introduction," 5.

25. Sinisalo, *Core of the Sun*, 115. All citations are taken from Lola Rogers's translation, except where noted.

26. In 2014, the law legalizing same-sex marriage in Finland was passed, and the debates preceding this decision can be seen as influences on Sinisalo's novel. Furthermore, Finnish masculinists and antifeminists such as Henry Laasanen and Timo Hännikäinen have claimed that women have more sexual power in the contemporary society and thus control the "marketplace of sex." See Laasanen, *Naisten seksuaalinen*; and Hännikäinen, *Ilman*.

27. *Kalevala*, 15.

28. In Finnish folklore, a human being or an animal may disappear into the forest cover when the surrounding forest suddenly changes. The one who disappears into the forest cannot be seen by other people and sometimes cannot find a way back home and is lost in the forest forever.

29. Siikala, *Suomalainen šamanismi*, 54–57.

30. Siimets, "The Sun, the Moon," 133.
31. Baccolini and Moylan, "Introduction," 7.
32. Ibid., 7.
33. Tatar, "Introduction," 4–5; Zipes, *Trials and Tribulations*, 9–10, 16.
34. Zipes, *Trials and Tribulations*, 1.
35. Zipes, *Why Fairy Tales Stick*, 28, 39.
36. Bacchilega, *Postmodern Fairy Tales*, 58.
37. Dällenbach, *Mirror*, 61–62.
38. Sinisalo, *Auringon ydin*, 54. We use our own translation here because Rogers's translation does not mention that the size of the wolf's ears helps him hear the thoughts of Redianna.
39. Sinisalo, *Core of the Sun*, 42.
40. Ibid., 331.
41. Samola and Roine, "Discussions of Genre."
42. Griffin, *Satire*, 67.
43. Ibid., 71.

Bibliography

Atwood, Margaret. *The Handmaid's Tale*. Toronto: McClelland and Stewart, 1985.

Bacchilega, Christina. *Postmodern Fairy Tales: Gender and Narrative Strategies*. Philadelphia: University of Pennsylvania Press, 1997.

Baccolini, Raffaella. "Finding Utopia in Dystopia: Feminism, Memory, Nostalgia, and Hope." In *Utopia Method Vision. The Use Value of Social Dreaming*. Ed. Tom Moylan and Raffaella Baccolini. Bern: Peter Lang, 2007. 159–91.

———, and Tom Moylan. "Introduction: Dystopia and Histories." In *Dark Horizons: Science Fiction and the Dystopian Imagination*. Ed. Raffaella Baccolini and Tom Moylan. New York: Routledge, 2003. 1–13.

Burdekin, Katharine. *Swastika Night*. London: Victor Gollancz Ltd., 1937.

Conrad, Joseph. *Heart of Darkness*. London: Penguin, 1994.

Dällenbach, Lucien. *The Mirror in the Text*. Trans. Jeremy Whiteley with Emma Hughes. Cambridge: Polity Press, 1977.

Fowler, Alastair. *Kinds of Literature: An Introduction to the Theory of Genres and Modes*. Oxford: Clarendon Press, 1982.

Gordon, Joan. "Hybridity, Heterotopia, and Mateship in China Miéville's *Perdido Street Station*." *Science Fiction Studies* 30.3 (2003): 456–76.

Griffin, Dustin. *Satire: A Critical Reintroduction*. Lexington: University Press of Kentucky, 1994.

Grimm, Jacob, and Wilhelm Grimm. "Rotkäppchen" [Little Red Riding Hood]. In *Kinder- und Hausmärchen*. Berlin: Realschulbuchh, 1812.

Haldane, Charlotte. *Man's World*. London: Chatto and Windus, 1926.

Hännikäinen, Timo. *Ilman: Esseitä seksuaalisesta syrjäytymisestä* [Without: Essays on sexual exclusion]. Turku: Savukeidas, 2009.

Huxley, Aldous. *Brave New World.* London: Chatto and Windus, 1932.

Iron Sky. Dir. Timo Vuorensola. Finland, Austria, and Germany: Energia Productions, 2012.

Järvinen, Outi. Rev. of *Auringon ydin* [The core of the sun], by Johanna Sinisalo. Trans. Ruth Urbom. *FILI.* Accessed August 4, 2017. http://www.finlit.fi/fili/en/books/the-core-of-the-sun/.

Kalevala. Helsinki: Suomalaisen Kirjallisuuden Seura, 1849.

Kivistö, Sari, and H. K. Riikonen. *Satiiri Suomessa* [Satire in Finland]. Helsinki: Suomalaisen Kirjallisuuden Seura, 2012.

Krohn, Leena. *Tainaron: Postia toisesta kaupungista* [Tainaron: Mail from another city]. Helsinki: Sanoma, 1985.

Laasanen, Henry. *Naisten seksuaalinen valta* [Women's sexual power]. Vantaa: Multikustannus, 2008.

Le Guin, Ursula K. Introduction to *The Left Hand of Darkness.* New York: Ace Books, 1976. n.p.

———. "Ursula K. Le Guin's Speech at National Book Awards: 'Books Aren't Just Commodities.'" *The Guardian,* November 20, 2014. Accessed August 4, 2017. http://www.theguardian.com/books/2014/nov/20/ursula-k-le-guin-national-book-awards-speech.

Lyytikäinen, Pirjo. "Realismia fantasian ja allegorian maisemissa. Erich Auerbach, 'Helvetin' realismi ja Johanna Sinisalon *Linnunaivot*" [Realism of fantasy and allegory: Erich Auerbach, the realism of Dante, and Johanna Sinisalo's *Little Brain*]. *Kirjallisuudentutkimuksen aikakauslehti Avain* 1 (2015): 11–29.

Mendlesohn, Farah. "Introduction: Reading Science Fiction." In *The Cambridge Companion to Science Fiction.* Ed. Edward James and Farah Mendlesohn. Cambridge: Cambridge University Press, 2003. 1–14

Mieville, China. *Perdido Street Station.* London: Macmillan, 2000.

Mohr, Dunja M. *Worlds Apart? Dualism and Transgression in Contemporary Female Dystopias.* Critical Explorations in Science Fiction and Fantasy, vol. 1. Jefferson, N.C.: McFarland and Co., 2005.

Perrault, Charles. "Le Petit Chaperon Rouge" [Little Red Riding Hood]. In *Histoires ou contes du temps passé, avec des moralités.* Paris: Émile Guérin, 1697.

Raevaara, Tiina. *Eräänä päivänä tyhjä taivas* [One day, an empty sky]. Helsinki: Teos, 2008.

———. *Yö ei saa tulla* [Deny the night]. Helsinki: Teos, 2015.

Roberts, Adam. *Science Fiction.* London: Routledge, 2000.

Samola, Hanna, and Hanna-Riikka Roine. "Discussions of Genre Interpretations in Johanna Sinisalo's *Auringon ydin* and Finnish Weird." *Fafnir—Nordic Journal of Science Fiction and Fantasy Research* 1.3 (2014): 27–35.

Scholes, Robert. *Structural Fabulation: An Essay on Fiction of the Future.* Bloomington: Indiana University Press, 1975.

Siikala, Anna-Leena. *Suomalainen šamanismi* [Shamanism in Finland]. Helsinki: SKS, 1992.

Siimets, Ülo. "The Sun, the Moon, and Firmament in Chukchi Mythology and on the Relations of Celestial Bodies and Sacrifice." *Folklore: Electronic Journal of Folklore* 32

(2006): 129–57. Accessed September 29, 2017. https://www.folklore.ee/folklore/vol32/siimets.pdf.

Sinisalo, Johanna. *Auringon ydin* [The core of the sun]. Helsinki: Teos, 2013.

———. *Birdbrain*. Trans. David Hackston. London: Peter Owen, 2010.

———. *The Blood of Angels*. Trans. Lola Rogers. London: Peter Owen, 2014.

———. *The Core of the Sun*. Trans. Lola Rogers. New York: Black Cat, 2016.

———. *Not before Sundown*. Trans. Herbert Lomas. London: Peter Owen, 2003.

———. "Rare Exports." In *Finnish Weird*. Ed. Toni Jerrman and J. Robert Tupasela. Helsinki: Helsinki Science Fiction Society, 2014. 3–4.

———. *Sankarit* [Heroes]. Helsinki: Tammi, 2003.

Suvin, Darko. *Metamorphoses of Science Fiction: On the Poetics and History of a Literary Genre*. New Haven, Conn.: Yale University Press, 1979.

Tatar, Maria. "Introduction: Little Red Riding Hood." In *The Annotated Classic Fairy Tales*. Ed. Maria Tatar. New York: W. W. Norton and Co., 1999. 3–10.

VanderMeer, Jeff, and Ann VanderMeer, eds. *The New Weird*. San Francisco: Tachyon Publications, 2008.

Wells, H. G. *The Time Machine*. London: William Heinemann, 1895.

Zipes, Jack. *The Trials and Tribulations of Little Red Riding Hood: Versions of the Tale in Sociocultural Context*. London: Heinemann, 1983.

———. *Why Fairy Tales Stick: The Evolution and Relevance of a Genre*. New York: Routledge, 2006.

Arkady and Boris Strugatsky

The Science-Fictionality of Russian Culture

YVONNE HOWELL

The Soviet Union was born in 1917 out of the chaos of a collapsing imperial autocracy, a political revolution, and a universal sense that, for better or worse, history had abruptly accelerated into a new kind of future. The Soviet experiment was meant to transform one of the most backwards countries in Europe (which stretched all the way through Siberia to the borders of China and Japan) into the world's first communist state. One of the most distinctive features of this radical twentieth-century experiment was its explicit allegiance to rational, scientific enlightenment as means of—and justification for—forcibly and radically transforming society. Soviet ideology did not make its claim on the shape of the future by invoking God's will or a mandate to recapture a "golden age" in the nation's (imagined) past. Instead, its claim to represent the most progressive, and therefore inevitable, vector of humanity's historical development was based on Enlightenment ideals (via Marx) having to do with the worth of man and faith in reason—along with a lot of strikingly science-fictional rhetoric, such as Lenin's famous dictum that "communism equals Soviet Power plus the electrification of the entire country." There was something essentially "science fictional" about the Soviet project, which superimposed a hyperrational, materialist, and stridently future-oriented official ideology onto deeply embedded premodern epistemologies, not to mention onto the simple fact of backwards conditions in many areas of the vast country.[1]

The enormous significance of the Strugatsky brothers' science fiction lies well beyond the fabled popularity of their key novels among Soviet readers, who reacted to government censorship of the arts and intellectual life by cultivating a heightened sensitivity to the power of real literature to give voice to things that matter. Over the course of three decades, from the late 1950s through the late 1980s, the Strugatskys helped turn science fiction into a genre more explicitly suited than any other to anticipate and interrogate the major currents of their generation's intellectual life. The constantly evolving body of work they created not only mirrors the development of Russian science fiction as a genre in the late Soviet period, it famously mirrors the shifting contours of Soviet reality with uncanny precision.[2] The following essay shows how the Strugatskys shaped their science fiction in a way that could record the distinctive tensions in the Soviet cultural Zeitgeist of their times. I will suggest that the Strugatskys' stories and novels ultimately expose the peculiar "science fictionality" of Soviet culture in the twentieth century and even beyond, as one sees in the "neo-cosmism" of nationalist conservatives in the current Putin era.[3]

The Strugatskys' influence on the development of Soviet and international science fiction extends beyond their books. Boris Strugatsky actively mentored writing workshops for aspiring young authors for decades, and in the last decade of his life he was one of the most broadly respected public intellectuals in post-Soviet Russia. The number of famous films that have been inspired (even unwittingly, in the case of James Cameron's *Avatar*) by the Strugatskys' touchstone themes and characterizations (for instance, a sentient forest populated by post-human beings called Nave) is a testament to the proleptic reach of their imagination.[4] Films adapted from the Strugatkys' novels have taken on a life of their own, most notably Andrei Tarkovsky's internationally renowned art film *Stalker* (Stalker; 1979) and, in a very different vein, Konstantin Bromberg's perennially popular New Year's Eve musical rom-com *Charodei* (The magicians; 1982). Aleksei German's long-awaited cinematic incarnation of the Strugatskys' novel *Trudno byt bogom* (Hard to be a god; 1965) was released in 2013, provoking polarized reviews from contemporary Russian liberals (positive) and Russian nationalist neoconservatives (negative). A collection of essays in *Science Fiction and Film Studies* offers ample evidence that the Strugatskys' cinematic influence is profound. As of this writing, the well-known director Aleksei Fedorchenko is filming a version of the Strugatskys' 1970 story "Malysh" (The kid; translated that same year as "Space Mowgli"). The Strugatskys' science fiction, in other words, has not gone out of date since the collapse of the Soviet Union. How can we attribute the Strugatskys' once and future relevance to the way in which their understanding of science fiction continued to evolve in the space between local and global developments?

Science Fiction in the Russian Empire and Early Soviet Union

We can justifiably call the period stretching from the very end of the nineteenth century to the mid-1920s a golden age of science-fiction production in Russia. The sudden emergence of this kind of fantastical literature—one that imagines a future profoundly altered by the application of new scientific and technological knowledge—occurred during the last two decades of the faltering Tsarist empire and picked up even more speed just after the Bolshevik Revolution of 1917, which led to the establishment of the world's first officially "communist" state. In other words, science fiction proved to be a form of imagination that points to some unexpected continuities between the seemingly antithetical worlds of pre-revolutionary Russia and the radical new state created by the Soviets.[5] The Strugatsky brothers were born in the interwar years, just *after* the first golden age of Russian science fiction had come to an end. They themselves were not yet aware of the (mostly banned) legacy of this era when they began writing in the late 1950s. Yet the first flourishing of science fiction in pre-revolutionary Russia and the early Soviet Union was tremendously important to the later development of the genre.

The most important "science-fictional" mind in late nineteenth-century Russia belonged to the erudite philosopher and Russian Orthodox visionary Nikolai Fedorov (1829–1903). Fedorov's voluminous writings (never published in his lifetime) advocate the use of advanced scientific technologies to overcome the discrepancy between the human body (frail, mortal, subject to the forces of nature) and the human spirit (infinite, immortal, beyond nature). He believed that all of humanity should join together in the "common cause" of overcoming death, resurrecting our ancestors, and populating other planets in the cosmos. These fantastical goals were nevertheless grounded in scientific premises that prefigure today's discourse of transhumanism. According to Fedorov, human beings can develop artificial and bioorganic prostheses that will infinitely renew and prolong our essential selves. Fedorov served as a tutor and mentor to the self-taught aeronautical engineer Konstantin Tsiolkovsky (1857–1935), whose successful experiments in rocketry design led directly to the Soviet Union's preemptive victory in putting the first man into orbit in outer space. Thus, the Soviet space program was born not only in the throes of military-technological competition between the United States and the USSR, but also in the lack of clear boundaries between Fedorov's late-nineteenth-century scientific-philosophical fictions and his legendary pupil's "applied futurism" in the form of calculations and technical blueprints for machines that would allow us to escape gravity and pursue immortality.[6]

This pattern is repeated several times in the revolutionary decades at the beginning of the twentieth century. In technologically backwards Russia, of all places, there was a very porous boundary between what could be imagined—in vivid fictional scenarios—and what the new Bolshevik commissars would actively fund in terms of scientific research.[7] The highly trained, European-educated scientific elite of Tsarist times quickly realized that the Bolsheviks needed their skill and expertise, especially to make good on promises made to the masses. The new Soviet leaders intended to abolish religion and replace it with scientific modernity: the wonders of ubiquitous electricity, vastly improved health care, automated transportation (cars, airplanes), radio communications, and x-ray technologies. In many cases, real scientific research, science fiction, and an energetic popular press touting the virtues of "Soviet progress" creatively reinforced each other.

Despite the Bolsheviks' favorable attitude and mostly favorable policies towards scientific research and development, it was impossible to leap over centuries of underdevelopment and the devastation left by Russia's involvement in World War I, a revolution, and a protracted civil war (1918–21). On the ground, there was famine, ruined infrastructure, orphans roaming the countryside in droves, and the spectacle of a conservative, nearly feudal social order suddenly being roused to new consciousness of itself as "the most radically progressive society in the world." Under these conditions, Russia's finest writers started writing some of the world's first modern science fiction, and they did so in a stunning variety of styles. Alexander Bogdanov's *Red Star* (1908) is an earnest, action-packed, emotionally evocative utopian tale about a man's journey to Mars and his love affair with one of the truly communist, truly enlightened, sexually androgynous Martian people. Andrei Platonov's story "Lunnaia bomba" (Lunar bomb; 1926) is filled with haunting, surrealistic images of a threadbare population dreaming of scientifically induced spiritual harmony:

> Kreuzkopf was guided by a secret thought: there were a lot of humans on earth, passing the days of their unrepeatable lives in stifling crowds that gathered around the shriveling veins sustaining the earth. Kreuzkopf hoped to open up new virgin sources of sustenance for life on earth, run hoses from these sources to the earth, and use them to swallow up the meanness and

the burdened, cramped feeling of human life. And then, when the endless depths of the alien celestial gift were opened, people would feel more of a need for other people.[8]

Evgeny Zamiatin's groundbreaking dystopia, the modernist masterpiece *My* (We; 1920), pursues the implications of state-mandated "universal happiness" in a far-future world. While English-language editions of *We* directly influenced George Orwell's *1984* (1949) and Ursula K. Le Guin's *The Dispossessed* (1979), the Russian version of *We* would not be published in the Soviet Union until 1988, more than a half-century later. The stylistic diversity and intellectual boldness of early Soviet science fiction was not in tune with the party's strategies for constructing a stable yet pliable national consciousness.

Science Fiction under Stalin

Throughout the 1920s, Soviet society changed dramatically and often unpredictably, as radical social reorganization and rapid scientific-technological developments occurred simultaneously. Still, the 1920s were characterized by a great deal of improvisation and cultural leniency. The government supported the arts and scientific development. It tried to control both, but in fact it did very little to control either. This changed when Joseph Stalin came to full power in 1930. Stalinism put an end to revolutionary improvisation and fantasies of colonizing other planets or perfecting full-body transplants. Stalinism had much more nearsighted goals: the country needed to industrialize rapidly, collectivize agriculture, and build up its military might. The arts and sciences would also be forcibly harnessed to the tasks of industrialization and militarization, in part by strictly constraining the subject matter of books and films to uplifting, patriotic themes and descriptions of real-life achievements in the Soviet workforce. Science fiction was left with the rather un-science-fictional mandate to depict the "near goals" of Stalinism. In the early 1930s, almost all of the most significant and challenging science fiction produced by modernist writers in the previous generation disappeared. Writers like Zamiatin, Platonov, and Bulgakov were banned. Works deemed incompatible with the new political culture were pulled from circulation. The Strugatskys grew up in the Stalin era.

Arkady Strugatsky was born in 1926 in the Georgian city of Batumi, and his younger brother Boris was born seven years later, in 1933, after the family had relocated to Leningrad. Tragedy struck in the winter of 1942, four months into the long siege of Leningrad. Sixteen-year-old Arkady and his forty-nine-year-old father were active in the city's resistance against the Nazi offensive, and both were dying from malnutrition. The only hope was to place them on an evacuation convoy that would travel in January over a frozen corridor of Lake Ladoga out to areas not yet controlled by the Germans. The truck they were in fell through the ice. Arkady Strugatsky was the only passenger to miraculously survive the ordeal in sub-zero temperatures. He was eventually nourished back to health and placed in the foreign-languages division of the military academy, in order to learn Japanese. He spent the immediate postwar years as an interpreter for accused Japanese war criminals on the Eastern Front. Later in life, he continued to translate classical Japanese literature into Russian.[9]

By the time Arkady was reunited with his mother and brother in 1956, Boris was working at the renowned Pulkovo Observatory and completing a dissertation on stellar astronomy. At this point in their lives, the extroverted translator of Japanese and the precise, dryly humorous astronomer belonged to a layer of postwar Russian society that identified with Enlightenment ideals, which were once again emphasized in the years after Stalin's death in 1953. The Strugatskys had come of age—and discovered in each other a shared desire to write fiction—at a moment when Soviet culture was entering an era of liberation and new optimism about the future, a period known as the "Thaw." The short-lived Thaw was signaled by two science-fictional events: In 1957, the Soviet Union launched Sputnik, the first man-made satellite to orbit the Earth successfully. In the same year, Ivan Efremov published *Tumannost Andromedy* (*Andromeda: A Space-Age Tale*), an epic novel set in the far-future world of cosmic communism, thus ending a long ban on imagining the radical otherness (even in a positive way) of perfected communism.

Noon: 22nd Century

The Strugatskys published their first novella, *Strana bagrovykh tuch* (Land of the crimson clouds), in 1957. This rather clumsy first effort describes the hardships (and the technical details) of trying to send a manned flight to Venus. Over the course of the next few years, they sought to unlock for themselves—and their readers—the hidden potential of the genre. They had grown up on boyish adventure and history novels (Jack London and Alexander Dumas were favorites) but sensed that the fantastical dimensions of science fiction would be necessary for uncovering the "social-philosophical foundations" of the issues they wanted to address.[10] In a series of increasingly innovative stories and linked novellas, they created a future history known as *Polden' XXII veka* (Noon: 22nd century). In this far-future world, perfect communism has united all of earthly humanity, thus freeing up our collective creativity to explore the cosmos and encounter other civilizations. The stories are not linked chronologically; instead, different episodes in the "Nooniverse" are united by the reappearance of familiar characters. For decades, Russian fan groups have been meticulously reconstructing and reinterpreting the exact chronology of the Nooniverse stories and their connections to each other.

When the Strugatskys conceived of the *Noon: 22nd Century* cycle in 1960, the most striking thing about their far-future universe was its combination of utopian optimism (hunger, poverty, and inequality have been abolished; the world is "nearly perfect") and disarmingly down-to-earth human characters. In later years, Boris Strugatsky explained what distinguishes their utopian vision from the others: "In the classical [Marxist] texts, communism is a society with no classes, no government, no exploitation of Man by fellow Man, no poverty, no social inequality.... So [we asked], what *is there?*"[11] At the height of the Thaw, it seemed worthwhile to depict the socialist future as a "well-equipped world" in terms of material and technological conveniences, but above all, as a world "in which we would find it comfortable and interesting to live."[12] By this they meant, in effect, a world in which everyone is free-thinking, intellectually curious, devoid of ethnic or class prejudice, and immune to bureaucratic stupidity. Official critics accused them of populating future communism with overly complicated characters who use too much crude language; in other circles they were accused of sticking to the naive aesthetics of "the good versus the even better."

In fact, the Strugatskys had launched their writing career just as they, along with many of their generation, began to uncover the hidden realities festering beneath the surface of society. With each new attempt at a novella, the Strugatskys found themselves confronting an enormous gap between the romanticized ideal of a progressive socialist society with a "human face" and the reality of deep, unresolved rents in the social fabric that had only deepened since the revolution. In his memoirs, Boris Strugatsky noted that "our life was such that you didn't have to be one of its miserable victims to understand the vast abyss that existed between the real world and the 'Noon' world we had tried to depict."[13] Thus, after *Dalekaia raduga* (Far rainbow; 1962), a poignant but ultimately humanely resolved fable of a physics experiment gone awry that threatens to wipe out a planet, the Strugatskys ceased to fantasize about the far future "as we would like it to be."

Encountering the Other: Progressorism and Its Discontents

The "real world" turned out to be more pertinent and more suggestive of science-fictional scenarios. Nikita Khrushchev was ousted in 1964; his successor, Leonid Brezhnev, subsequently presided over a period of gray bureaucratic and political repression that lasted all the way into the 1980s. The real world raised questions that needed to be addressed in a form that could circumvent increasingly restrictive censorship, while also exploring painful ethical questions. At the time, these questions seemed to arise directly out of the trauma of Soviet historical experience and the unspoken falsehoods undergirding the Brezhnev-era status quo. Later, it turned out that these same questions were just as relevant to rest of the world: *Is it ever admissible to confront barbaric cruelty with retaliatory violence? If so, when does the circle of violence ever stop? Is it ever admissible for a more advanced, more enlightened society to interfere in the affairs of a primitive and corrupt society? If so, what will be the unintended side effects?*

Over the next two decades, the Strugatskys repeatedly formulated these questions as a dramatic encounter between two technologically and spiritually incommensurable civilizations. The contradictions they encountered in their own society on a daily basis turned out to be inherently science fictional in this formulation: on the one hand, you perceive yourself as belonging to a cultivated, technologically advanced, humane civilization; on the other hand, you are confronted with entrenched ignorance, brutality, and the kind of misery that breeds fanaticism. It doesn't matter if the face of irrational cruelty is wearing a suit and wielding the stamp of official power, or if it exists in some godforsaken village where nobody has asked for (or even heard of) indoor plumbing. The point is that it appears to you as a clash of worlds that are alien to each other. In their memoirs, the Strugatskys bring up small, seemingly trivial episodes that seem to have "opened their eyes" and pointed them towards an articulation of deeper causes. For example, in the early 1960s, the astronomer Boris is sent on an expedition to Soviet Central Asia to survey possible sites for an observatory. He is asked to provide an introductory lecture about astronomy to the local workers. Two of them look at him blankly, one sees no difference between a planet and a star, and one insists the earth is flat and circled by the sun. Boris is astonished that these four young men, who have completed a full ten years of school in the country that is winning the space race, are completely content to believe that a naked shepherd sits in the moon and gives it its "face." In roughly the same years, back in Moscow, impulsive, emotional Arkady goes to a routine meeting for members of the Writer's Union and listens to a powerful member of the conservative faction using anti-Semitic slurs to condemn one of the most inventive writers of new science fiction. Arkady nearly explodes in amazement and horror.[14] Such encounters would consistently be reflected in later works, such as *Hard to Be a God, Gadkie lebedi* (*Ugly Swans*; 1972, translated in 1986), and *Otiagoshchennye zlom, ili sorok let spustia* (Burdened by evil; 1988).

At first, adventures in the Nooniverse modeled the encounter between ideally advanced humanity from twenty-second-century Earth and primitive, barbaric societies (usually ruled by corrupt dictators) existing on other planets. In this scenario, enlightened humanity sends "Progressors" to encourage advancement in benighted civilizations. A Progressor is defined as "someone who embodies the intellectual, moral, and physical virtues of an elite civilization (to which he belongs), and is therefore willing and able to secretly infiltrate a less developed civilization in order to effect social change; specifically, the Progressor will manipulate the local system in various ways so that social processes begin to move towards a better, more enlightened future."[15] Thus, unlike the Prime Directive in the *Star Trek* universe, the Progressorist stance at first asserts the desirability of (covert) interference. Over time, however, both the Strugatskys' Progressorism and the Starfleet's mandate of "noninterference" prove to be vulnerable when faced with deeply ambiguous results.

Hard to Be a God is the first fully realized example of what came to be called the "Progressor" problematic. Anton, a highly trained historian from ideally socialist Earth, goes undercover as Don Rumata, an entitled, swashbuckling nobleman in the feudal society of Arkanar. He conceals his squeamishness when consorting with the foul aristocrats of his (assumed) class. He finds it alarmingly easy to play his role in disdaining the ordinary people, even though he knows—in theory—that they are not in control of the circumstances that make them filthy, drunk, ignorant, and complacent. The Arkanar mission allows him to observe the dynamics of an earlier historical stage of humanity's social development and covertly to foster small glimmers of enlightenment by trying to protect the lives of a few persecuted book lovers and knowledge-seeking healers. As Don Rumata's nemesis, the powerful monk Don Reba, manipulates the tide of fascist violence in his society with increasing success, Arkanar's proto-intellectuals end up in torture chambers, and the fearsome, brawling Gray Order is overthrown by a fanatically purist and therefore even more cruel Black Order. Don Rumata is strictly forbidden to use his earthly superpowers to change the course of history. So what can he do? The reader is put in the same position as the Progressor hero, wondering whether it is possible or even morally defensible to maintain "professional objectivity" when soldiers from the Black Guard accidentally shoot his Arkanar girlfriend. We are put in the position of cheering on a furious outburst of violence as he fights his way through the guards to kill the evil Don Reba. But in the epilogue, after Anton has been reintegrated into his enlightened cohort on Earth, we are put in the uncomfortable position of feeling his best friend cringe when she sees strawberry juice on his hands—she has involuntarily mistaken the juice for fresh blood. Can any "Progressorist" society get rid of the blood on its hands?

Unexpected Encounters: Enlightenment Fails

In 1968, after the Soviet military suppression of the Prague Spring in Czechoslovakia, any lingering hopes for internal liberalization within the Soviet Union were laid to rest. In Europe and the United States as well, the end of the 1960s was marked by a sense of unease, as the cold war continued and proxy wars in Vietnam and elsewhere heated up. On both sides of the Iron Curtain, optimism and faith in scientific rationality gave way to skepticism and disillusionment about the efficacy of technological "solutions." Accordingly, the late 1960s recorded a new interest in religious philosophy, esoteric traditions, and seeking in the realm of the nonrational. The British writer J. G. Ballard described the shift in mood as a change from interest in Outer Space to interest in Inner Space.[16] The change in zeitgeist from rational optimism to inner reckoning registered in the Strugatskys' work of this period as well.[17] They wrote three superficially disparate works in close succession: *Otel' u pogibshego al'pinista* (Dead mountaineer's hotel; 1969, translated in 2015 as *Dead Mountaineer's Inn*), *The Kid*, and *Piknik na obochine* (*Roadside Picnic*; 1971, translated in 2014). *Hotel* is framed as a murder mystery, and it takes place in a peculiar version of the present (roughly 1970) in an alpine location that is vaguely Western, perhaps a version of Slovenia. *Roadside Picnic* is also set on present-day Earth, where the only thing that has changed is proof that an alien intelligence has actually visited Earth. *The Kid*, although it belongs to the Nooniverse series and takes place on an unexplored planet, shares with the other two the primary features of "heterotopia": its location in time/space (chronotope) is purposely elusive, denoting neither a good place (utopia) nor a bad place (dystopia); neither identifiable past nor imagined future. The primary feature of the heterotopia is that it is *not here*, and it is *not exactly now*.[18]

Hotel was the Strugatskys' attempt at detective fiction, which then took on the features of a hybrid genre incorporating strong gothic features (haunted hotel, unsolved mysteries; sexually ambiguous, androgynous characters; a sense of doom) and superficially science-fictional ones (are some of the other guests humanoid aliens or cyborgs?). Despite the presence of a good Soviet police detective (Inspector Glebsky) at the scene, the sudden disappearance (murder?) of a guest is never solved. Glebsky's rational methods prove to be utterly ineffective in the face of stubbornly irrational, inexplicable events. In short, in this version of the "alien encounters" scenario, the encounter is unexpected, and the would-be hero is utterly incapable of making sense of it.[19]

Likewise, the Nooniverse Progressors (a crew of four) who land on the eponymous kid's planet in the *The Kid* do not expect to find anyone. The planet is supposed to be dead. Instead, as the crew's more sensitive female member quickly realizes, the planet is "actively necrotic," and it has the "smell of former life." It is also inhabited—by the orphaned child of previous human explorers who perished there in a crash. The story shares aspects of Robert Heinlein's *Stranger in a Strange Land* and Stanislaw Lem's *Solaris*. The kid has been raised by the planet's unfathomable planetary consciousness. He is at once a savage (raised not even by wolves, but by something like "a giant squid with superhuman cognitive powers") and an alien so advanced that he can conjure optical and auditory illusions, fly, breathe underwater, and change the color and temperature of his body. The four Progressors no longer agree on how to handle contact across a civilizational divide. After all, the kid is a de facto "civilization of one." The crew's rational scientist wants to force him to communicate as a human, so that humans can learn the secret of his super-advanced capabilities. The kid holds the keys to our desire to evolve towards "galactic man." The others see that the kid cannot split himself into two without losing his alien perfection as an adapted product of his planet. Many readers saw *The Kid* as a postcolonial parable criticizing the Soviet occupation of Eastern Europe. The scientific rationalist came off as a Soviet handler, demanding that the more advanced "colonized person" hand over his riches and his essential identity.[20] However, as indicated in this essay's conclusion, in the first decades of the twenty-first century, a neonationalist strain of Russian transhumanism has emphasized a different message in this previously less-noticed tale.

The most famous novel in the Strugatsky oeuvre appeared a year later. In *Roadside Picnic*, human beings wake up one morning to discover that a clearly delineated stretch of territory—seemingly in a part of North America that might be Canada—has been altered. Within the Zone (as it comes to be called), all known laws of physics and even metaphysics have changed. The Zone is littered with debris whose purpose and function is incomprehensible, although a brisk black market in lucrative trade of these objects is quickly established. Naturally, the military-industrial complex has cordoned off the Zone for the exclusive purpose of allowing scientists to study its dangerous technologies. Daring and desperate "Stalkers" make a living entering the Zone illegally, at enormous risk to their own lives, in order to poach its physics-defying objects for sale outside. The novel's protagonist, a Stalker named Red, has learned to live with the Zone's uncanny power. Red's daughter is a mute, golden-furred "child" with strange psychic gifts; his own father has become one of the undead that does not stay buried in the Zone—those who were laid to rest there have reappeared in town as zombies. For its part, the town—representative of the great majority of ordinary humans—has long since ceased to care about what does not directly affect its pursuit of business and daily pleasures. Most people no longer care to ponder the central enigma posed by the Zone itself: Who are the hypothesized intergalactic aliens that made a quick stop on Earth for a roadside picnic and left their mind-boggling equivalent of candy wrappers and corkscrews to bedevil us? Are they evidence of a far more advanced race? Or are they representatives of a less advanced race, no more conscious than Red's daughter Monkey, who stupidly litter the galaxy with dangerous super-technologies?

Roadside Picnic succeeds as a profoundly "open work" (in Umberto Eco's formulation) that is able continually to spawn new meanings, new interpretations, and new understandings of our own times. The most famous interpretation of the novel is certainly Andrei Tarkovsky's film *Stalker*, a three-hour work of art that turned the Strugatskys' rough-and-tumble sci-fi quest novel (will Red evade the "witch's jelly" that dissolves limbs? will he escape the zombies?) into a cinematic search for God. *Roadside Picnic*'s memes have also spread in other ways. When a Soviet nuclear reactor exploded in Chernobyl in 1986, the area surrounding the accident was cordoned off, and it was assumed that its extreme radioactivity would kill off all higher life for decades to come. The deadly area was immediately dubbed the Zone, and those who went back in (with protective suits) to build the "sarcophagus" enclosing the damaged reactor were called Stalkers. In 2007, GSC Game World released the first of their massively popular S.T.A.L.K.E.R. series. The "first-person shooter/survival horror" video games conflate aspects of the Strugatskys' Zone with other postapocalyptic nuclear-disaster scenarios. Yet, in a twist that the Strugatskys would have appreciated, contemporary scientists have been more baffled by the Chernobyl Zone's oddly regenerative "rewilding." After the Soviet Union collapsed, old women stubbornly returned to their homes in the Zone. They did not want to die in the ugly urban apartment blocks to which they had been evacuated. The Zone seems to have rewarded them—scientists recently discovered that the old women who returned have, on average, survived longer than those who stayed in the resettlement projects. As in each of the Strugatskys' "threshold" works discussed above, all interpretations point to a tenuous source of hope and redemption in the sphere of the irrational, where only what we don't know makes sense.

The Universe Defends Itself

As we have seen, the first Progressorist scenarios were inspired by an Enlightenment faith in the power of reason and human decency to lift up and improve the lot of all humanity. The stubborn resistance of ignorance and brutality could be figured as a form of "alien intelligence" that might still be infiltrated, prodded forward, and humanely conquered. The Strugatskys' science-fictional models showed that this could not be the case. Thus, in the final phase of their work, the encounter between humans and aliens is turned on its head: the "Progressors" are superhuman aliens so far ahead of us in technological and spiritual advancement that we cannot fathom their intentions. The imperfect humanity of our existing civilization is portrayed as somehow defendable in the face of transhuman or superhuman alternatives. (Or is it? See the conclusion.)

The first highly ambiguous portrait of the superhuman "other" occurs in a work that the Strugatskys had already completed but couldn't publish at the end of the 1960s. *The Ugly Swans* is in many ways indicative of the dominant strain in all their later work: there is no need for other planets, technogadgetry, or time travel in order to create an eerily recognizable science-fictional scenario.[21] The protagonist Banev is a writer in a "softly" totalitarian regime that might be located anywhere in Europe. Most of the town's inhabitants content themselves with a dissipated lifestyle that is made possible by the government's willingness to provide consumer comforts while ignoring behaviors that do not constitute a genuine challenge to its authority. Banev is in equal measure depressed by his acute awareness of government censorship and disgusted by his tendency to drown his sorrows in debauched living, just like nearly everyone else. Moreover, it rains all day, every day (at the time, the rain seemed like a metaphor for Banev's damp spirits; with time, it seems like the logical consequence of climate change brought on by a decadent and shortsighted civilization). Banev's generation occupies a dead end: cynical adults trapped in a fairly comfortable yet repressive social order. The only alternative to this feeble form of late twentieth-century humanity comes in the shape of the town's strange "slimies"—preternaturally intelligent and oddly affectless children who seem already to belong to some kind of higher and different future. In this way, the vector of Progressorism is inverted, and it now seems as though some kind of uncomfortably transhuman intelligence may have infiltrated the human planet for its own reasons.

The liberal intellectuals who composed the heart of the Strugatskys' assumed audience chaffed against the "soft totalitarianism" of the Brezhnev years throughout the 1970s and 1980s. It was easy to read every new Strugatsky publication as an allegory of one's discontent. *Za milliard let do kontsa sveta* (One billion years before the end of the world; 1976, translated in 2014 as *Definitely Maybe*) offered yet another brilliant, pitch-perfect evocation of the intellectual's plight. This time the hero is right smack in Moscow, in his sweltering apartment on a July day, when the rest of his small family—wife and young son—are taking a holiday out of town. Our hero is an astrophysicist working on space-energy contours. He is on the verge of an enormous conceptual breakthrough. He has worked long and hard on this problem, and suddenly he catches a glimpse of the solution. He knows he is close to a magnificent discovery, and he can't help but indulge in a slightly premature feeling of triumph: "My God, that's pretty clever! Go Malianov! What a mind! Finally, you're getting there. Knock on wood. OK, this integral. . . . Damn the integral, full speed ahead!"[22] It soon becomes apparent that this is not a novel about creative inspiration, but about the forces that thwart discovery. The story veers off in a direction that can be compared to other unusual fables of stalled creativity, such as Frederich Pohl's "Speed Trap" and Orson Scott Card's "Prior Restraint."

Everything seems to conspire against Malianov's final effort to conjure up the key set of equations. The obstructions to the creative process seem benign and comic at first: it's too hot in the un-air-conditioned apartment; the refrigerator is empty, and the cat is yowling for food; the phone keeps ringing with a wrong number. It turns out that several of Malianov's acquaintances in very different fields are all experiencing something similar—a near-breakthrough interrupted by a series of bizarre annoyances and coincidences. The plot takes on an ominous tone. Something or somebody seems to be deliberately obstructing the individual scientists' most compelling creative trajectories. In order to soothe their rattled nerves, a biologist, a cultural historian, a computer programmer, and a mathematician converge in Malianov's cramped apartment to discuss the mysterious events. The plot is further animated by the protagonists' enjoyment of one the distractions that interrupted Malianov's thinking earlier—the surprise delivery of a large box of cognac and chocolates. In an atmosphere of growing panic (as well as inebriation), the researchers discuss a pattern of breathtaking intellectual progress in which the closer one gets to the goal, the more serious the harassment—the murder of a physicist colleague, the sudden appearance of a heretofore unsuspected illegitimate child, threats to the safety of Malianov's own child.

Although it was quite possible in the mid-1970s to read *One Billion Years before the End of the World* as a veiled allegory of state-sponsored censorship and persecution of dissident thinkers, the Strugatskys went out of their way to complicate this interpretation. The forms and targets of the harassment seem both arbitrary and much more universal in intent than any given political agenda. After rejecting any plausible "realistic" reasons for their plight, the protagonists briefly entertain the familiar science-fictional scenario whereby they find themselves the victims of a hostile super-civilization that wants to hold humans back. The novella then sidesteps the temptation to metaliterary spoof. Instead, the protagonists come to a different conclusion; namely, they have unintentionally run up against the principle of the Homeostatic Universe. This force is neither a friend nor an enemy but an expression of the cybernetic paradigm that had taken hold in Soviet science in the late 1960s. The mathematician explains: "If only the law of non-decreasing entropy existed, the structure of the universe would disappear and chaos would reign. But on the other hand, if only a constantly self-perfecting and all-powerful intelligence prevails, the structure of the universe based on homeostasis is disrupted. . . . The universe is defending itself."[23]

Malianov is at a loss to understand how his work and the work of his friends has so enraged the "principle of homeostasis," but the outcome is not happy. One of the five researchers vows to continue the fight for scientific advancement on behalf of all of them—but his heroism is construed as absurd and almost diabolical. Malianov's final capitulation to the "homeostatic universe," however, can be read as something other than a moral failing.

> He [Malianov's colleague] will go to the Pamir [mountains] to struggle with Weingarten's revertase, Zakhar's fadings, with his own brilliant math, and all the rest. They will be aiming balls of fire at him, sending ghosts, frozen mountain climbers, especially female ones, dropping avalanches on him, tossing him in space and time, and they will finally get to him there. Or maybe not. . . . But I will stay at home, meet my mother-and-law and Bobchik at the airport tomorrow, and we'll all go buy bookshelves.[24]

Malianov does not give up his cutting-edge work to "go shopping," as long as it is still possible to imagine a form of resistance. Yet one by one, the scientists give in to the notion that the principle of self-regulating homeostasis is destiny, and the old ideals of reason and secular humanism are obsolete in the face of a philosophical *cum* scientific figure of eternal closure.

The Strugatskys' late works came out in the final decades of the twentieth century, but they do not fit easily into the popular genre categories of that time. They contain structural elements of the space opera, future history, and dystopian/postapocalyptic imagining but, philosophically, they seem to anticipate a future in which all easy dichotomies between good and evil, moral and immoral, rational and irrational have been hopelessly confused. In the "Max Kammerer" trilogy, consisting of three linked novels that take place in an imperfect far-future world, societies (on various planets) still consist of feuding, fallible people. The universe does contain other, far more advanced intelligences, but these so-called Wanderers are never seen. Their interference into the (lower) human order is probably motivated by their own version of Progressorism, but the end goal is not made clear.

Forest, Bureau, and the Fate of Transhumanism
in Putin's Russia

In 1965, at the early peak of the Strugatskys' official favor with the regime, they were afforded a "working holiday" at one of the writer's colonies that belonged to the Writer's Union. They were delighted with this token of their success and set off to work on a new novel.[25] The resulting writer's block precipitated a revelation that turned out to be fundamental to the larger story of their intellectual influence. According to Boris, the idea of a sentient, fertile, and febrile matriarchal forest-planet called Pandora was born at this time. The resulting novella was initially published as *Ulitka na sklone* in a rather obscure journal in 1966 (translated as *Snail on the Slope* in 1980). That journal issue was subsequently pulled from the shelves, and the story was banned. Its companion piece, *Skazka o troike* (*Tale of the Troika*; 1967, translated in 1977), was also briefly published then banned. Its unauthorized appearance in an émigré journal prompted a nasty official censure of the Strugatskys in their own country.

Together, the twin pieces depict two evolutionary polarities. The overwhelming female, biologically polymorphic, relentlessly absorbent, inarticulate Forest represents one version of alterity. Unlike the superficially similar forest-worlds depicted in Le Guin's *The Word for World Is Forest* and James Cameron's *Avatar*, the Strugatskys' Forest is not figured as a potentially edenic society living in harmony with nature. While it stands in stark contrast to the Kafkaesque Bureau that tries to control it, neither world is figured as morally superior. The Bureau is harshly hierarchical, hyperverbal ("the proclamation to proclaim the termination of terminal proclamations"), entirely male-dominated, and committed to overcoming all obstacles with technological fixes. In the Forest and the Bureau, the Strugatskys seem to have created two archetypes of social-evolutionary end-points they detested but might be powerless to avert.

Today's Russian neoconservatives reread the Strugatskys as a vindication of the necessary "third way" that Russian transhumanist philosophy offers the world. In their interpretation, the "Forest" archetype represents the rejection of progress in the name of eco-harmony with animals and earth; the "Bureau" archetype represents technocratic Western neoliberalism. The "third way" suggested by Russian neoconservatives once again suggests a science-fictional erasure of the present in order to conjure up a future that is imminent (at least rhetorically), even as it draws (also rhetorically) on a nostalgic reinvention of past glories. In short, it is a call to a nationally specific transhumanism whereby science allows us to have the superpowers of *The Kid*, but Russian Orthodox Christian philosophy gives us all the right spiritual values. As one critic of the neoconservative movement puts it, "the current historical period, in which the victory of technological rationality coexists with the rapid archaisation of countries and entire regions, makes Russian science fiction artists, writers, and political philosophers revisit the legacy of the Strugatsky brothers. The sociopolitical questions they formulated half a century ago remain integral to Russia's present and future."[26]

However, as I hope to have demonstrated here, the Strugatskys' lasting value rests on the way they insist on a mode of intellectualism that foregrounds rationality, yet privileges empathy; engages in public debate, yet resists dogmatism; strives to entertain, yet prods the moral imagination of three generations of readers. The Strugatskys' place in Russian and global literature is secured by the universality of the questions they address and the exquisitely polysemic nature of the texts themselves.

Notes

1. "Science fictional" is used to describe more than a genre. In the twentieth century, it becomes a "mode of awareness," and the cognitive paradigm we use to confront an everyday reality that is universally shaped by technoscience—from "smart" devices to rapidly changing climate patterns. See Csiscery-Ronay, *Seven Beauties* and "What Do We Mean."

2. See Howell, *Apocalyptic Realism.*

3. Birgit Menzel, Michael Hagemeister, and Bernice Glatzer show the persistence of pre-revolutionary occultist and esoteric strains in Russian cultural thought throughout the Soviet period. The striking resurgence of various "cosmist" and "Eurasianist" ideas and their opportunistic reformulation in the ideological projects of post-Soviet right-wing radicals can be traced in the contemporary Russian media. See Menzel, Hagemeister, and Glatzer, *New Age of Russia.* See also Laruelle, "Alexander Dugin"; and Bassin and Kotkina, "*EthnoGenez* Project."

4. The overlap of certain themes, names, and images in James Cameron's *Avatar* (2009) and the Strugatskys' 1966 novella *Snail on the Slope* suggests an interesting convergence, not a case of inadvertent plagiarism.

5. See Banerjee, *We Modern People.*

6. Michael Holquist remarked on "The Philosophical Bases of Soviet Space Exploration" in *The Key Reporter* (1985–86). Subsequent studies of Tsiolkovsky include Andrews, *Red Cosmos*; Hagemeister, "Konstatin Tsiolkovsky"; and Andrews and Siddiqi, *Into the Cosmos.*

7. See Krementsov, *Revolutionary Experiments.*

8. Platonov, "Lunar Bomb," 161.

9. His first attempt at fiction, however, was a novel about the 1954 "test" detonation of an American thermonuclear hydrogen bomb in the Bikini Atoll and its effect on a Japanese ship crew that is exposed to the fallout.

10. Strugatsky, *Commentary*, 69. Boris commented extensively on Arkady's literary life and times (but not on their private lives) in the book *Kommentarii k proidennomu* [Commentary on what happened]. All translations from this text are mine.

11. Ibid.

12. Ibid., 68.

13. Ibid., 66.

14. Ibid., 108. The conservative faction's politicized and racist condemnation was directed against the science-fiction author Genrikh Al'tshuller, who today is best known in the West for his TRIZ method for innovative thinking.

15. *Miry brat'ev Strugatskikh*, 199.

16. Cederlöf, *Alien Places*, 2.

17. See ibid.

18. Ibid., 17.

19. See Cederlöf and Näripea, "Genre and Gender."

20. See Cederlöf, *Alien Places*; and Engström, "Scent of a Former Life."

21. Unauthorized publication in West Germany in 1972 caused a lot of trouble for the authors at home. They were not able to publish the work officially in the USSR until the dissolution of censorship under Gorbachev in 1986.

22. Strugatsky and Strugatsky, *Definitely Maybe*, 6.

23. Ibid., 103.

24. Ibid., 142.

25. Strugatsky, *Commentary*, 150.

26. Engström, "Scent of a Former Life," 196.

Bibliography

Andrews, James T. *Red Cosmos: K. E. Tsiolkovsky, Grandfather of Soviet Rocketry*. College Station: Texas A&M University Press, 2009.

——, and Asif Siddiqi. *Into the Cosmos: Space Exploration and Soviet Culture*. Pittsburgh: University of Pittsburgh Press, 2011.

Avatar. Dir. James Cameron. United States: Twentieth Century Fox, 2009.

Banerjee, Anindita. *We Modern People: Science Fiction and the Making of Russian Modernity*. Middletown, Conn.: Wesleyan University Press, 2012.

Bassin, Mark, and Irina Kotkina. "The *EthnoGenez* Project: Ideology and Science Fiction in Putin's Russia." *Utopian Studies* 27.1 (March 2016): 53–76.

Bogdanov, Alexander. *Red Star: The First Bolshevik Utopia* (1908). Ed. Loren Graham and Richard Stites. Trans. Charles Rougle. Bloomington: Indiana University Press, 1984.

Card, Orson Scott. "Prior Restraint." In *Maps in a Mirror*. New York: Tor Books, 1990. 74–81.

Cederlöf, Henriette. *Alien Places in Late Soviet Science Fiction: The "Unexpected Encounters" of Arkady and Boris Strugatsky as Novels and Films*. Studies in Russian Literature 42. Stockholm: Acta Universitatis Stockholmiensis, 2014.

————, and Eva Näripea. "Genre and Gender in *The Dead Mountaineer's Hotel*." *Science Fiction Film and Television* 8.2 (2015): 145–66.

Charodei [The magicians]. Dir. Konstantin Bromberg. USSR: Odessa Film Studio, 1982.

Csicsery-Ronay, Istvan. *The Seven Beauties of Science Fiction*. Middletown, Conn.: Wesleyan University Press, 2008.

————. "What Do We Mean When We Say 'Global Science Fiction'? Reflections on a New Nexus." *Science Fiction Studies* 39.3 (2012): 478–93.

Efremov, Ivan. *Andromeda: A Space Age Tale*. Trans. George Hannah. 1957–58; reprint, Amsterdam: Fredonia Books, 2004.

Engström, Maria. "The Scent of a Former Life: The Czech Adaptation of the Strugatskiis' Story *The Kid*." *Science Fiction Film and Television* 8.2 (2015): 179–98.

Hagemeister, Michael. "Konstatin Tsiolkovsky and the Occult Roots of Soviet Space Travel." In *The New Age of Russia: Occult and Esoteric Dimensions*. Ed. Birgit Menzel, Michael Hagemeister, and Bernice Glatzer. München: Verlag Otto Sagner, 2012. 135–50.

Heinlein, Robert. *Stranger in a Strange Land*. New York: Putnam, 1961.

Holquist, Michael. "The Philosophical Bases of Soviet Space Exploration." *Key Reporter* 51.2 (Winter 1985–86): 1.

Howell, Yvonne. *Apocalyptic Realism: The Science Fiction of Arkady and Boris Strugatsky*. New York: Peter Lang, 1994.

————, ed. *Red Star Tales: An Anthology of Russian and Soviet Science Fiction*. Montpelier, Vt.: RIS Press, 2015.

Krementsov, Nikolai. *Revolutionary Experiments: The Quest for Immortality in Bolshevik Science and Fiction*. Oxford: Oxford University Press, 2013.

Laruelle, Marlene. "Alexander Dugin: A Russian Version of the European Radical Right?" Washington, D.C.: Kennan Institute Occasional Paper no. 294, 2001.

LeGuin, Ursula K. *The Dispossessed: An Ambiguous Utopia*. New York: Harper and Row, 1974.

————. *The Word for World Is Forest*. 1972; reprint, New York: Berkley, 1976.

Lem, Stanislaw. *Solaris* (1970). Trans. Joanna Kilmartin and Steve Cox. San Diego: Harcourt Brace and Co, 2002.

Maguire, Muireann, and Andrei Rogachevsky, eds. "Filming the Strugatskiis." Special issue of *Science Fiction Film and Television* 8.2 (2015).

Menzel, Birgit, Michael Hagemeister, and Bernice Glatzer, eds. *The New Age of Russia: Occult and Esoteric Dimensions*. Munich: Verlag Otto Sagner, 2012.

Miry brat'ev Strugatskikh. Entsiklopediia v 2-kh tomakh [The worlds of the Strugatskys: An encyclopedia in 2 volumes]. Russia: AST Publisher, 1999. Accessed August 7, 2017. http://www.rusf.ru/abs/abs_meta/m_010185.htm.

Orwell, George. *1984*. New York: Harcourt Brace and Co., 1949.

Platonov, Andrei. "Lunnaia bomba" [Lunar bomb]. In *Red Star Tales*. Ed. Yvonne Howell. Trans. Keith Blasing. Montpelier, Vt.: RIS Publications, 2015. 158–80.

Pohl, Frederik. "Speed Trap." *Playboy*, November 1967. 159.

Stalker [Stalker]. Dir. Andrei Tarkovsky. USSR: Mosfilm, 1980.

S.T.A.L.K.E.R. Video Game. Released March 20, 2007. GCS Game World, THQ.

Strugatsky, Arkady, and Boris Strugatsky. *Beetle in the Anthill* [Zhuk v muraveinike]. Trans. Antonina W. Bouis. New York: Macmillan, 1980.

———. *The Dead Mountaineer's Inn* [Otel' u pogibshego al'pinista]. Trans. Josh Billings. Brooklyn, N.Y.: Melville House, 2015.

———. *Definitely Maybe* [Za milliard let do kontsa sveta]. Trans. Antonina W. Bouis. Brooklyn, N.Y.: Melville House Publishing, 2014.

———. *The Doomed City* [Rad obrechennyi]. Trans. Andrew Bromfield. Chicago: Chicago Review Press, 2016.

———. *Far Rainbow* [Dalekaia raduga]. Trans. Antonina W. Bouis. New York: Macmillan, 1979.

———. *Hard to Be a God* [Trudno byt bogom]. Trans. Olga Bormashenko. Chicago: Chicago Review Press, 2014.

———. *Monday Begins on Saturday* [Ponedelnik nachinaetsia v subbotu]. Trans. Leonin Renen. New York: DAW Books, 1977.

———. *Noon: 22nd Century* [Polden' XXII veka]. Trans. P. L. McGuire. New York: Macmillan, 1978.

———. *Otiagoshchennye zlom, ili sorok let spustia* [Burdened with evil, or forty years later]. Moscow: Prometei, 1988.

———. *Prisoners of Power* [Bitaemyi ostrov]. Trans. Helen Saltz Jacobson. New York: Macmillan, 1977.

———. *Roadside Picnic* [Piknik na obochine]. Trans. Olga Bormashenko. Chicago: Chicago Review Press, 2014.

———. *Snail on the Slope* [Ulitka na sklone]. Trans. A. Meyers. London: Bantam Books, 1980.

———. "Space Mowgli" [Malysh]. Trans. Roger DeGaris. In *Escape Attempt*. New York: Macmillan, 1982.

———. *Strana bagrovykh tuch* [Land of the crimson clouds]. USSR: Detgiz, 1959.

———. *Tale of the Troika* [Skazka o troike; 1967]. In *Roadside Picnic/Tale of the Troika*. Trans. Antonia Bouis. New York: MacMillan, 1977. 147–244.

———. *The Time Wanderers* [Volny gasiat veter]. Trans. Antonina W. Bouis. New York: St. Martin's Press, 1986.

———. *Ugly Swans* [Gadkie lebedi]. Trans. Alice Stone Nakhimovsky and Alexander Nakhimovsky. New York: Collier-Macmillan, 1980.

Strugatsky, Boris. *Kommentarii k proidennomu* [Commentary on what happened]. St. Petersburg: Amfora, 2003.

Zamiatin, Evgeny. *We* [My]. Trans. Natasha Randall. New York: Modern Library, 2006.

Contributors

ALEXIS BROOKS DE VITA holds degrees in comparative literature studying African and Diaspora works in English, French, Italian, and Spanish. Her scholarly books include *Mythatypes: Signatures and Signs of African/Diaspora and Black Goddesses*, *The 1855 Murder Case of Missouri versus Celia, an Enslaved Woman*, her translation of *Dante's Inferno: A Wanderer in Hell*, and essays on African/Diaspora, gothic, and horror media. Her fictional publications include *Left Hand of the Moon* and the *Books of Joy* dark fantasy trilogy: *Burning Streams*, *Blood of Angels*, and *Chain Dance*. She is a contributing editor for the anthologies *Tales in Firelight and Shadow* and *Love and Darker Passions*.

PAWEŁ FRELIK is associate professor in the Department of American Literature and Culture at Maria Curie-Skłodowska University, Lublin, and at the American Studies Center, University of Warsaw, Poland. His research and writing interests include science-fiction visualities, contemporary experimental fiction, unpopular culture, and cross-media storytelling. He has published widely in these fields, including *Kultury wizualne science fiction* [Visual cultures of science fiction; 2017], *Playing the Universe: Games and Gaming in Science Fiction* (2007), and recent chapters in *Parabolas of Science Fiction*, *The Liverpool Companion to World Science Fiction Film*, and *Oxford Handbook of Science Fiction*. He serves on the boards of *Science Fiction Studies*, *Extrapolation*, and *Journal of Gaming and Virtual Worlds*.

YVONNE HOWELL studied biology and Russian language at Dartmouth College and interned for a year with Russian ornithologists at Leningrad State University (former USSR). She is the author of *Apocalyptic Realism: The Science Fiction of Arkady and Boris Strugatsky* and editor of *Red Star Tales: An Anthology of Russian and Soviet Science Fiction.* She has also written extensively on the intersections between scientific and literary culture in the twentieth and twenty-first centuries. She is professor of Russian and international studies at the University of Richmond, Virginia, and a member of the executive board for the Southern Conference of Slavic Studies.

DALE KNICKERBOCKER is the McMahon Distinguished Professor of Foreign Languages and Literatures at East Carolina University. His publications include *Juan José Millás: The Obsessive-Compulsive Aesthetic,* as well as numerous articles on Spanish and Latin American fantasy and science fiction. He is associate editor of the *Journal of the Fantastic in the Arts* and *Alambique* and serves on the boards of the journals *Extrapolation, Brumal,* and *Abusões.*

YOLANDA MOLINA-GAVILÁN is professor of Spanish at Eckerd College in St. Petersburg, Florida. Her research centers on science-fiction literature from the Spanish-speaking world. Main works by her in this field include *Ciencia ficción en español: una mitología moderna ante el cambio* [Science fiction in Spanish: A modern mythology before change], *Cosmos Latinos: An Anthology of Science Fiction from Latin America and Spain,* "Chronology of Latin American SF 1775–2005," and *The Time Ship: A Chrononautical Journey.*

AMY J. RANSOM is professor of French at Central Michigan University. She has authored nearly two dozen articles on sf, the fantastic, and horror writing from Québec, published in such venues as *Science Fiction Studies, Journal of the Fantastic in the Arts* (forthcoming), *Extrapolation, Foundation, Canadian Literature, Studies in Canadian Literature, Études francophones,* and the online journal *Temporalités.* Her 2009 book *Science Fiction from Quebec: A Postcolonial Study* is the first monograph devoted to the scholarly analysis of French-Canadian science fiction and fantasy in French or in English. She also publishes on popular music and film from Quebec, with articles appearing in *Quebec Studies, American Review of Canadian Studies,* the online journal *Glottopol,* and in her 2014 book, *Hockey PQ: Canada's Game in Québec's Popular Culture.* Her recent scholarship, including an essay on Jean-Baptiste Cousin de Grainville's *The Last Man* in *Science Fiction Studies,* deals with nineteenth-century French sf. She is associate book-review editor for the *Journal of the Fantastic in the Arts* and vice president of the Science Fiction Research Association (2012–14).

HANNA-RIIKKA ROINE works as a postdoctoral researcher at the University of Helsinki. Her doctoral dissertation, "Imaginative, Immersive, and Interactive Engagements: The Rhetoric of Worldbuilding in Contemporary Speculative Fiction" (2016), pursues speculative worldbuilding as a rhetorical and communicative practice beyond textual fictions to digital, interactive, transmedial, and fan fictions. Roine has also worked as an editor-in-chief of *Fafnir—Nordic Journal for Science Fiction and Fantasy Research* and published numerous articles on speculative fiction.

VIBEKE RÜTZOU PETERSEN received her Ph.D. in German Studies from New York University. She is associate professor of women's studies at Drake University in Iowa. She is the author of *Women and Modernity in Weimar Germany: Reality and Its Reflection in Popular Fiction* and *Kursbuch, 1965–1975: Social, Political and Literary Perspectives of West Germany*. She is coeditor of *Detectives, Dystopias, and Poplit: Studies in Modern German Genre Fiction* and *Gender and German Cinema: German Film History/German History on Film*, vol. 2: *Feminist Interventions*.

HANNA SAMOLA works as a senior lecturer in Finnish literature and as a postdoctoral researcher on the project "Darkening Visions: Dystopian Fiction in Contemporary Finnish Literature" at the University of Tampere, Finland. In her dissertation, she examined the generic combination of dystopia and fairy tale in contemporary Finnish literature. Samola has published articles on totalitarian and feminist dystopias and the generic combinations of dystopias with other genres. Her current research interests include fairy-tale and dystopian studies, genre studies, and critical plant studies.

MINGWEI SONG is an associate professor of Chinese literature at Wellesley College. He is the author of *Young China: National Rejuvenation and the Bildungsroman, 1900–1959* and numerous articles on modern Chinese literature and culture. He has been researching Chinese science fiction since 2010. He is the coeditor of a special issue of *Renditions* on science fiction, a special issue of *China Perspective* on utopia and dystopia in Chinese literature, and an anthology, *The Reincarnated Giant: Twenty-first Century Chinese Science Fiction*.

TATSUMI TAKAYUKI is professor of English at Keio University, Tokyo. He is the sixteenth president of the American Literature Society of Japan and is a member of the editorial board of *Science-Fiction Studies*, the *Edgar Allan Poe Review*, *Mark Twain Studies*, and the *Journal of Transnational American Studies*. His major books are *Cyberpunk America*, the winner of the JAPAN-U.S. Friendship Commission's American Studies Book Prize; *New Americanist Poetics*, winner of the Yukichi Fukuzawa Award; and *Full Metal Apache: Transactions between Cyberpunk Japan and Avant-Pop America*, the winner of the 2010 IAFA Distinguished Scholarship Award. Coeditor of the "New Japanese Fiction" issue of *Review of Contemporary Fiction* and the "Three Asias—Japan, S. Korea, China" issue of *PARA*DOXA*, he has also published a variety of essays such as "Literary History on the Road: Transatlantic Crossings and Transpacific Crossovers" and "Race and Black Humor: From a Planetary Perspective."

JUAN CARLOS TOLEDANO REDONDO works on the fantastic in contemporary narrative written in Spanish. His previous academic production includes "Recuerdos que curan: Memoria y ciencia ficción en Chile" [Memories that cure: Memory and science fiction in Chile], with Kaitlin Sommerfeld; "Una cartografía de la CF cubana a través del trabajo de Yoss" [A cartography of Cuban science fiction through the work of Yoss]; "The Many Names of God: Christianity in Hispanic Caribbean Science Fiction"; and "From Socialist Realism to Anarchist Capitalism: Cuban Cyberpunk," among others. Toledano Redondo is coeditor of the academic journal *Alambique* and professor of Hispanic studies at Lewis and Clark College in Portland, Oregon.

NATACHA VAS-DEYRES is docent and research associate at the Laboratoire pluridisciplinaire de recherches sur l'imaginaire appliquées à la littérature (Multidisciplinary Research Laboratory on the Imaginary Applied to Literature, Lapril/ CLARE) at the Université Bordeaux-Montaigne. She has published dozens of articles on literature of social anticipation, most notably that written between the two world wars, but also on contemporary science fiction. She has edited or co-edited four collections of essays: *L'Imaginaire du temps dans le fantastique et la science-fiction* [The imaginary of time in fantasy and science fiction]; *Régis Messac, l'écrivain-journaliste à re-connaître* [Régis Messac, a writer-journalist to rediscover]; *Les Dieux cachés de la science-fiction française et francophone, 1950–2010* [The hidden gods of French and Francophone science fiction]; and, most recently and notably, *Ces Français qui ont écrit demain. Utopie, anticipation et science-fiction au XXème siècle* [The French who write tomorrow: Utopia, anticipation, and science fiction of the twentieth century], which won the Grand Prix de l'Imaginaire for 2013 in the catgory of essays. She is also currently vice president of the Centre d'études et de recherches sur les littératures de l'imaginaire (Center for Studies and Research on Literatures of the Imaginary).

Index

The University of Illinois Press
is a founding member of the
Association of American University Presses.

Composed in 10.75/13 Arno Pro
with Adrianna Extended Pro display
by Lisa Connery
at the University of Illinois Press
Cover designed by Tamara Shidlauski
Cover illustrations: Astrostar/Shutterstock.com, Vectomart/
Shutterstock.com

University of Illinois Press
1325 South Oak Street
Champaign, IL 61820-6903
www.press.uillinois.edu